I0018478

Dennis Wiebusch

Reusability for Intelligent Realtime Interactive Systems

Dennis Wiebusch

Reusability for Intelligent Realtime Interactive Systems

Würzburg
University Press

Dissertation, Julius-Maximilians-Universität Würzburg
Fakultät für Mathematik und Informatik, 2015
Gutachter: Prof. Dr. Marc Erich Latoschik, Prof. Dr.-Ing. Samuel Kounev

Impressum

Julius-Maximilians-Universität Würzburg
Würzburg University Press
Universitätsbibliothek Würzburg
Am Hubland
D-97074 Würzburg
www.wup.uni-wuerzburg.de

© 2016 Würzburg University Press
Print on Demand

Coverdesign: Jakob Löffler
Zeichnung: Francis Kaiser

ISBN 978-3-95826-040-5 (print)
ISBN 978-3-95826-041-2 (online)
URN urn:nbn:de:bvb:20-opus-121869

Except otherwise noted, this document—excluding the cover—is licensed under the
Creative Commons Attribution-ShareAlike 3.0 DE License (CC BY-SA 3.0 DE):
http://creativecommons.org/licenses/by-sa/3.0/de/

The cover page is licensed under the Creative Commons
Attribution-NonCommercial-NoDerivatives 3.0 DE License (CC BY-NC-ND 3.0 DE):
http://creativecommons.org/licenses/by-nc-nd/3.0/de/

Acknowledgments

Finishing this thesis would not have been possible without many of the people who accompanied me during the time of its creation. Some of them directly influenced my work, while others accompanied me in life beyond. To each and everyone of them I owe the fact that I was able to successfully make it through my PhD time.

First and foremost, I am very grateful to my supervisor, Prof. Dr. Marc Erich Latoschik, for providing me with the opportunity to pursue my thesis. He always allowed me to follow my own ideas, providing helpful discussions and advice whenever needed. Moreover, I am thankful for being given the opportunity to support the establishment of his professorial chair and for the trust he placed in me during the past years.

Undoubtedly, this thesis would not exist the way it does, if I had not been supported by my friend and colleague Martin Fischbach, who was a constant companion all the time. Besides co-development of the Simulator X framework and countless productive discussions, he cared about my fitness (going to the gym and playing squash) as well as physical and mental well-being (cooking and playing console games). I am sincerely grateful for his support and I hope that I have been—and will be—as helpful to him on his way to his PhD.

Although she turned her back on academic life before my thesis was finished, Anke Giebler-Schubert is probably the second most important person to help me making it through my PhD time. For one, many aspects of the created software are the result of very fruitful discussions with her. Much more importantly, she was always there for me to talk when I needed to have a weep over life at and beyond work.

I am grateful to Henrik Tramberend and Stephan Rehfeld, who have influenced my work from the start in their roles as colleagues and members of the SIRIS project, in the context of which the foundation for this thesis was established. Moreover, I want to thank my colleague Jean-Luc Lugrin for helping me with valuable comments during work on publications and especially for his dry sense of humor. I also want to thank Benjamin Eckstein, who served as a self-proclaimed beta tester for the late aspects of the Simulator X framework during his master thesis (he thus had little choice, all the more I am thankful for his support).

My brother Nico has been a source of inspiration and always helped me to divert my thoughts to other topics of scientific nature when I was stuck, needed some distraction, or simply when he felt like it. Each time I needed a safe haven, my mother Marita and my sister Ines provided me with a place to return to and to feel understood.

I would especially like to thank my dear friend Carl David Mildenberger and his wife Anna, who took the burden to migrate to Scotland to provide me with a place to get away from it all. Even more, they decided to get two children to entertain me in those days. Although I have the feeling that I am not the only reason for this, I am glad that both of them are very likable and it thus turned out to be a good decision, anyway. All jesting aside, I am deeply thankful for our friendship, for the supportive conversations, and for all the good times we shared.

I feel lucky to have found a friend in Friederike Meyer. No matter where she was living, she always was open to a visit by me. Over the time, she became my personal cultural and nutritional adviser, a familiar, and someone I do not want to miss. I also wish to thank Claudia Hänel, who supported me with encouraging words in the late phases of writing and kept me believing in myself. I owe her large parts of the motivation to finish this thesis and am very glad to call her a friend.

I am much obliged to those who took the time to proofread this thesis, in whole or in part, and provided me with suggestions and corrections: Sebastian Oberdörfer, Julia and Christian Fröhlich, Regina Roßmann, and Magdalena Hartmann. Special thanks go to my friend of many years, Francis Kaiser, for creating the cover image for this book.

And last, but most certainly not least, I want to mention those, who have been there when I hit rock bottom and needed someone to talk to: Lara Luttmer who made me take a deep breath and relax my mind every time I was close to stumble. Simon and Alexandra Claßen who, no matter what, always were on hand with help and advice for me, and Maha Salem and Melanie Hey who, knowing what I was going through, have supported me with empathy and words of understanding.

Many thanks to all of you!

Preface

At the time of this writing, the acquisition of Oculus by Facebook for an equivalent countervalue of approximately 2 billion dollars is 18 month old. A major player in the social web industry buys itself into a start-up company for consumer head-mounted displays (HMDs). HMDs are one vital periphery for an idea which gained momentum during the late 60th and in various science fiction stories: Virtual Reality (VR). VR research underwent a staggering process and in general, the expectations of many people were not met so far and hence many thought of VR as being dead. In contrast to these prophecies, the idea of VR, while so far not being successful commercially, has always been an active field of research and science. Once a domain of specialized (and very expensive) hard- and software, researchers all over the world worked at the necessary technology and its improvement constantly.

Today, the public view and expectation of VR (again) changed drastically. First, the necessary high quality graphics systems became affordable (thanks to the gaming industry). Second, consumer-grade tracking systems were developed (again, targeting entertainment). Third, after the Facebook deal (thanks to the mobile industry for cheap high resolution displays), there seems literally to be no big player in the industry, from game companies to simulation and robotics etc. who does not revive at least some ideas of applying VR to their own products or to built new complete VR products.

Dr. Wiebusch came to the field long before the new hype started and he thoroughly analyzed the existing state-of-the-art of VR systems since then. VR researchers have produced impressive results over the years despite the ups and downs of the field and the general public recognition. Still, many of the sometimes very impressive demos and software systems built over the years could today only be analyzed by the papers published or the videos produced. They could no longer be executed or tried out.

The general problem: VR system often combine many different hard- and software parts and they often tend to become very complex due to their manifold underlying functionality. The well-known fact that "software ages" is stubbornly dominant for many VR systems. Reusability, a very important software quality, is often low for VR systems, a problem for which Dr. Wiebusch developed an interesting and promising solution. He proposes a knowledge-based model to describe the relevant aspects and software interfaces of highly interactive and intelligent human-computer systems. So called real-time interactive systems (RISs) combine complex functional requirements with very specific non-functional requirements: Multimodal and multimedia input/output has to be realized given user-oriented psychophysical constraints in real-time. RIS systems comprise VR and many other related domains, e.g., augmented reality (AR), mixed reality (MR), computer games, robotics, or telepresence.

The proposed solution of Dr. Wiebusch presents a promising approach to increase software quality, specifically reusability, of RIS in general. In addition, his knowledge-based approach establishes an implicit semantics layer not only beneficial in terms of software quality. Many interesting state-of-the-art human-computer interaction paradigms, e.g., multimodal (speech and gesture etc.) interfaces, virtual agents, or social robotics, are based on algorithms which require a representation of the semantics of the environment (the interaction domain) and the communicative content. The approach by Dr. Wiebusch fulfills this central requirement as an implicit feature of the system architecture and makes it continuously available throughout the software development process. Given the current regained interest in VR in general, it seems that Dr. Wiebusch presents his work just at the right time.

Marc Erich Latoschik
Chair IX – Human-Computer Interaction
Insitiute of Computer Science
University of Würzburg

Contents

Acronyms

3DUI	3D User Interface
ABox	Assertional Box
AI	Artificial Intelligence
AOP	Aspect Oriented Programming
API	Application Programming Interface
CBSE	Component-Based Software Engineering
COTS	components-off-the-shelf
CWA	Closed World Assumption
DAML	DARPA Agent Markup Language
DL	Description Logic
DSL	Domain Specific Language
ECS	Entity-Component-System
FOL	First-Order Logic
GUI	Graphical User Interface
IDE	Integrated Development Environment
IRI	International Resource Identifier
IRIS	Intelligent Realtime Interactive System
IVA	Intelligent Virtual Agent
IVE	Intelligent Virtual Environment
KB	Knowledge Base
KRL	Knowledge Representation Layer
LOC	Lines of Code
MR	Mixed Reality
OOP	Object-Oriented Programming
OWA	Open World Assumption
OWL	Web Ontology Language
PDDL	Planning Domain Definition Language
RDF	Resource Description Framework
RIS	Realtime Interactive System
SPARQL	SPARQL Protocol And RDF Query Language
SVE	Semantic Virtual Environment
UNA	Unique Name Assumption
UML	Unified Modeling Language
UUID	Universally Unique Identifier
TBox	Terminological Box
VE	Virtual Environment
VR	Virtual Reality
VRPN	Virtual-Reality Peripheral Network
W3C	World Wide Web Consortium

List of Figures

List of Tables

Listings

Chapter 1

Introduction

The major cause [of the software crisis] is ... that the machines have become several orders of magnitude more powerful! To put it quite bluntly: as long as there were no machines, programming was no problem at all; when we had a few weak computers, programming became a mild problem, and now we have gigantic computers, programming has become an equally gigantic problem. In this sense the electronic industry has not solved a single problem, it has only created them—it has created the problem of using its products. To put it in another way: as the power of available machines grew by a factor of more than a thousand, society's ambition to apply these machines grew in proportion, and it was the poor programmer who found his job in this exploded field of tension between ends and means.

The Humble Programmer
Dijkstra (1972)

1.1 Motivation

As Edsger W. Dijkstra pointed out in his above-quoted 1972 ACM Turing Award lecture, the complexity of computer programs as well as their development is strongly linked to the technical capabilities created by technological advance. Although he probably will neither have had the computational power, that is provided by modern devices, nor their currently experienced availability in mind, his statement is still pertinent.

The number and diversity of programmable machines used in everyday life remains growing, as does the complexity of implemented software. For example, fifteen years ago mobile computing was mostly limited to the utilization of rather expensive laptop computers, whereas nowadays smartphones and tablet computers, which easily outperform those earlier devices, have become affordable for many people. As predicted by Dijkstra, such devices are employed ever more and lately even used to facilitate daily life.

Accordingly, the complexity of the software running on such devices has increased immensely. While in the 1990's the use of computers mainly involved office-based applications, recent software ranges from dictionaries, encyclopedias, communication software, navigational software, and realistic computer games to VR and Mixed Reality (MR) applications. To make things even worse, the hardware in use today is much more diverse than it was in 1972, and new generations of devices are released much more frequently. In this regard, when analyzing the difficulties related to software engineering, Brooks (1987) stated that "[...] we must observe that the anomaly is not that software progress is so slow but that computer hardware progress is so fast."

Getting back to Dijkstra's statement, one reason for difficulties in the area of software development is that created systems are used by more and more people in most different areas of application. Accordingly, expectations on software have increased: whereas earlier computer programs were meant to plainly organize and store data, nowadays they are expected to support a user in his or her tasks in an understandable, intelligent, and convenient way.

In doing so, applications benefit from additional information on the data being processed. Hence, the integration of semantics, knowledge representations, and services depending thereon plays a major role. In this context, new technologies and ideas, such as the *Semantic Web* and the *Web Ontology Language* (OWL), have been brought up. Such techniques allow for automatized access to information and communication between applications. Recent developments include the integration of semantic web services and natural language interfaces. For instance, Apple's *Siri* provides the user with a speech interface to query information, as does Google's *Google Now*. The *Hummingbird* search algorithm, also developed by Google, is a text based service, relying on semantic information, that provides so-called semantic search and allows users to enter fully formulated questions instead of searching for keywords.

Virtual Environments (VEs), as one possible type of future human-computer interfaces, have experienced similar developments. For example, interaction with supportive virtual agents often is based on speech and gesture interfaces. Similar to the examples mentioned above, agents and gesture interfaces benefit from the existence of semantic information. In this context, the term *Intelligent Virtual Environment* (IVE) was introduced, describing the "combination of intelligent techniques and tools, embodied in autonomous creatures and agents, together with effective means for their graphical representation and interaction of various kinds" (Luck & Aylett, 2000, p. 4). In this work, the more comprehensive term *Intelligent Realtime Interactive System* (IRIS) is used, denoting a system that simulates a virtual environment the elements of which support their utilization in intelligent ways. In this regard, an element can be any part of the VE, including software modules that perform the necessary simulations.

Such systems are increasingly becoming part of everyday life. For example, current computer games largely include the visualization of some virtual environment, modern navigational systems overlay the view of the street with the calculated route, and applications for interior design allow to integrate virtual furniture into a customer's home, using smartphones and most recently even consumer-grade VR hardware.

Seen from a rather philosophical point of view every software in fact simulates some kind of VE. While this is quite obvious for computer games and most mixed reality applications, counting a word processor as a VR application seems rather odd. Nevertheless, such software does simulate a virtual piece of paper, which may be seen as a very limited virtual environment. In a sense, this admittedly uncommon perspective is reasonable: due to its nature, a computer inevitably has to internally represent and simulate whatever it shall process. With this in mind, the scope of this work is not limited to VEs but can be applied to many other types of software. Yet, VR systems pose one of the most complex types of software (regarding both functional and non-functional requirements) and thus provide a reasonable domain for this work.

In addition to the appropriateness of emerging examples and growing use in various areas of daily life, a third incentive to focus on such systems is the fact that the games industry has created a huge market that is addressed by this field. Simplifying work in this domain could reduce development costs and increase profit in that area of industry.

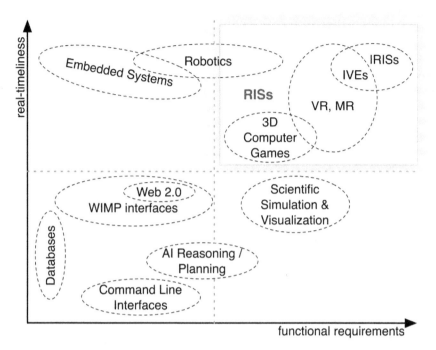

Figure 1.1: Classification of the addressed application area (visualized by the blue rectangle). Real-timeliness relates to expected response times, whereas the functional requirements commonly manifest in the number of input and output modalities as well as the variety of interacting software modules.

But, as desirable as such systems may seem as complex is their development, extension, and maintenance, requiring high efforts and often generating huge expenses. One of the reasons for this is the large number and variety of software modules that have to interact in order to satisfy the expectations that are imposed on an up-to-date Realtime Interactive System (RIS). As opposed to many other software systems, the aspects that are addressed by such modules tend to overlap. For example, the position of a virtual object is concurrently accessed by multiple modules. Such systems' inherent request for interactivity imposes realtime requirements, e.g., varying update rates of displays or haptic feedback devices, which complicate an implementation even more. Figure 1.1 provides the context for application areas that are impacted by this work (edged in blue).

Due to its inherent complexity, multiple developers and designers commonly collaborate to create a RIS, each of them being an expert in one or multiple project-related areas. These involve, for example, physical simulation, (stereoscopic) realtime 3D graphics rendering, sound rendering, artificial intelligence (e.g., reasoning and planning), object and human body tracking, sensor data processing, multimodal interaction, development of application logic, 3D user interfaces, 3D modeling, game design, and many more.

Besides well-known software engineering- and project management-related problems, the development of RISs underlies additional requirements: they inevitably need to make full use of the available hardware resources to guarantee maximum interactivity, involving both performance and usability. As a result, an implementation often is tailored to the capabilities of the available hardware. However, the aforementioned speed of innovations results in frequent hardware replacements and possibly in the need for new interaction methods, thus calling for modularity.

In the absence of a proper middleware the combined modules are often closely coupled and their compilation is customized to fulfill the specific use case of the application. Maintaining such software requires a holistic understanding of the interrelationship of involved modules. Accordingly, the initial development of an Intelligent Realtime Interactive System (IRIS) is complicated by possible communication difficulties between the involved individuals, whereas later maintenance and possible extensions necessitate preserving the holistic understanding that was obtained by the initial development team.

This changes for the better by the utilization of current RIS middleware. Nonetheless, these frameworks often involve a fixed set of simulation modules and render the integration of additional modules or exchange of existing ones difficult, maybe even impossible. Moreover, even in the presence of such middleware, the application logic itself often exhibits high internal coupling, wherefore reusing single elements of the implementation remains difficult. Reasons for this include the fact that provided software interfaces allow to decouple the application from the utilized simulation modules, but little assistance is provided to cope with application-related issues.

So far, these issues resulted in applications being reimplemented almost from scratch, over and over again. Multiple frameworks have been developed to ease the creation of virtual environments, but only few have put their focus on extensibility and maintainability of created applications. Yet, especially in research environments, it is necessary to be able to *reuse* software created before, since the structure of the development team changes frequently but developed systems are required to stay up-to-date. This work aims at providing methods that facilitate the creation of reusable IRISs in order to overcome these problems.

1.2 Reusability for Intelligent Realtime Interactive Systems

This work is closely related to the field of software engineering and the idea of *software reuse*. Furthermore, it involves virtual environments and intelligent realtime interactive systems. The following sections give an overview of related concepts, whereas a more detailed discussion is presented in chapter 2.

1.2.1 Software Reusability and Software Reuse

In general, the term reusability denotes the extent to which some asset is suited to be reused. To reuse, in turn, means to use something that was used before. In this regard, the title of this work is quite vague, since reusability itself does not specify in which way assets—in this case parts of an eventual IRIS—are reused. This ambiguity is intentional: neither does the word reusability completely capture the intention of this work nor is the scope of reused parts clearly defined.

A short explanation is required: a central goal of this work is to increase the extent to which parts of an existing RIS can be reused. In this context, 'parts' can denote a subset of the system. This would require the elements of which the software is composed to be *modular* and *loosely coupled*, allowing to easily extract a subset of a RIS and reuse it in a different context (re-use case 1). Note that software modules that are used to simulate the VE, which subsequently will be called *simulation modules*, as well as the content of the simulation can be subject to reuse.

Alternatively, 'parts' could relate to the whole system, meaning that the existing system itself is reused (re-use case 2). For example, new functionality or new content could be added. In that case, the system is required to be *extensible*.

Norms and Definitions　The ISO/IEC 9126 (2001) and ISO/IEC 25010 (2011) standards define the following characteristics,[1] which are closely related to software reusability:

maintainability	portability
modifiability	*adaptability*
reusability	*replaceability*
modularity	
functionality	**usability**
suitability	*understandability*
interoperability	*learnability*

Table 1.1: Software reusability related terms defined in the ISO/IEC-9126 and ISO/IEC-25010 standards.

In fact, with regard to these standards, this work does rather address maintainability than reusability: not only should a system be reusable, but also changeable (especially extensible) and maintainable. A second characteristic that is addressed by this work is portability: software that was developed for one hardware setup has to easily work with different systems. In addition, the term replaceability is applicable to some extent: although the whole system is not required to replace another system, this holds true for the modules it consists of. Finally, usability is related to this work, since a lack of understandability often leads to a decrease in reusability. Hence, of the nine aspects of software reuse at least seven are addressed by this work.

However, the principal idea remains to reuse single components and their functionality or parts thereof in order to create maintainable software. On a related note, H. Mili, Mili, and Mili found that "maintenance has been recognized by a number of researchers as a particular form of reuse" (H. Mili et al., 1995, p. 556). All in all, even though none of the mentioned concepts fully covers the intended scope of this work, reusability and the corresponding term *software reusability* are believed to fit best.

Software Reusability　First ideas concerning the systematic reuse of software were brought up by McIlroy (1968) in conjunction with the so-called *software crisis*. The growing complexity of software and diversity of hardware required to rethink the way software was created.

---

[1] The presented terms are a subset of the terms defined in the ISO/IEC 9126 (2001) standard. Reusability and modularity were added in the superseding ISO/IEC 25010 (2011) standard.

The term *software reusability* originates from the field of software engineering and refers to the reuse potential of a software module. Although not being the same, it is often synonymously used with the term *software reuse* or *code reuse*. For both software reusability and software reuse multiple definitions exist, such as

- "The degree to which a software module or other work product can be used in more than one computer program or software system" (p. 64 Radatz, Geraci, & Katki, 1990, on reusability),

- "Reusability is a measure of the ease with which the resource can be reused in a new situation" (Kim & Stohr, 1998, p. 116),

- "Software reuse is the process of creating software systems from existing software rather than building software systems from scratch" (Krueger, 1992, p. 131),

- "Software reuse is generally defined as the use of previously developed software resources from all phases of the software life cycle, in new applications by various users such as programmers and systems analysts" (Kim & Stohr, 1998, p. 115), and

- "Software reuse is about methods and techniques to enhance the reusability of software, including the management of repositories of components" (Clements, 2001, p. 2).

In this work, the following definition, which is adapted to the development of RIS frameworks, is used:

Definition 1.1. *Reusability* denotes the degree to which a software system supports adding, removing, or replacing assets without necessitating further changes to either the system or the asset. Assets, in this context, are the software modules which the system consists of as well as the objects that are processed by these modules.

1.2.2 Intelligent Realtime Interactive Systems

Given the definition of reusability, the aforementioned terms Realtime Interactive System and Intelligent Realtime Interactive System remain to be clearly specified. In this work, they will be used to denote the following concepts:

Definition 1.2. A *Realtime Interactive System* (RIS) is "an interactive system with multiple timings partly subject to enhanced real-time timing conditions (stronger than soft real-time) due to high reactivity requirements" (Latoschik, 2015).

Definition 1.3. An *Intelligent Realtime Interactive System* (IRIS) is a RIS that involves software assets which facilitate their utilization in intelligent ways.

A further definition is required to specify the different facets that are addressed by the simulation modules that a RIS is composed of:

Definition 1.4. A *simulation aspect*, or an *aspect* for short, is a subset of the simulation state that is associated with a single facet of the simulation.

Such aspects can overlap. For example, the position of an object is part of both the visual as well as the physical aspect of the simulation. Moreover, an aspect can concern a subset of the simulation state, i.e. multiple properties of one object or of a group of such. Hence, it is suitable to refer to, e.g., the physical nature of objects.

Regarding reusability, the field of IRISs and their development is particularly challenging since multiple aspects complicate the reuse of such software:

1. The diversity and complexity of utilized software modules requires to convene developers who are specialists in most different areas. Due to the overlap of simulation aspects addressed by different developers, a combination (and therefore reuse) of developed modules is rendered difficult.

2. The skills of these developers may be highly diverse, depending on their particular profession. Thus, specialized concepts used by one group of developers may be completely unknown to others.

3. The real-time nature of a VE often favors close coupling of involved software modules regarding both data structures and execution schemes, which contradicts the concept of reusability.

4. The applied Artificial Intelligence (AI) methods, the update rates of which do commonly not comply with realtime requirements, require access to a potentially all-encompassing representation of the application state, and thus impede modularity.

Interactive 3D computer games are one popular example of RISs, in the context of which the demand for graphically rich representation, physical simulation of the environment, animation of virtual avatars, and many other features arises. Such applications suffer from the fact that the utilized simulation components often are developed for a particular hardware platform, which complicates both keeping the application compatible to updated hardware resources as well as making the most of that hardware. Hence, the following typical example for the re-use case 1, which is concerned with partial reuse of a RIS, will recurrently be investigated throughout this work:

Use Case 1.1. In an existing RIS application, a platform-dependent 3D graphics renderer is assumed to be replaced with one that is more up to date and that allows the application in question to be used on a different hardware platform.

This use case is affected by at least three of the above-mentioned aspects: the highly optimized nature of a 3D rendering module requires specialized data structures that have to be connected to different data structures, used by other modules that address the same aspects (1). In the use case, the previous renderer conceivably uses an octree, whereas the new module uses a scene graph data structure. An application developer may be unfamiliar with both, wherefore the lack of a simple interface complicates the replacement process (2). Finally, the execution scheme of the rendering module is most likely coupled to those of the modules that update the simulation state (3).

Recently, new types of devices are becoming available to the public that previously were reserved for research groups (e.g., the *Oculus Rift* or Razer's *Hydra* and *Stem*). With these, new ways of human-computer interaction are introduced, which are not supported by existing applications. Similarly, mixed reality applications benefit from the utilization of most up to date sensors, which are required to correctly integrate real content into the virtual world (and vice versa). A current example is given by the field of smart home applications, which need to monitor the resident's state and desires. This area provides the second running example, relating to the above-mentioned re-use case 2, in which existing systems need to be extended by further modules:

Use Case 1.2. A heart-rate monitor module, the data of which shall be utilized to reinforce the system's knowledge about the user's physical condition, is said to be integrated into an existing IRIS application.

This use case is impeded by the complex data provided by the module (2) and the interference with other modules' data structures to integrate the obtained data (3). Moreover, other modules have to become aware of the added data without being modified themselves (4).

Some applications utilize online access to integrate information located on the Internet or special servers. The latter approach is often adopted by IRIS applications that employ knowledge bases from the Semantic Web. Examples for such applications are virtual environments that are inhabited by Intelligent Virtual Agents (IVAs), which serve as tour guides, cooperative partners in construction scenarios, etc. In such systems, interaction with agents tends to be multimodal, mostly involving speech and gesture interfaces. Given a sufficient understanding of the VE, these interfaces allow for natural interaction between users and agents. But even in the absence of such embodied agents, elements could intelligently react to inputs, e.g., by knowing which other elements they can be combined with. This type of RISs serves as a third example, which will be used throughout this work to address the utilization of integrated of semantics:

Use Case 1.3. An AI rule engine, a semantic reasoner, and an action planning module are assumed to cooperate in order to enable an IRIS to react to state updates in an intelligent way.

In this situation, especially the access to an all-encompassing representation of the simulation state is required (4), since it is unpredictable which information is required by the AI modules. Furthermore, the execution schemes of such modules have to be decoupled from others, since lengthy calculation would block realtime features of the application (3). Finally, the data that is accessed by the modules cannot be highly specialized but has to be processable by AI methods (2).

1.3 Problem Statement

Whereas in the beginning of RIS and VR research it was justifiable to create custom-made solutions for the set of specialized devices located in a single research lab, current and future RIS software requires to be flexibly adjustable to the multitude of constantly emerging devices and areas of application. This way, non-RIS experts will be able utilize the new technology in various settings, e.g., in smart homes, experiments in psychological research, or in the context of computer games.

Although the set of possible RIS applications are highly diverse, most of them share subsets of the specialized software modules they use. But, as discussed before, high performance requirements and use of specialized devices often result in close coupling of these modules, thereby hindering reuse. Furthermore, the recently increasing desire to create RISs and VEs that intelligently react to user input requires information about the elements involved in the interaction. All in all, the central problem is the existing lack of a uniform approach to integrate simulation modules and AI methods into IRISs, eventually resulting in inflexible, custom-made solutions.

Thus, simulation module developers as well as IRIS application developers face the problem that reusing parts of existing IRISs is highly complicated. In consequence, despite common functionality, applications often are reimplemented when a module has to be added, removed, or exchanged.

1.4 Objectives

This work will create a methodology that allows to provide reusable elements for intelligent realtime interactive systems. The presented approach is concerned with decoupling the involved elements:

O1. **Decoupling Simulation Modules**: The very first step towards reusable intelligent realtime interactive systems is to decouple the elements that the underlying software is made of. Since there are no clearly defined boundaries to a simulation module, a flexible representation is required.

O2. **Decoupling Application Content**: Given decoupled simulation modules, the content of an eventual application has to be decoupled from those modules. In order to replace a module the content must not depend on the specific implementation of a module but (at most) on the simulation features that it provides.

O3. **Decoupling Application Logic**: Assuming that neither the simulation basis nor the static content directly depend on their specific composition, the logic that defines a specific application should not rely on both (and vice versa).

It is important to mention that the elements to be decoupled are not meant to be developed from scratch. Especially the above-mentioned simulation modules are assumed to exist in advance.

In this context, the terms *software component* and *component model* as defined by Councill and Heineman (2001) are appropriate:

- "A *software component* is a software element that conforms to a component model and can be independently deployed and composed without modification according to a composition standard.

- A *component model* defines specific interaction and composition standards. A *component model implementation* is the dedicated set of executable software elements required to support the execution of components that conform to the model."

(Councill & Heineman, 2001, p. 7)

With regard to these terms, a subgoal of this work is to create a component model that allows to turn preexisting simulation modules into *simulation components* that can easily be reused. Obviously, this does not exclude the implementation of new modules either, but— living up to the idea of reuse—decoupling and reusing existing elements is considered even more desirable.

As mentioned before, an IRIS requires a flexible representation of the application state that is accessible by AI methods. Since, depending on the purpose of the implemented system, every element of the architecture as well as every element of the simulation could potentially be relevant for AI modules, the approach builds upon an extensible Knowledge Representation Layer (KRL). The contents of this layer reflect the above-mentioned decoupled simulation modules, application content, and application logic. Thereby, a generic interface for symbolic AI methods is created.

In this way, the developed methods address the detected lack of a uniform way to couple simulation modules and AI methods. The contribution of this work is twofold:

1. An approach to semantically augment the essential elements of an IRIS application is proposed. It builds on a deeply integrated, extensible KRL that provides the foundation for integrating symbolic AI methods. By means of the established set of symbolic identifiers a concise, human-readable interface, which facilitates access to different simulation aspects, is created. This interface constitutes the basis for decoupling simulation modules and application content, thereby fostering extensibility, maintainability, and understandability of an application.

2. A component model for intelligent realtime interactive systems is developed. It involves an interface that builds on the above-mentioned KRL, providing uniform, semantic-type based access to the simulation state. The latter is represented in a centralized way, whereby overlapping simulation aspects are addressed. Moreover, the adoption of a message-based architecture allows to decouple simulation loops of applied modules and thus to enable concurrent calculations and differing update rates (realtime-related issues are not addressed in this work, though). This way, simulation modules are turned into black-box components, which can easily be added, removed, and replaced. By combining multiple of such components, modular applications are created, which can easily be extended, e.g., by input device handling, interaction modules, behavior simulation, and many more.

In this way, a novel approach to the development of reusable IRIS applications is pursued. It allows to face upcoming developments in RIS-related areas, like virtual, mixed, and augmented reality, intelligent virtual environments, multimodal interaction, and many more.

1.5 Structure

The main part of this work is divided into six chapters: Chapter 2 enlarges upon related work in the related areas of research. For this purpose, section 2.2 surveys related aspects in the area of software engineering and especially software reuse. Section 2.3 reviews aspects of prominent VR frameworks, putting special focus on Intelligent Virtual Environment (IVE) frameworks.

Content	Publication
The world interface that is implemented in the Simulator X framework, acting as a central registry and providing symbol-based access to the architecture elements (cf. sections 4.3.3 and 5.2.8)	Wiebusch, Latoschik, and Tramberend (2010)
First ideas to decouple architecture elements of RIS applications by incorporating an ontology, influencing sections on the reusable knowledge representation model (3.3), code generation (3.4.2), and entity creation (4.5.2 and 5.2.6)	Wiebusch and Latoschik (2012)
Reflections on the design decisions that were taken in the development of the Simulator X framework (cf. section 5.2)	Wiebusch, Fischbach, Latoschik, and Tramberend (2012)
The foundations of the uniform access model that is presented in section 4.3, also affecting the definitions relating to state and events (cf. section 3.2.4)	Wiebusch and Latoschik (2014)
The concept of semantic traits as introduced in section 4.2.3	Wiebusch and Latoschik (2015)
Applications that were built using the Simulator X framework (cf. section 6.3)	Fischbach et al. (2011) Fischbach, Wiebusch, Latoschik, Bruder, and Steinicke (2012b, 2012a)

Table 1.2: Publications including aspects that are presented in this work.

Afterwards, section 2.4 briefly overviews relevant forms of knowledge representation. Finally, a summary is given in section 2.5.

Extending on the observations regarding related work, chapter 3 will focus on the creation of a knowledge representation model for IRISs. In order to establish its foundations, reflections about semantics of IRIS frameworks are presented in section 3.2. Building on these, the knowledge representation model is proposed in section 3.3. By means of this model, information about architecture elements and the simulation state become accessible. Finally, its integration into an IRIS framework is discussed in section 3.4 before the chapter is summarized in section 3.5.

Chapter 4 presents different methods to increase the reusability of IRIS simulation modules. These methods include the integration of the model from the previous chapter, in order to create an KRL. This semantics based approach is presented in section 4.2. To access the KRL and the current simulation state, a uniform access model is proposed in section 4.3. In order to achieve decoupling of simulation modules, the adoption of the actor model is discussed in section 4.4. The combination of these methods leads to the component model for IRIS frameworks, which is presented in section 4.5 before the chapter is concluded in section 4.6.

Subsequently, chapter 5 presents the integration of the proposed model into the Simulator X framework. For this purpose, section 5.2 overviews the architecture of the framework. Afterwards, noteworthy features that are facilitated by the proposed models are discussed in section 5.3. Section 5.4 overviews the organization of a Simulator X application. This structure is unrelated to the proposed model, but yields aspects that facilitate reusability in an IRIS project. Use cases 1.2 and 1.3, which were mentioned above, are covered by the discussion of representative Simulator X simulation components in section 5.5.

Parts of the results presented chapters 4 and 5 have been presented on different national and international workshops and conferences (see table 1.2).

Chapter 6 discusses results that were achieved by applying the model. In section 6.2 a case study that covers use case 1.1 is presented, pointing out the applicability and benefits of the proposed approach. Moreover, section 6.3 lists the applications and contexts in which the framework was used. Section 6.4 presents results from a prestudy that was conducted to evaluate the usability of the Simulator X framework and therefore of the proposed model.

Chapter 7 concludes this thesis and provides an overview of directions for future work.

Chapter 2

Related Work

We are like dwarfs on the shoulders of giants, so that we can see more than they, and things at a greater distance, not by virtue of any sharpness of sight on our part, or any physical distinction, but because we are carried high and raised up by their giant size.

attributed to Bernard of Chartres
in *Metalogicon* by John of Salisbury (1159)

2.1 Overview

Due to the large number of involved modules, creating IRISs is a highly complex and tedious task. The implementation of each of those modules requires expert knowledge in a field that constitutes an area of research on its own. Building on the achievements in these areas, different frameworks, which are composed of multiple of these modules, have been created to ease the process and reduce the amount of expert knowledge required by an application developer.

The endeavor to develop methods that facilitate composition of highly specialized simulation modules, and thus the creation of reusable software, in the context of IRIS development and in particular of IVE development, addresses multiple areas of research:

- The field of software engineering and therein especially contributions regarding software reusability, maintainability, and extensibility are of high importance.

- Achievements in the area of development of Virtual Reality (VR) frameworks and Realtime Interactive Systems (RISs) are crucial for this work. In this context, existing frameworks for the creation of Intelligent Virtual Environments (IVEs) and related applications are of particular importance, since they pose a representative example for this kind of systems.

- Since the latter highly depend on the availability of knowledge about the simulated environment, existing methods from the field of knowledge representation pose the third aspect that is related to this work.

In order to put this work into the context of those fields, the following sections will provide an introduction to each of these. This chapter is structured corresponding to the above-mentioned three areas: software reusability, frameworks for intelligent virtual environments, and methods for knowledge representation.

2.2 Software Reusability

Reuse is the default problem-solving strategy in most human activities (Prieto-Díaz, 1993). For example, in the fields of architecture and engineering reusing artifacts and knowledge is a commonly observed approach.

Accordingly, *software reusability* has been an important topic in the area of software engineering since the rise of the so-called *software crisis*, which was envisioned to be overcome by means of *software reuse*. In this context, McIlroy (1968) proposed what has become termed *commercial off-the-shelf* or *components-off-the-shelf* (COTS): industrially produced software assets that can be reused by software developers.

Extensive overviews of the topic of software reuse were written in the past (Krueger, 1992; H. Mili et al., 1995; Kim & Stohr, 1998), shedding some light on this many-faceted area of research. The next section presents an overview of definitions that have been used in the literature and provides an introduction to related concepts.

2.2.1 Definitions

According to the *Systems and software engineering – Vocabulary* (software) reusability is defined as the "degree to which an asset can be used in more than one system, or in building other assets" (ISO/IEC/IEEE 24765, 2010, p. 307). Similarly, Kim and Stohr define software reusability as "a measure of the ease with which the resource can be reused in a new situation" (Kim & Stohr, 1998, p. 116). Clearly, the definition of software reusability depends on the definition of software reuse.

The most obvious aspect of software reuse, which mainly focuses on the reuse of program source code, is often called *code reuse*. While all definitions of software reuse include this aspect, some leave it that general (e.g., Krueger, 1992), whereas others are more specific. For example, some authors stress that not only developed components but also the tools and resources created during software development are associated with the concept of software reuse (Prieto-Díaz, 1993; Kim & Stohr, 1998). Others explicitly attribute the acquired knowledge and employed techniques to the term (Prieto-Díaz, 1989; Dusink & van Katwijk, 1995; Clements, 2001; Frakes & Kang, 2005). The creation of software that is reusable by design is part of a definition by H. Mili et al. (1995). Morisio, Ezran, and Tully (2002) emphasize that reuse is a systematic practice and add the aspects of productivity, quality, and business performance.

The latter relates to the observation by Prieto-Díaz, who states that "the problem we face in software engineering is not a lack of reuse, but a lack of widespread, systematic reuse" (Prieto-Díaz, 1993, p. 61). Thereby the fact that so-called *ad-hoc* reuse (see section 2.2.3) is not as fruitful as systematic reuse is addressed.

Related Concepts

Since 2011 the term reusability is part of the ISO/IEC 25010 (2011) standard on *Systems and software Quality Requirements and Evaluation*. In replacing the ISO/IEC 9126 (2001) *Software engineering - Product quality* standard it was added—alongside of *modularity*—as a sub-characteristic of *maintainability*. Both concepts, modularity as well as maintainability, are closely related to this work, as discussed below. Regarding these and other below-mentioned

Term	Definition	Page
asset	an item that has been designed for use in multiple contexts	25
cohesion	the manner and degree to which the tasks performed by a single software module are related to one another	57
coupling	the manner and degree of interdependence between software modules	83
extendability	the ease with which a system or component can be modified to increase its storage or functional capacity	136
flexibility	the ease with which a system or component can be modified for use in applications or environments other than those for which it was specifically designed	144
maintainability	the ease with which a software system or component can be modified to correct faults, improve performance or other attributes, or adapt to a changed environment	204
modularity	1. the degree to which a system or computer program is composed of discrete components such that a change to one component has minimal impact on other components, 2. software attributes that provide a structure of highly independent components, and 3. the extent to which a routine or module is like a black-box	223
reusability	the degree to which an asset can be used in more than one system, or in building other assets	307
understandability	the ease with which a system can be comprehended at both the system-organizational and detailed-statement levels	385

Table 2.1: Definitions of related concepts from the *Systems and software engineering – Vocabulary* standard ISO/IEC/IEEE 24765 (2010).

concepts that are related to software reusability, this work utilizes the definitions from the *IEEE Systems and software engineering – Vocabulary*, which are shown in table 2.1.

Maintainability rather is concerned with environmental changes and corrections of errors, whereas the linked concepts of *extendability* and *flexibility* are related to adapting to unforeseen environments. Both are relevant for IRISs: the ever-changing hardware setup requires to maintain the functionality of previously implemented applications. For instance, in the introductorily mentioned use case 1.1 on page 7, all parts of the adapted application (except for the replaced rendering module) are desired to remain unchanged. Consequently, maintainability is of high importance for the development of reusable RISs.

The defined goal of this work is to develop methodologies that facilitate reuse of parts of such systems in order to create new ones (cf. section 1.4), emphasizing flexibility and extendability. A common situation that exhibits the importance of these concepts is the extension of a RIS by the integration of alternative sensor modules (cf. use case 1.2). Maintaining as well as extending a complex software system require it to exhibit high *understandability*.

In the specific context of Virtual Reality (VR) applications, Allard, Lesage, and Raffin (2010) suggest the aforementioned concept of *modularity* to be a key idea to handle complexity. Regarding the definitions of modularity that are shown in table 2.1, especially the aspect of a module being of black-box nature is relevant in the context of this work: the replacement of a rendering module in use case 1.1 becomes more difficult, if internal modifications to such module are required to reuse it.

Modularity has been seen as a means to overcome the complexity of large software systems and is said to enable reusability (Haefliger, Von Krogh, & Spaeth, 2008). It led to popular software engineering approaches, like component-based software engineering and creation of software frameworks, which are discussed in section 2.2.4. As the above-mentioned definition suggests, modular program structure benefits understandability, flexibility, and reusability by fostering low *coupling* and high *cohesion*.

While the benefits of low coupling are quite obvious, this is not necessarily true for high cohesion. It is rather the absence of cohesion which exhibits the problem: if the program code that is concerned with a specific task is distributed rather than locally specified, it will be difficult to maintain the system or to reuse parts of it.

This is especially problematic in the situation of use case 1.3: if AI functionality is implemented into each object, possible side-effects tend to be incomprehensible and later modifications become extremely complex.

Coupling and Cohesion

Other researchers observed that strong coupling can lead to non-reusability (Bachmann, Kunde, Litz, & Schreiber, 2010) and that low coupling and high cohesion increases reusability (Van Vliet, 1993). Moreover, in a study of 16 open source projects, Beck and Diehl (2011) observed that the principle of low coupling and high cohesion indeed was one of the dominating principles used to modularize software systems. Colburn and Shute (2011) consider the concept of decoupling as a fundamental value for computer science in general. They argue that change is a fundamental feature of reality, wherefore close coupling is undesirable since it prohibits adaption: in order to allow systems that model parts of reality to adapt to change, their internals have to be decoupled as much as possible.

In the context of VR applications, early frameworks already emphasized decoupling (C. Shaw, Liang, Green, & Sun, 1992; C. Shaw, Green, Liang, & Sun, 1993). Yet, more recent work expresses concerns that too few attention is given to these two principles, since still special purpose data structures, e.g., scene graphs, are often utilized to capture out-of-context data (Latoschik & Tramberend, 2010).

On a related note, Bachmann et al. (2010) report on experiences in the context of developing a scientific simulation workflow system in the German Aerospace Center (DLR). They state that no all-in-one solution existed for their needs, wherefore they had to integrate multiple, partly incompatible tools. Hence, the concepts of reuse and decoupling were of high importance.

This is owed to the fact that their work environment required to connect existing software libraries and visualization tools. In this context, they found the utilization of a common data format to be beneficial, an idea that was also proposed by M. Shaw (1995) and that will be seized in later sections.

2.2.2 Benefits and Inhibitors of Software Reuse

Software reuse has regularly been mentioned as an important means to approach the problems related to the aforementioned software crisis (for example, by Boehm, 1987; Krueger, 1992; Sametinger, 1997; Ezran, Morisio, & Tully, 2002; Haefliger et al., 2008; Manhas, Vashisht, Sandhu, & Neeru, 2010). Mili et al. even state that "several decades of intensive research in software engineering and artificial intelligence left few alternatives but software reuse as the (only) realistic approach to bring about the gains of productivity and quality that the software industry needs" (H. Mili et al., 1995, p. 528).

Benefits of Software Reuse

The high interest in the topic is owed to the many benefits of software reuse reported by various researchers. For example, Sametinger (1997) mentions quality improvements and effort reduction as the main benefits of software reuse. In addition, rapid prototyping support and expertise sharing are named. Ezran et al. (2002) add business performance improvements and, in turn, higher profitability, growth, greater competitiveness, increased market share, and entry to new markets to this list.

Motivated by these incentives, software companies have carried out software reuse programs, some of which have been successful while others failed. Studies have been conducted to examine the extent of software reuse, e.g., by Bieman and Zhao (1995), Morisio et al. (2002), and Heinemann, Deissenboeck, Gleirscher, Hummel, and Irlbeck (2011). Amongst the successful reuse programs, high improvements concerning all of the above-mentioned beneficial aspects have been reported. Some examples of such results (taken from Sametinger, 1997) are:

- NEC Software Engineering Laboratory
    - *productivity*: 6.7 times higher
    - *quality*: 2.8 times higher

- Hewlett-Packard
    - *reduction in defect density*: 24% to 76%
    - *increase in productivity*: 40% to 57%

- Fujitsu
    - *projects on schedule*: increased from 20% to 70%

Sametinger (1997), Ezran et al. (2002), Mohagheghi and Conradi (2007), as well as Leach (2012) compile more results from different studies.

While such findings suggest that software reuse is a beneficial concept in general, the related problems are of higher importance for its application in the context of IRISs development, since they provide valuable insight into avoidable issues and improvable aspects.

Inhibitors of Software Reuse

Even though reuse programs and software reusability are considered highly effective in many regards, various barriers were found that complicate conducting a successful reuse program and achieving efficient reuse. Huge efforts have been made to identify inhibitors of software reuse (cf. Griss, 1993; Fichman & Kemerer, 2001; Morisio et al., 2002; Sherif & Vinze, 2003) and book chapters have been written on the topic (e.g., by Sametinger, 1997). This section provides a brief overview of different aspects obstructing the path to reuse.

Inhibitors of reuse can be divided into three categories (for similar categorizations see Sametinger (1997) or Sherif and Vinze (2003)):

- incentive-related inhibitors
    - management related
    - developers' reluctance

- organizational inhibitors
    - planning / structure
    - misconceptions

- technical inhibitors
    - conflicting methodology
    - missing technical support
    - incompatible assets

It is worth mentioning that the reasons for reuse programs to fail mostly involved disregard of not only one but multiple of these aspects. The next paragraphs describe these categories in more detail.

Incentive Related Inhibitors   Most studies have investigated inhibitors of reuse adoption in the context of commercially developed software. It was found, that the most crucial factors are incentive-related ones (Sherif & Vinze, 2003):

Multiple studies found that commitment of the management is essential for the success of a reuse program (Tracz, 1988; Morisio et al., 2002; Sherif & Vinze, 2003). For this group especially cost-benefit related aspects are important factors. Researchers found that the establishment of a reuse program can create high costs before coming to fruition, e.g., adding 30-50% (Tracz, 1995) and even up to 200% (Haefliger et al., 2008) of the initial costs. Consequently, a reuse program often is seen as an investment with no significant short-term returns (Sherif & Vinze, 2003).

Software developers, on the other hand, sometimes struggle to participate in a reuse program, too. Partly, this is due to the so-called *Not Invented Here* syndrome (Sametinger, 1997):

the externally developed components are often thought to be less fitting for the current problem than custom-made solutions. In addition, reusing external assets requires trust in their developers' abilities, especially in the case of black-box reuse (Sherif & Vinze, 2003).

In the context of this work it is assumed that both developers and management have committed themselves to the reuse program and, hence, inhibitors regarding management issues and incentives are not investigated any further. For more detailed discussions of these topics see, e.g., Sametinger (1997), Fichman and Kemerer (2001), Sherif and Vinze (2003), or Haefliger et al. (2008).

Organizational Inhibitors The second major category of inhibitors is concerned with the organization of a particular reuse program. For a reuse program to be successful, the scope in which reuse shall be applied has to be carefully planned. On a related note, McCain states that "the lack of planned accommodation of future needs and reuse in an initial software development effort contributes immensely to high software costs and low software development productivity" (McCain, 1985, p. 125). Especially the misconception that the application of Object-Oriented Programming (OOP) or similar techniques in its own is sufficient to achieve reusability was found to be related to eventual failures (see Sametinger, 1997; Morisio et al., 2002; Sherif & Vinze, 2003).

These aspects mostly escape the scope of this work, wherefore readers are directed to Sherif and Vinze (2003) who list different propositions addressing multiple aspects of this issue. Nevertheless, the possibility to adapt the developed framework to unforeseen future needs has to be taken into account during its design.

Even in a well-conceived setting further barriers to reuse may arise. For example, the search for reusable assets already creates a considerable amount of costs. In this context, Ravichandran and Rothenberger (2003) state that "search cost is inherent in reuse". Similarly, a lack of regulations on how to store and classify reusable assets was found to be an obstructive factor (Sherif & Vinze, 2003).

Discussing the modification of reusable assets H. Mili et al. (1995) claim that with poorly planned or unanticipated changes of the reused assets the productivity and quality advantages of reuse may be defeated. Also related to the modification of reused assets, Sherif and Vinze (2003) state that the absence of periodical updates to improve asset quality poses a barrier to reuse adoption. More generally, the authors suggest that the lack of supportive technology, e.g., a well-organized software repository, poses a barrier to reuse adoption.

These aspects are addressed in this work by the well-considered utilization of version control software (see section 5.6). The proposed repository structure allows to store created software modules and perform the mentioned periodical updates. At the same time, it allows different projects to link to an older version of a module, eliminating possibly negative effects of unanticipated changes. Aside from that, the utilization of a central mechanism to automatically resolve dependencies on (external) software libraries reduces the issues that arise in the context of searching and retrieving reusable assets.

Technical Inhibitors For this work, the most relevant category of inhibitors is the one concerning technical issues. According to Sherif and Vinze (2003), these revolve around building assets, the assets themselves, and the support for utilizing and maintaining them.

Building reusable assets is connected to aforementioned misconceptions and found to mainly be in conflict with traditional development methodology, since systematic reuse rather requires a mixture of traditional methodologies (Sherif & Vinze, 2003). To overcome this issue, new approaches, such as domain engineering and component-based software engineering (see section 2.2.4), have emerged.

Reusing assets first of all requires the developer to find a candidate asset. Hence, missing technical support for searching and accessing reusable assets is another reason for aversion to the adoption of reuse (Sametinger, 1997). The search for an asset is closely related to understanding the context in which it can be used. Availability of information on the usage of an asset therefore is of huge importance, as is the possibility to announce recently added assets (Sherif & Vinze, 2003). Another important fact is that the software that is found is not necessarily designed to be reused, and hence reusing it may be more expensive than reimplementing it from scratch (Sametinger, 1997).

All of these retrieval-related aspects assume that a software asset is searched for, retrieved, and afterwards integrated into the application being developed. In contrast, this work aims at semantically annotating assets, wherefore an alternative way of component retrieval can be achieved: instead of manually retrieving an asset that fits the respective situation, automatic retrieval by specifying the desired characteristics or effects of the asset can be supported.

Regarding the third barrier—support for an asset's use—Aoyama (1998) found that the aspect of interoperability between assets is a major issue. Similarly, an obstructive lack of support for the integration of assets was reported by developers (cf. Sherif & Vinze, 2003). On a related note, Garlan, Allen, and Ockerbloom (1995) mention that nearly all the problems they observed were related to assumptions about the structure of systems and the environment in which they operated.

When analyzing "the rise and fall of CORBA," Henning (2006) identifies the complexity of Application Programming Interfaces (APIs) to be the most obvious technical problem. Both aspects, problems integrating modules and problems understanding modules, were found to be amongst the most common ones encountered in reuse attempts (cf. Frakes & Fox, 1996).

The reported lack of interoperability between software assets is one of the major issues addressed by this work, since interoperability has to be maximized in order to be able to exchange software modules. Aside from interoperability, reducing the complexity of software interfaces, and thus to increase understandability, is a further pursued objective.

2.2.3 Facets of Software Reuse

There are two main forms of software reuse. These are termed *ad hoc* (or *opportunistic*) *reuse* and *planned reuse* (Kim & Stohr, 1998) the latter of which is also called *systematic reuse* (cf. Prieto-Díaz, 1993).

Ad hoc reuse denotes reuse in an incidental manner. It is often performed by applying a technique that is called *code scavenging* (Krueger, 1992), where a developer searches existing program code for reusable elements. Although being said to be less fruitful, ad hoc reuse is a very common form of software reuse. As opposed to this, systematic reuse relies on well prepared processes and standards, which are applied during the development process. According to these categories, this work aims for systematic reuse of black-box components.

Reuse Strategies

Irrespective of the form of reuse, the process of reusing assets is defined by the reuse strategy. The terms used in the literature for such strategies are (Ezran et al., 2002):

- *white-box reuse* describes the situation in which the developer has to modify an asset in order to reuse it.

- *gray-box reuse* is similar to white-box reuse, yet limiting modifications to parametrization only.

- *glass-box reuse* describes the situation where a developer is required to look at the internals of a reused asset but does not modify it.

- *black-box reuse* denotes situations in which an asset can be reused without further adoption.

Depending on the respective author, the definitions of these strategies slightly differ. For example, black-box reuse may explicitly exclude the option to inspect the asset's code and gray-box reuse can allow minor modifications instead of parametrization only (Sametinger, 1997).

While each strategy has its advantages and disadvantages, the amount of available information on the reused resources often restricts the choice of reuse strategies to be adopted. For white-, gray-, and glass-box reuse access to the source code is required. If a piece of software is available in binary form only, the developer is limited to black-box reuse. Hence, white-, gray-, and glass-box reuse are commonly found in open source projects. Similarly, commercial projects are more often limited to black-box reuse.

With black-box reuse developers have no options to adapt reused program code to their needs and the reused assets are left untouched. Therefore, their capability of being reused by other projects is maintained. Modification of such assets is thus reserved to its maintainers. This corresponds to the benefits of software reuse, which include the enhanced quality of software that was built using carefully maintained software libraries (Haefliger et al., 2008). On a related note Ravichandran and Rothenberger state that "code modification is also a key source of problems encountered during reuse" (Ravichandran & Rothenberger, 2003, p. 110). Other researchers (e.g., H. Mili et al., 1995) report similar observations.

According to Fayad and Schmidt (1997), frameworks foster modularity, reusability, extensibility, and inversion of control. The latter, however, has to be treated with care in the context of RISs, since it could introduce unexpected runtime-behavior. Nevertheless, they provide a perfect fit for the intention of reusable software. The authors moreover state that white-box frameworks "tend to produce systems that are tightly coupled to the specific details of the framework's inheritance hierarchies" (Fayad & Schmidt, 1997, p. 35). As opposed to this, black-box frameworks are said to be more difficult to develop but easier to use and extend.

Consequently, this work is concerned with developing a framework that allows to create black-box assets, which can easily be exchanged and reused. Nevertheless, access to and modification of source code is not discouraged, as long as the headline goal of decoupling is pursued.

The Software Reuse Process

According to Kim and Stohr (1998), the software reuse process can be divided into the following categories:

- Producing reusable resources
    - Identification
    - Classification

- Consuming reusable resources
    - Retrieval
    - Understanding
    - Modification
    - Integration

The authors use these categories in an eight-step model of reuse-based software development. In that model, no difference is made between internally and externally developed assets.

The first two steps are concerned with the creation of a reuse repository: first, reusable assets are (1) identified and afterwards they are (2) classified and inserted into the repository. The subsequent steps are concerned with the utilization of the created repository. Initially, the requirements for the new system have to be (3) specified. Afterwards, assets have to be (4) retrieved and their functionality has to be (5) understood. In most cases, an asset will not exactly fit the specific needs of the developer and hence has to be (6) modified. If no suitable assets could be retrieved new ones have to be (7) built. Finally, the assets are (8) integrated into the target software system.

This model corresponds to the observation by Cheng and Jeng, who state that "the major objectives of a reuse system are to classify the reusable components, to retrieve them from an existing library, and to modify the retrieved components to satisfy the query specification" (Cheng & Jeng, 1997, p. 341).

However, in this work a further step is added before an asset is inserted into the repository: the software resource has to be adapted to match the architecture of the proposed framework. In this way, the efforts that arise during the modification step can be minimized. This is a reasonable approach, since an asset is usually inserted only once, but reused multiple times.

2.2.4 Reuse Techniques

There are two general principles of reuse: *composition* of assets and *generation* of assets (Biggerstaff & Richter, 1989).

Composition-based techniques depend on repositories of reusable software modules, e.g., software libraries, that can be reused either with or without modification. With compositional reuse the form of the reused asset usually ranges from single lines of code that are copied to arbitrarily sized software modules.

Generative techniques do not directly rely on the reuse of program code or binaries but rather an abstraction thereof. Examples for generative techniques are application generators, language-based generators, and transformation systems (Sametinger, 1997).

Composition Techniques

Composition-based techniques rely on repositories of reusable software modules. Since the concept of composition is—by definition—related to the concept of modularity (see section 2.2.1), early approaches naturally relied on modular programming (Parnas, 1972) and function libraries.

Language Level Aspects A key aspect of the modular programming paradigm is the *separation of concerns*, a term introduced by Dijkstra (1982). A module should be dedicated to a single concern of the program and have as few interconnections with other modules as possible. In this sense, each module should be a logically independent part of a software system. This is especially difficult in the context of RIS development due to overlapping simulation aspects, as indicated in the first chapter of this work.

Extending the modular programming paradigm, Object-Oriented Programming (OOP) adds the concept of information hiding by means of its encapsulation features, hence enforcing modularity. Additional concepts like inheritance and polymorphism foster modularity of created programs. Armstrong (2006) presents an overview of the fundamental concepts of OOP.

However, OOP techniques are widely considered as an enabling technology for creating interchangeable and reusable software components (Meyer, 1987; H. Mili et al., 1995; Sherif & Vinze, 2003) and with the definition of *design patterns* (Gamma, Helm, Johnson, & Vlissides, 1994) a classification of reusable object-oriented elements emerged.

Despite all positive aspects and its wide use, OOP techniques also have been criticized (e.g., by Cardelli, 1996). In an investigation of 19 commercial products Potok, Vouk, and Rindos (1999) found no improvement of productivity in software development teams that were using OOP techniques.

OOP languages encourage the developer to make excessive use of the features of inheritance and information hiding. While this strategy is beneficial in some cases, it exhibits some issues regarding RIS development: the enforced tree-like structures often do not match the many-faceted nature of the simulated objects. In order to allow to choose composition over inheritance, the concepts of mixin-based inheritance (Bracha & Cook, 1990) and traits (Ducasse, Nierstrasz, Schärli, Wuyts, & Black, 2006) were introduced.

Similarly, the imposed fixed type hierarchies do not account for the dynamic nature of an IRIS. Considering use case 1.3 from page 8, the type of a represented entity may change according to its composition, as may the actions that it can be involved in. For instance, a previously inoperative object might be attached to a power source and thereby fundamentally change its behavior.

Further negative aspects of OOP in terms of reusability for VR frameworks will be analyzed in section 4.1.

Component-Based Software Engineering (CBSE) Building upon OOP techniques, CBSE has become the most commonly applied development model in the context of software reuse. The idea of CBSE has been proposed by McIlroy (1968): "My thesis is that the software industry is weakly founded, in part because of the absence of a software components subindustry."

According to Aoyama (1998), CBSE fosters the avoidance of monolithic design. Linking CBSE with "the dawn of a new age of software development", he distinguishes between conventional software reuse (software architecture, design patterns, and frameworks) and CBSE as follows:

1. "Plug & Play: Component should be able to plug and play with other components and/or frameworks so that component can be composed at run-time without compilation.

2. Interface-centric: Component should separate the interface from the implementation and hide the implementation details so that they can be composed without knowing their implementation.

3. Architecture-centric: Components are designed on a pre-defined architecture so that they can interoperate with other components and/or frameworks.

4. Standardization: Component interface should be standardized so that they can be manufactured by multiple vendors and widely reused across the corporations.

5. Distribution through Market: Components can be acquired and improved through competition market, and provide incentives to the vendors."

Aoyama (1998, p. 2)

These aspects provide guidelines for the software framework that is developed in the context of this work. While the fifth item (distribution through market) is not really applicable for this thesis, the first four aspects definitely are.

Clements (2001) suggests to use precisely defined software interfaces in order to overcome the problem of mislead assumptions regarding the intended way of compositing particular components. Since this is difficult to achieve for complex components, especially if these are not built by one single software firm, he proposes a layered architecture. He concludes his work with a list of possible pitfalls that can arise with CBSE, mainly addressing the incompatibility of different off-the-shelf components, causing problems when they have to be exchanged for any reason.

These findings are addressed by the framework that is developed in this work in that it uses a layered architecture on multiple levels. The effects of possible incompatibility between components is addressed by decoupling them by means of an ontology as well as by message-based interfaces.

When analyzing issues in the context of CBSE, Nierstrasz, Gibbs, and Tsichritzis (1992) state that a mechanism that supports the organization of component retrieval is a mandatory feature. Similarly, they observe that one of the issues with CBSE is that there is too few emphasis on the actual composition of an application. Finally, they note that "the design of reusable frameworks is an iterative, evolutionary process, so it is necessary to manage software and software information in such a way that designs and implementations can evolve gracefully" (Nierstrasz et al., 1992, p. 160).

As mentioned before, the careful design of a version controlled repository for software modules is applied to address these issues. Furthermore, an ontology that contains knowledge about resources supports the description and retrieval of assets is integrated.

Generative Techniques

As opposed to composition techniques, generative techniques do not use existing components but rather build on encoded domain knowledge, which can be parametrized and used to generate an application or parts of it (for a categorization of generative techniques see Krueger (1992) and H. Mili et al. (1995)).

Frakes and Kang summarize the concept of generative methods as follows: "New systems in the domain are created by writing specifications for them in a domain specific specification language. The generator then translates the specification into code for the new system in a target language. The generation process can be completely automated, or may require manual intervention" (Frakes & Kang, 2005, p. 533).

In this regard, a plethora of systems has been developed and used. Some examples are the interface definition language (IDL) of CORBA (Vinoski, 1997), the transformation from the Unified Modeling Language (UML) to programming languages (e.g., to Java, see Nickel, Niere, & Zündorf, 2000), or generation of program code from Resource Description Framework (RDF) knowledge bases (Völkel & Sure, 2005). In addition, the field of conceptual modeling (cf. Pellens, 2007) and the concept of visual programming can be counted among this category. In the context of RISs and more specifically game engines the latter is, for example, implemented by the *Kismet* system of the Unreal Engine 3, the *Blueprint* system of the Unreal Engine 4 (Epic Games, 2015), and the *FlowGraph* system of the CryEngine 2 and 3 (Crytek, 2015).

According to Krueger the utilization of a generative approach is appropriate when

- "many similar software systems are written,

- one software system is modified or rewritten many times during its life-time, or

- many prototypes are necessary to converge on a usable product."

Krueger (1992, p. 156)

Hence, implementing a generative approach is highly reasonable in the context of this work: the created systems are frequently modified during their life-time, which is one of the reasons why they become unusable. Furthermore—since especially systems in the academic area are addressed—development heavily depends on the implementation of many research prototypes. The first item, however, does only apply in part, as the created systems are not similar but highly diverse. Nevertheless, the modules they comprise tend to be similar, as indicated by use case 1.1. Whereas the underlying application may have arbitrary content, almost all of the features of the rendering module that shall be exchanged are shared by other 3D rendering modules. Consequently, at least the interfaces between them are a subject to a generative approach.

Domain Engineering

Instead of focusing on the implementation of single assets, domain engineering aims at capturing the essentials of a whole application domain. This way, software reuse is highly facilitated, since the initial analysis of the domain allows for well-informed implementation of reusable components. Rugaber (2000) provides an extensive overview of the use of domain knowledge in program understanding.

The concept of domain engineering is motivated by an observation by Sherif and Vinze, who state that "the creation of reusable assets is basically a question of finding the commonalties that exist between systems in a specific domain. This depends on the availability of domain knowledge (detailed information about the entities and relationships between them) and the technical experience of staff to analyze and design solutions for a window of applications rather than just one" (Sherif & Vinze, 2003, p. 167). Furthermore, it accounts for the finding that most software is not completely new but instead a variant of a system that existed before (Frakes & Kang, 2005).

Domain engineering consists of three main phases: *domain analysis*, *domain design*, and *domain implementation*. The first phase aims at the creation of a domain model that contains vocabulary, concepts, as well as varying and consistent features of that domain. According to H. Mili et al., "domain models should identify: 1) the entities and operations on those entities that are common to the application domain, 2) relationships and constraints between the entities, and 3) "retrieval cues", i.e. properties of objects that are likely to be used by developers in the process of searching for reusable components" (H. Mili et al., 1995, p. 5). In order to provide a well-founded basis, existing documents, knowledge, and systems are reviewed.

The thus created domain model is used in the subsequent domain design phase. In this phase the gathered concepts are transformed into architectural patterns that can be used to address problems that are common in the domain. Using these patterns facilitates the creation of systems for the addressed domain. In the third phase, tools and the software that finally allows for the creation of a software in the specific domain are implemented.

For all of these aspects the integration of semantic annotations, as proposed in this work, is highly beneficial. This way, the results of the domain engineering process become available to the application at runtime. This is addressed by the integration of a knowledge layer that encourages developers to model the contents of the respective domain before an actual application is developed (see chapter 3). In this way, developers of a specialized software module can provide their knowledge about the domain together with the module to its users. Thereby, non-experts can benefit from the knowledge of experts more easily.

Use case 1.3 provides an example for such advantages, in which a module that is capable of interpreting data from different sensors could include rules that prescribe the implications of certain readings. For instance, the observation of an overly high heart rate in a situation that was rated 'frightening' by a different module can result in the conclusion that the user is in an anxious state. An application developer might not be aware of the details and relationships between these observations, but will still be capable to interpret the user's state and make the application react appropriately.

2.2.5 Measuring Reusability

In order to evaluate the reusability of a software framework and express results in a comparable way a standardized approach has to be applied. Commonly, reusability of software is measured by means of an appropriate metric that is applied to program code. Multiple metrics have been proposed to measure maintainability and reusability of software components (Frakes & Terry, 1996). Yet, these metrics are not directly applicable in the context of this work, since their main intent is to measure the reusability of existing software modules, whereas this work aims at providing a framework to combine such modules.

However, the measures that are applied can be used as guidelines for the conceptual design of the framework. In this context, Cardino, Baruchelli, and Valerio (1997) provide a list of criteria for framework reusability. Each of them is associated with one of the four high-level factors presented in the context of the *REBOOT* approach (Sindre, Conradi, & Karlsson, 1995), namely *portability*, *adaptability*, *understandability*, and *confidence*, which affect the reusability of a framework.

Also based on the *REBOOT* approach, Washizaki, Yamamoto, and Fukazawa (2003) provide five metrics to measure *existence of meta information*, *observability*, *customizability*, and *external dependencies*. The metrics are implemented and tested to evaluate Java Beans components. Moreover, a metric is provided that combines the results of the previous five. These metrics are found to be able to effectively identify black-box components with high reusability.

More recently, Hristov, Hummel, Huq, and Janjic (2012) composed a list of eight core elements of reusability, which contains *availability*, *documentation*, *complexity*, *quality*, *maintainability*, *adaptability*, *reuse*, and *price*. Moreover, they indicate qualitative and quantitative (mostly Lines of Code-based) metrics for each of these elements. On a related note, but not directly concerned with measuring reusability, Riaz, Mendes, and Tempero (2009) present a survey on the literature of software maintainability prediction and metrics.

In conclusion, the commonly applied measures to evaluate the reusability of software cannot be applied to the approaches proposed in this work without modification. Nevertheless, they constitute guidelines for design decisions to be taken: A framework should foster low coupling and high cohesion (Gui & Scott, 2006), facilitate customizability of components at a rational level (Washizaki et al., 2003), as well as provide support for searching for components, reduce the complexity of using them, and ease upgrading to newer versions (Hristov et al., 2012). It furthermore should be portable (i.e. platform-independent), modular, well-documented, and mature (Cardino et al., 1997). Different consequences for the designed component model, as well as the implementation and perception of the created framework will be discussed in later chapters.

2.2.6 Intermediate Conclusion

Previous sections indicated that software reuse can be highly beneficial, but achieving reusability is all but an easy task. It is of high importance that components are originally designed to be reused (McCain, 1985; Sametinger, 1997). In this context, the abstraction level of reusable components is required to rise, to considerably improve productivity (Sametinger, 1997).

The stakeholders at some companies, surveyed by Sherif and Vinze (2003), believed that a layered architecture that would be sufficiently transportable to be applied to different situations is a critical success factor. In such settings, "perfect retrieval and effortless adaption are only possible if the relation between specifications and implementations has been completely formalized" (H. Mili et al., 1995, p. 558).

Seeing the huge amounts of research and possible benefits related to software reuse, one could think that most of the problems regarding software reuse have been solved. However, it was observed that reuse in software development often still is ad hoc, whereas inter-project 'as-is' reuse was found to be rare (Fichman & Kemerer, 2001). More recent publications state that this still is true in the area of VE development (e.g., Wingrave and LaViola (2010) and Latoschik and Tramberend (2010)).

All in all, the implications for this work can be summarized with the words of Sherif and Vinze: "establishing a systematic reuse program requires an implementation strategy that identifies opportunities for reuse, analyzes domains, builds architectural structures, and develops built for reuse assets" (Sherif & Vinze, 2003, p. 160).

Reviewing different categories of inhibitors that have been found by other research, especially the observation that applying OOP techniques is not sufficient, affects this work. Instead of implementing another object-oriented framework, an approach that chooses composition over inheritance and extends beyond classical type hierarchies by the integration of semantics is taken. Besides such low-level decisions, a component-based approach is adopted, since it was reported to be beneficial for systematic software reuse. Although this work is not explicitly concerned with domain engineering, the means to integrate semantics enables users of a developed framework to make use of this concept more easily. In addition to the adoption of a component-based perspective, a generative approach is taken: encouraged by the mentioned appropriateness of such concept (cf. section 2.2.4), formalized knowledge about the system, which is provided by both the developed framework and associated components, is transformed into program code.

Regarding the creation, classification, and retrieval of reusable components (cf. section 2.2.3) a version controlled software repository is proposed. Although not fully implemented in the context of this work, the above-mentioned formalized knowledge about the system can be used support automatic component retrieval. According to the review of reusability measures, modular structure, low coupling and high cohesion, as well as reducing complexity of configuring and using components are the major goals regarding framework design.

2.3 Intelligent Realtime Interactive Systems

Having investigated the topic of reusability, this section surveys related work in the area of RIS and IRIS development. In doing so, special focus is put on VR and IVE frameworks, which serve as representative examples for those fields.

As stressed in the introduction of this work, the development of such systems is complicated by multiple aspects. Besides realtime constraints, the demand for interactivity, and utilization of most diverse hardware devices, IVEs additionally require the integration of AI-methods and appropriate forms of knowledge representation.

The term *Intelligent Virtual Environment* (IVE) was introduced by Luck and Aylett to denote the

> "combination of intelligent techniques and tools, embodied in autonomous creatures and agents, together with effective means for their graphical representation and interaction of various kinds [...]."
>
> Luck and Aylett (2000, p. 4)

In their publication, the authors put a special focus on issues that arise in the context of the integration of autonomous virtual agents in IVEs. Nevertheless, they also address the requirement of specifying knowledge about the virtual environment itself. In this context, they mention that the development of IVEs requires the incorporation of explicit knowledge representation facilities.

Although the concept of intelligent virtual agents does build upon the representation of their environment, most research has focused on the realistic simulation of the virtual agents' behavior. Environmental knowledge has largely been hardcoded or been achieved by means of annotating entities of the VE with semantic symbols. This works for a single application, but does not foster reusability. Thus, there are still few approaches regarding the systematic—and hence reusable—integration of knowledge facilities that reflect the simulation state, today.

One year after the introduction of the term IVE, Aylett and Cavazza (2001) provided an overview of the state-of-the-art in the area. As indicated by the covered topics, research was still mostly concerned with the simulation of virtual agent behavior.

Orkin (2004) discusses the symbolic representation of game world state for real-time planning in games. In the publication he overviews the workflow with designers, emphasizing the benefits of decoupled actions and goals. He reports about the integration of symbolic representations in the context of two games to enable action planning.

The lack of reusability regarding virtual objects is addressed by Otto (2005b), who introduces the term *Semantic Virtual Environment* (SVE). He suggests an RDF[2]-based approach (cf. section 2.4.2) to externalize knowledge and thus facilitate reuse of virtual entities. A similar issue is addressed by Gutierrez, Vexo, and Thalmann (2005). They state that semantics could be used at every stage of VE implementation, starting with content modeling. Yet, they focus on the representation of semantics at runtime, particularly regarding geometric information.

The *Virtual Reality – With Intuitive Specifications Enabled* (VR-WISE) approach (see, e.g., De Troyer, Kleinermann, Pellens, & Bille, 2007) puts special focus on semantic modeling of virtual environments. It is especially concerned with the creation and design of semantically annotated content of VEs as well as the specification of possible behaviors. The approach includes an ontology (cf. section 2.4.2) to store semantic concepts and relations. In a three step process the content of the ontology is specified, mapped to implementation primitives, and transformed into a VE application.

The benefits of semantics in games and simulations is also evaluated by Tutenel, Bidarra, Smelik, and Kraker (2008). The authors overview different aspects of semantics in the design phase as well as at runtime by surveying related work. In their conclusion, they call for a generic semantic specification layer:

> "An important challenge here, however, is the development of a generic specification layer for sharing the appropriate semantic data with all its potential client modules (e.g., AI, animation, rendering, physics, etc.). Among other problems, this will likely collide with many current practices, including the use of own ad hoc data and hard-coded scripts for expressing object behavior, features, and so on; however, as we noticed in Section 5, several research examples have proven that the use of semantic information can definitely bring about a considerable enrichment in many of these fields."

Tutenel et al. (2008, pp. 31–32)

The creation of such a layer is one of the main aspects that are addressed in this work. In this way, the results from the VR-WISE modeling approach can be made available to all other simulation modules, allowing for more effective utilization of the integrated semantics. In chapter 3 the theoretical basis of this approach is established, while chapter 5 discusses the details of the respective implementation.

---

[2] Resource Description Framework, Manola and Miller (2004)

2.3.1 Aspects of VE Development

As observed by multiple researchers (e.g, Coninx, De Troyer, Raymaekers, & Kleinermann, 2006) the development of VE applications is a highly complex task. This is owed to the fact that multiple modules, which put high demands on the utilized hardware, interact with each other. Wingrave and LaViola (2010) as well as Taylor et al. (2010) provide highly valuable insight on the issues that exist with the design and implementation of virtual environments. More particularly, Wingrave and LaViola (2010) identify a total of 67 issues related to the topic, which they categorize into eleven themes. Among these are issues regarding reuse of assets, the need for real-time operation, and the complexity of the overall topic. For example, they observe that, "despite community efforts to standardize and build better tools, it remains easier to build than to reuse, and models are not widespread in use" (Wingrave & LaViola, 2010, p. 182). Furthermore, they find that the set of tools used by one community of practitioners separates it from other communities using other tools, due to incompatibilities and the impossibility of sharing implementations.

As opposed to this approach, Taylor et al. (2010) report on the experiences gained in 20 years of VE development and provide 13 so-called *nuggets*[3] of related knowledge. Among others, their experiences include that a framework has to be easily understandable and support its user to achieve goals in different spaces (e.g., different coordinate systems). In this work, a uniform access model as well as an automatic type conversion mechanism are proposed, which allow for answering these desires. The authors also state that more information regarding the simulated objects than only geometry data may be desirable. This is in line with this work's intention to add semantic information to arbitrary elements of a VE.

Closely Coupled Simulation Modules

The above-mentioned findings often lead to close coupling of simulation modules. There is no single root cause for this, but rather a set of interdependent aspects, which largely address the performance of the implemented application. Since a VE application aims at high immersion, it is inherently required to be interactive. The associated requirement for high responsiveness necessitates highly optimized implementations (Wingrave & LaViola, 2010).

In order to make the most of current multi-core architectures, required computations are performed concurrently. Although single threads of computation are usually decoupled from each other, the access to shared data and the utilization of computed results requires communication with other parts of an application. This possibly results in an incomprehensible control flow, since synchronization mechanisms have to be applied to prohibit concurrent modifications (Lee, 2006). The opaque nature of dependencies between the different applied mechanisms complicates grasping a program's internals—and thus hinders reusability.

Regarding a single simulation module, the required real-time operations result in the implementation of highly optimized data structures. To retain the gained performance advantages, data duplication is undesirable and should be avoided. This, in turn, means that one simulation module has to access data that is associated with another module. In order to reduce this kind of coupling, VE frameworks often provide a centralized shared memory

---

[3] The authors define nuggets as "brief insights from current and past designers, describing features they found useful or describing hazards to be avoided" (Taylor et al., 2010, p. 163).

representation of the simulation state. Either way, a simulation module in such frameworks is coupled to the content of another module or to global data structures.

In use case 1.1 this would complicate the replacement of a rendering module: since synchronization mechanisms are required to prevent issues arising from concurrent access to shared data, the newly inserted module has to be adapted to each point of shared access. This is impeded even more, if the shared data structures do not match the module's internal representation, e.g., if one renderer employs a scene graph, whereas the other one conceivably implements an octree.

One approach to overcome this issue is to apply the actor model proposed by Hewitt, Bishop, and Steiger (1973). An implementation is presented by Fröhlich and Latoschik (2008), whose work will be discussed in section 2.3.4.

Involved personnel

Despite the problem of closely coupled simulation modules, the groups of developers involved in the process of creating a VE application as well as their knowledge and expertise are highly diverse. The developers can be broadly categorized into three groups (Ponder, 2004):

- *Component Framework Developers*, who develop the framework that provides the basis for composing an application from several components.

- *Component Developers* (in the sense of simulation modules or components), who are experts in the simulation module's domain.

- *Application developers*, who eventually develop an application using the work of the aforementioned groups. Members of this group often are not VR-experts (cf. Kleinermann et al., 2005).

In the context of IVE development, the group of knowledge engineers is joined to the above-mentioned ones. These are specially concerned with the computational representation of knowledge. More specifically, their task is to design and maintain the knowledge bases that underly an eventual IVE application.

This categorization does by no means match the previously observed close coupling of simulation modules but rather represents the desirable situation. Ideally, the above-mentioned categorization can be taken as a layered model in which the persons in one layer only access results from the previous layer.

Consequently, a framework that aims for reusability has to account for this structure. In the end this means that not only software assets, but also the work of persons who are concerned with their implementation has to be decoupled.

2.3.2 VR Frameworks

As a matter of fact, there currently is no widely accepted standard for the integration of simulation modules into VR applications. Consequently, multiple research frameworks were implemented over the last decades (see table 2.2 for some prominent examples). Few of these were (re-)used by others than the research group they were developed by. In the field of IRIS research, this does apply even more: due to highly application specific content almost every IVE application is custom-made. Of course, preexisting simulation modules are reused, but after their integration further modification or replacement is not intended. Consequently, results are based on custom-made solutions, wherefore their replication is virtually impossible.

This situation is partly owed to the fact that the field of intelligent virtual environments is situated in between multiple others. For example, in most cases an IVE involves computer graphics, which is a highly active field of research in its own. Similarly, other aspects that are related to the simulation of virtual environments, e.g., physics simulation or 3D sound rendering, require highly elaborate computations. All of these are unrelated to the field of artificial intelligence, wherefore the links that are necessary to create the required knowledge representation have to be established manually. As a result, intelligent behavior in IVEs is mostly restricted to a single aspect, for example, the simulation of a virtual agent and its knowledge, representation and utilization of knowledge about the content of the virtual environment, or knowledge about physical processes that take place in the virtual environment. For use case 1.3 this means that the combination of a reasoning mechanism that infers knowledge regarding specific sensor information with a rule engine that processes rules that concern the laws of physics is impeded by shortage of shared, semantically annotated information.

The hence existing lack of a common ground hinders the possibility of interoperability of developed applications. In order to create such common ground, the next section surveys architectures of prominent frameworks. In addition to the frameworks that were developed in the academic area, two game engines that recently gained attention in the context of VR development are reviewed.

Common Architectures

There is no commonly accepted categorization of VR frameworks, which partly is due to the fact that the implemented features cannot be clearly distinguished. In most cases a framework mixes in multiple architecture concepts. For example, graph-based architectures often are combined with event systems, which allow for communication between simulation modules without obeying the graph structure. The examination of frameworks and reviews by others revealed the categories of VE framework architecture concepts described below. Table 2.2 provides an overview of the properties of some prominent VR research frameworks.

Micro-kernel based: Micro-kernel based architectures, e.g., VR Juggler (Bierbaum et al., 2001), provide a plugin system that enables the registration of simulation modules. The kernel orchestrates these modules, which have to implement certain interfaces. Accordingly, the fixed execution schemes are imposed upon developers.

As opposed to other architecture types, no specific form of state representation is enforced by micro-kernel architectures. While this leaves the developer the freedom to decide on the best form of representation, it also potentially reduces reusability of such application, since each application defines its own software interfaces.

Component-based: Component-based architectures, such as NPSNET-V (Kapolka, Mc-Gregor, & Capps, 2002) and VHD++ (Ponder, Papagiannakis, Molet, Magnenat-Thalmann, & Thalmann, 2003), depend on the features provided by the object-oriented programming

Name	MK	DG	MB	CB	ES	EM	IS	Publication
MR Toolkit			x					C. Shaw, Green, Liang, and Sun (1993)
DIVE			x	(x)	x	x		Carlsson and Hagsand (1993), Frécon (2004)
VR Juggler	x							Bierbaum et al. (2001), Allard, Gouranton, Lecointre, Melin, and Raffin (2002)
I4D			x	x	x			Geiger, Paelke, Reimann, and Rosenbach (2000)
NPSNET-V				x	x	x		Kapolka, McGregor, and Capps (2002)
VHD++			x	x	x			Ponder, Papagiannakis, Molet, Magnenat-Thalmann, and Thalmann (2003)
FlowVR		x						Allard et al. (2004)
SCIVE		x	x	x		x	x	Latoschik, Fröhlich, and Wendler (2006), Fröhlich (2014)
AvangoNG		x						Kuck, Wind, Riege, and Bogen (2008)
instantReality		x						Behr, Bockholt, and Fellner (2011)
REVE	x				x	x	x	Anastassakis and Panayiotopoulos (2011)
MASCARET	x					x	x	Chevaillier et al. (2012)

Table 2.2: Comparison of popular existing VR research frameworks (MK = Micro-Kernel based, DG = Data Flow Graph-based, MB = Message-based, CB = Component-based, ES = Event System, EM = Entity Model, IS = Integrated support for Semantics)

paradigm. If designed thoughtfully, components are loosely coupled simulation modules that can be exchanged if they conform to the interfaces defined by the framework. In this regard, a component-based framework is very similar to the micro kernel-based architecture mentioned above. However, no predefined execution scheme is imposed upon the components but they can run in parallel or use specific configurations.

The benefits of component-based architectures especially lie in their flexibility, since they enable components to apply their own execution schemes. On the downside, such frameworks tend to impose complex interfaces on the developer of a simulation module, reducing understandability.

Graph-based: VR frameworks that adopt a graph-based architecture focus on modularization by means of single nodes, which are connected via so-called routes. The input- and output-ports of such nodes are often called fields, the values of which are propagated along the application graph. Application logic is implemented inside the nodes, which can instantly react on new data that arrives on the input field or postpone calculations to the invocation of a dedicated *evaluate* method. Some examples for systems that apply a graph-based architecture are FlowVR (Allard et al., 2004; Limet, Robert, & Turki, 2009), Avango (Tramberend, 1999), and its successor Avango NG (Kuck, Wind, Riege, & Bogen, 2008).

A graph-based architecture fosters modularity in the way that it requires parts of the application logic to be coherently implemented in graph nodes. The fact that nodes can be rearranged and thus be reused in different contexts exhibits the beneficial nature of graph-based architectures regarding decoupling. Furthermore, this kind of structure facilitates the implementation of visual programming methods (even inside the virtual environment, cf. Biermann and Wachsmuth (2003)). On the downside, application graphs tend to become incomprehensible as more nodes are added.

Message-based: Similar to the graph-based approach, message-based architectures allow to send data from one module to another. Accordingly, the propagation of field values can be implemented in the form of messages that are exchanged between simulation modules. However, as opposed to a graph-based architecture, the execution scheme of simulation modules is not necessarily defined by the order in which messages are dispatched. Moreover, simulation modules do not have to be coupled explicitly, since message broadcast and the application of a publish/subscribe model can be supported.

Representatives of the message-based architecture are DIVE (Carlsson & Hagsand, 1993), I4D (Geiger, Paelke, Reimann, & Rosenbach, 2000), and the MR Toolkit (C. Shaw et al., 1993). This kind of architecture is especially encountered in the area of distributed virtual environments, since it inherently supports client/server architectures.

The benefit of message-based communication between simulation modules lies in the inherently low coupling of the approach. A problem that arises in this context is the missing support for compile-time verification of message support. More precisely, the capability of a receiver to process a certain type of message cannot be ensured at compile-time. This is especially the case if messages are marshalled in the dispatching process. Moreover, additional mechanisms are required to specify the underlying execution scheme, wherefore this approach is often combined with a component-based one.

Event Systems: Steed (2008) observed that an event system is a highly beneficial feature. This is not exactly a type of architecture to be found in VR frameworks but rather an additional concept that is added on top of the applied architecture.

An event can be regarded as a completely independent piece of information. Implemented similar to a message-based architecture, an event system allows for communication between simulation modules, ignoring execution schemes and thus rendering coupling between event source and event destination unnecessary. Therefore, only changes to the message interface result in the requirement for global changes to the application, whereas local changes remain local. Consequently, the application of an event system fosters low coupling and high cohesion.

However, Wingrave and LaViola (2010) argue that the application of callbacks and events lacks a mechanism to organize system complexity and thus negatively affects extensibility and maintainability. Similarly, the drawbacks of message-based architectures apply.

Entity Model: A second aspect that was found beneficial is the application of an entity model (Mannuß, Hinkenjann, & Maiero, 2008; Taylor et al., 2010). As opposed to a scene graph centered representation of the objects in the VE this approach regards them as individual entities. This is in line with the observation by Latoschik and Tramberend (2010), who identified scene graphs to have negative effects on coupling and cohesion.

A related approach, which is used in recent frameworks for virtual environments (e.g., Unity 3D), is the Entity-Component-System (ECS) pattern. Under its application simulated objects are represented as *entities* that are composed of so-called *components*. Such a component contains the data that is required for multiple aspects of the simulation. This could, for example, be the position and orientation of the entity or its representation as a rigid body. These components are accessed by *systems*, which simulate certain aspects of the virtual environment. Examples for systems are physics engines and rendering modules.

The systems that operate on a particular entity are identified depending on the components it aggregates. This facilitates decoupling, since each aspect of the simulation can be treated individually. Furthermore, it enables the possibility to dynamically add and remove components—and hence functionality—at runtime.

The idea behind the ECS pattern is to reduce the impact of the strict type hierarchy that is imposed by the OOP paradigm. By composing entities by means of aggregation instead of inheritance an entity's nature is determined by its content instead of its position in the type hierarchy. As a result, modifications to its character and thus the roles it assumes in the environment are simplified.

However, the approach has some drawbacks. First, the order in which systems modify data is required to be fixed, to avoid unexpected behavior. Hence, the simulation modules are still coupled, since components introduce the concept of shared memory.

Second, a component constitutes an interface that a related simulation module has to comply with. This hinders reusability, since an independently developed simulation module still has to be adapted manually to match these interfaces. At this point, the fixed hierarchy of components and associated systems creates a further restriction: there is no way to reuse a certain component for a newly implemented system without involving the system it was originally designed for (except if that system is disabled completely), because adding and removing a certain component does implicitly associate an entity with a system. Consider the following situation: if the aforementioned rigid body component shall be reused with an optimized collision detection system, but an affected entity must not be simulated physically, some effort has to be made to create an adequate component without eliminating the possibility of reusing both the physics system and the new collision detection. This is owed to the fact that, with OOP, it is hard to retrospectively insert elements into an existing class hierarchy.

Implications

All of the identified architectures exhibit advantages and disadvantages. As already mentioned, this often results in the combination of multiple architectural concepts in a single framework. With regard to coupling a message-based architecture is beneficial, especially since it inherently supports the implementation of an event system. Furthermore, the notification mechanism that is indirectly introduced with graph-based architectures (i.e. the calculation of a new value is propagated along the graph) as well as the associated mechanism to specify the execution scheme is desirable. Consequently, an eventual architecture should support message-based communication.

As opposed to this, a component-based architecture, which allows for replacement of conceptually coherent functionality (e.g., a rendering module or a physics engine), is also desirable. A common way to represent the simulation state in such systems is the utilization of an entity model, which has been found to be superior to scene-graph data structures. It allows to overcome possibly incomprehensible application graphs and creates an understandable view on the contents of the simulation.

In order to address the identified drawbacks of the ECS pattern, the approach proposed in this work does require the programmer to explicitly specify so-called *aspects* of the simulation, which define an entity's association with a certain simulation module (cf. section 4.5). Furthermore, the problem of inserting new elements into an existing class hierarchy is addressed by means of *semantic traits* (cf. section 4.2.3).

2.3.3 Game Engines

In the last decade game engines are being more and more used in the context of VE development in order to create highly realistic VEs in different application areas (Lewis & Jacobson, 2002; Juarez, Schonenberg, & Bartneck, 2010; Lugrin et al., 2012). The two most popular of these engines are the Unity platform (Unity Technologies, 2015) and the Unreal Engine (Epic Games, 2015). Reacting to the request of developers in the academic area as well as other non-commercial users, the licensing models of both engines have been changed to monthly subscription and even free packages. This way, the engines that previously only were available to game development companies are now getting more and more popular in the area of research.

Unity

Unity, currently in its fifth version, provides the developer with the opportunity to integrate C#, JavaScript, and Boo code. One of the major advantages of Unity's architecture is the implementation of the ECS pattern, which was discussed in section 2.3.2. As opposed to its pure version, in Unity components do also contain functionality. At runtime, components

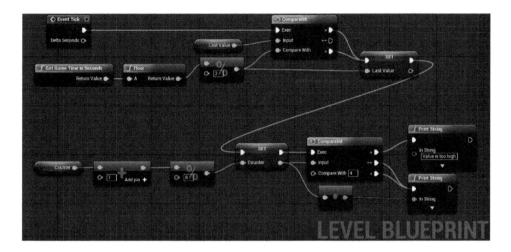

Figure 2.1: An Unreal Level Blueprint that is invoked every frame. Scala code that provides the same functionality is shown in listing 2.1.

can be added to entities, which essentially are subclasses of the `GameObject` class. In this way, Unity's architecture facilitates highly modular design.

Said architecture is beneficial for the Unity editor, which allows the developer to design a virtual world and inspect the current world state at runtime. New content can be easily imported, either from local sources (via drag & drop) or the Unity Asset store. The latter also allows for reuse of program code that was implemented by other developers. Due to the growing community, multiple add-ons to Unity exist, which facilitate its use in the context of VR development. Furthermore, documentation is available in the form of tutorial videos, code examples, and a well documented API.

However, some important features required for IVE development are missing. First of all, a Knowledge Representation Layer (KRL, Cavazza & Palmer, 2000) has to be added manually. Moreover, no uniform way of observing modification to a component's property is provided by the engine. Many events can be reacted on by registering callback methods, but no means to broadcast an event to a set of registered subscribers is provided. Instead, events have to be passed down the scene graph when recipients are unknown to the sender. Since this leaves the implementation to the users, it introduces a possible source for incompatibilities. Apart from this, Unity imposes a fixed execution scheme that can only be intersected at prescribed points using a respective callback.

Unreal Engine

The Unreal Engine, in the current fourth version, provides the developer with a powerful editor that consists of multiple modules. Similar to Unity, (C++) program code can be added by a developer to implement application logic. In addition, the Unreal Engine 4 introduces *Blueprint*, a visual scripting tool that allows for graph-based modeling of application logic. An exemplary visual script is shown in figure 2.1. The flow of data can be inspected at runtime,

```
def EventTick(deltaSeconds : Float) = {
   if (gameTime.toInt % 2 != LastValue){
      LastValue = gameTime.toInt % 2
      Counter   = (Counter + 1) % 8
      if (Counter > 4) println("Value is too high")
      else println(Counter)
   }
}
```

Listing 2.1: Scala equivalent to the Unreal Blueprint from figure 2.1: A counter is increased each second and reset to zero when it reaches the value eight. Depending on its value, different output is printed.

which is a highly valuable feature that is not inherently supported by any of the other presented frameworks. In contrast to Unity, the Unreal Engine does also provide the possibility to publish events and subscribe to them.

Visual programming with Blueprint is not always more comprehensible than writing program code, as the comparison between figure 2.1 and listing 2.1 indicates. Especially computations involving plain numbers can be expressed in a much more concise way using program code. The Unreal Engine allows to implement functionality using C++ and to utilize the implemented function in Blueprint. However, due to the high amount of macros that are used in the C++ API of the Unreal Engine, this approach is much more complex to understand and requires a lot more training than the visual programming.

Similar to Unity, content can easily be imported from local files into the Unreal Engine Editor and an asset store can be accessed to download additional content, like 3D models or scripts. Also, video tutorials, code examples, and API documentation are available.

Unfortunately, the Unreal Engine does not provide integrated support for semantics or elaborate AI methods. Furthermore, registering callbacks for value changes is not supported and a fixed execution scheme is prescribed.

Benefits and Drawbacks

One of the major benefits of the utilization of a game engine are the features it provides to generate believable virtual worlds. The highly optimized visual rendering modules, which are maintained by the engine's manufacturer, implement state-of-the-art methods that can impossibly be matched by custom-made solutions. Similarly, the editing facilities, which provide designers with easy to use interfaces, are highly beneficial for the creation of VEs.

On the downside, such engines prescribe fixed execution schemes and do not support the developer in breaking out of these. With both Unity as well as the Unreal Engine it is possible to start new threads of execution, but the developer has to manually sync the results with the engine's internal update loop. Furthermore, there is no support for the integration of semantic annotations, reasoning modules, rule engines, or similar modules that are required for the development of IVEs.

Regarding reusability the asset stores provide a means to access foreign content and program code. However, the possibilities provided for searching the store content are limited to text based search.

The application of the entity-component-system pattern in Unity provides a way to add and remove modules from an application without having to modify other part of the application than the entities. However, the data structures that are used are prescribed by the utilized components. Therefore, exchanging a component for a similar one does still require manual adaption of every affected application.

It is virtually impossible to achieve use case 1.1 with the presented game engines. They aim for highly realistic visualizations of the VE, wherefore the rendering module is the centerpiece of such an engine and, by no means, intended to be exchanged. The only (moot) option would be to add an additional rendering module while the initial one remains intact. Even though theoretically possible, this would require tremendous efforts.

Regarding use case 1.3 the situation is similarly desperate: due to a total lack of computationally accessible knowledge about the VE and relationships between entities therein, the introduction of advanced AI methods, which go beyond common game-AI like path-planning, requires high efforts. It is not impossible to achieve though, as, for example, work by Lugrin and Cavazza (2007) shows.

The most easy—but still complex—task to achieve is indicated by use case 1.2. Integrating an additional sensor, which represents a self-contained system, can be achieved by implementing an appropriate plugin to the engine. Utilizing the obtained data, however, often requires the utilizing module to be closely coupled to that plugin, since it constitutes a custom-made piece of software that was not provided for in the first place.

In summary, although game engines provide highly efficient and elaborate simulation modules, their utilization in the context of IRISs is rather inappropriate.

2.3.4 IVE frameworks

The number of frameworks dedicated to the creation of intelligent virtual environments is limited. Most research projects rather build on a VR framework and extend it by a Knowledge Representation Layer (KRL) that is tailored for the specific use case. The following paragraphs overview four frameworks that focus on the representation of semantics in VEs and thus are highly relevant for this work.

SCIVE

Latoschik, Fröhlich, and Wendler (2006) present the *Simulation Core for Intelligent Virtual Environments* (SCIVE), which later was extended by Fröhlich (2014). SCIVE builds on a central KRL, which is used to tie together the different simulation modules in use. Due to SCIVE's modular architecture and the adoption of the actor model, these modules can be executed concurrently.

An overview of this architecture is shown in figure 2.2: The central KRL is used to represent the current world state, which is accessed by multiple simulation modules. The latter are decoupled by means of the software interfaces that are provided by the SCIVE framework.

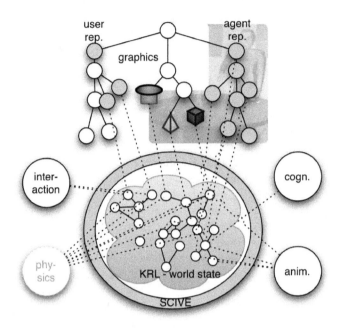

Figure 2.2: Conceptual overview of a SCIVE application involving a user and a virtual agent (figure from Latoschik & Fröhlich, 2007b, ©2007 SCITEPRESS).

In SCIVE, the propagation and integration of computed values is organized in a data-flow graph. The nodes of this graph are *filters*, which can modify the values and eventually integrate them into the KRL. Related to this, Heumer, Schilling, and Latoschik (2005) present a mechanism for automatic data exchange and synchronization by means of which the exchange of data between different simulation modules is facilitated.

The Actor Model   As mentioned above, concurrent execution of simulation modules is facilitated by the adoption of the actor model into the SCIVE framework (Fröhlich & Latoschik, 2008). In the actor model by Hewitt et al. (1973) an actor is an independent computational entity that can solely communicate via messages.

More specifically, an actor can perform the following actions:

- send messages

- create further actors

- change its behavior according to received messages

Besides message-based communication, an actor is completely restricted to local computations. Thus, the model inherently facilitates concurrent computations and avoids problems that commonly arise in the context of concurrency control mechanisms. Furthermore, the message-based communication allows for implementation of distributed systems, which is highly beneficial in the context of VR frameworks.

Semantic Reflection   During the development of SCIVE the concept called *Semantic Reflection* was introduced (Latoschik & Fröhlich, 2007b). With semantic reflection, semantic-based access to all levels of the application including its configuration, simulation modules, and simulated entities is enabled. This is facilitated by the integration of a KRL as a central data representation. Among the examined frameworks, SCIVE is the only one that incorporates a semantic representation of architecture elements to this extent.

For example, objects in the scene graph can be tagged at runtime to change their dynamic type (e.g., to `is_agent_perceptable`). This way, using the possibly inflexible type system of the underlying programming language can be avoided. Similarly, the configuration of simulation modules or the application can be changed at runtime.

Although the goals pursued by SCIVE are highly similar to those this work aims for, no methodology for decoupling simulation modules is provided by its authors. More precisely, the software interfaces that are mentioned to simplify replacement of simulation modules are not published. For example, it is not clear in which way new simulated objects are instantiated. Moreover, the structure of the employed semantic network remains unspecified.

SCIVE's KRL is implemented in the form of a semantic network (cf. section 2.4.1), which is processed by semantic traversers. While semantic networks provide a comprehensible form of representation, they lack formal semantics and thus often depend on custom-made implementations. Regarding reusability a more flexible representation is desirable. In this context, recent IVE frameworks implement formats that were developed in the context of the Semantic Web. One of these frameworks is ISReal, which is examined in the next section.

ISReal

The *Intelligent Simulated Realities* (ISReal) platform, which is more related to the field of Intelligent Virtual Agents, is presented by Kapahnke, Liedtke, Nesbigall, Warwas, and Klusch (2010) and Nesbigall et al. (2011). Its central building block is a *semantic world model*. ISReal utilizes a semantically annotated scene graph and ontologies for both semantic properties and services. Owed to its focus on IVAs, the ISReal platform emphasizes the semantic annotation of services and virtual objects.

The semantic world model builds on a scene graph that is used to represent the objects that exist in the virtual world. Each object is added high-level semantic annotations, which can contain information about its physical properties, semantic descriptions, and services it can be used with. The platform utilizes ontologies that are represented using the Web Ontology Language (OWL) (cf. section 2.4.2) to specify semantic content.

It furthermore uses so-called *semantic objects*, which contain URIs that refer to the associated semantic concepts, semantic services, and an OWL individual that represents its high-level description. In addition, a semantic object encompasses information on its geometry, animations, and its physical properties.

Since ISReal focuses on the integration of virtual agents, no further information on the integration of other modules that update the simulation state at high frequencies (e.g., a physics engine) is given. However, the utilization of OWL based service descriptions enables the creation of a distributed architecture. In this way, a centralized semantic representation of the simulated environment can be maintained, which is accessed by remotely executed services (e.g., graphics rendering).

As opposed to SCIVE, the ISReal platform does not support semantic representation of low-level concepts but rather encapsulates knowledge in the form of semantic objects, which are linked with high-level concepts. The restriction to high-level concepts is beneficial regarding extensibility, since program code has to be adapted to newly specified concepts. On the other hand, information in the semantic world model has to be explicitly linked with runtime information. This possibly results in a lack of information on particular aspects that might be required in an extended version of an application.

REVE

The *REVE* platform (Anastassakis & Panayiotopoulos, 2011) is one of the very few software frameworks that were explicitly developed for the creation of reusable Intelligent Virtual Environments. REVE is a set of software tools that allow for creation and simulation of IVEs as well as the integration of virtual agents.

The representation of virtual objects in REVE is based on an entity model in which entities are called *items* (Anastassakis & Panayiotopoulos, 2012). Such items consist of a set of *item aspects*, which model specific aspects of the entity. These aspects are similar to components in the ECS pattern mentioned in section 2.3.2. By default each item has a *physical aspect*, a *semantic aspect*, as well as an *access aspect*. In addition, depending on the requirements of a particular application, further aspects can be added. The data that is required for the simulation of the virtual objects is stored in a centralized *virtual world store*.

The framework was used to investigate the integration of a physics engine into existing virtual environments by Anastassakis, Panayiotopoulos, and Raptis (2012). In this scenario a *physics aspect* was added, which contained the elements that were required for physical simulation of the respective entity (e.g., mass and velocity). An implementation dependent adapter module was created, which connected the physics engine to be used with the aforementioned virtual world store. Updates were propagated via the frame event notification and response infrastructure, which is provided by the integrated rendering module. The authors emphasize that the integration neither required the adoption of the REVE platform nor of the newly integrated physics engine, which reveals the beneficial aspects of the architecture regarding extensibility and reuse.

Besides the difference of integrating a physics engine instead of a 3D rendering module, this example is very similar to the frequently discussed use case 1.1, which hence is supported by the architecture of the platform. However, REVE does hardcode semantic information in the above-mentioned aspects, wherefore such information cannot be reused easily. Moreover, the application of semantic reasoners or similar modules is hindered by this approach.

MASCARET

The only IVE framework that is available to the public is the *MultiAgent System for Collaborative, Adaptive & Realistic Environments for Training* (MASCARET), which has been presented by Buche, Querrec, De Loor, and Chevaillier (2003). As its acronym suggests, it was designed to support the creation of VEs that are inhabited by IVAs.

In MASCARET, semantic modeling builds on UML-based meta-models (Chevaillier et al., 2012). The authors justify their decision by stating that UML has the same abstraction level that a semantic modeling language for VR applications is required to have. In addition, they state that UML does not cover all of the requirements that arise in this context and propose corresponding extensions. This approach bears resemblance to the intention to implement *MOF Support for Semantic Structures* (Object Management Group, 2013).

Additional simulation modules can be added in the form of plugins, which are triggered once per simulation step (i.e. once per frame). In this regard, the framework's architecture can be considered to have a micro-kernel based nature.

MASCARET implements a signal/slot mechanism that allows to observe value changes of internal properties. Access to slots is achieved by means of their names, which are encoded in the form of strings. Moreover, virtual objects are represented by means of an entity model. Every entity in that model is assigned a set of slots, representing its attributes. In addition, an entity is assigned a state machine, which can be specified to react to certain events.

All of these concepts are beneficial regarding decoupling of simulation modules. On the downside, the framework does not employ a knowledge representation format that can be read by external modules. In addition, although the proposed UML-based modeling approach is built on a solid basis it does not involve logic-based semantics. Thus, to provide support for common AI modules, a connection between these meta-models, an appropriate formalism, as well as the application state would have to be implemented manually.

Implications

As indicated before, there is no uniform architecture that underlies existing IVE frameworks. Consequently, the employed forms of knowledge representation, software interfaces, and modeling mechanisms differ, thereby prohibiting reuse.

Encountered features include observability of arbitrary simulation aspects, externalized forms of knowledge representation, independence from underlying types, and decoupled simulation modules. The used technologies involve signal/slot systems, distributed ontologies using Semantic Web technologies, type conversion mechanisms, as well as the adoption of the actor model and its underlying message-based architecture. None of the examined systems provides all of these and implementation details often are not published.

Such features, however, are of high importance for the mentioned use cases: In order to create exchangeable modules it is necessary to observe and perform changes to relevant simulation aspects. In the example of use case 1.1 information about position and orientation updates could be sufficient to replace a rendering module.

However, depending on the rendering features that are used by the application, further information might be required. Aiming for exchangeability of arbitrary modules, the number of types to be observed can impossibly be foreseen. Especially the AI modules that are employed in use case 1.3 depend on such feature: depending on the particular application, any kind of information can become useful or even required for these modules.

Use case 1.2 (integrating a new sensor) requires a different point of view: in order to inform modules that were present in the application before the newly integrated module has to be able to provide information to the former ones. This can either be achieved by publish/subscribe patterns or by accessing the present aspects that are observed by existing modules.

In this context, the above-mentioned feature of externalized forms of knowledge representations are highly useful. Since a uniform naming scheme is required to ensure that two modules access the same properties, symbol-based access that is facilitated by an external, common vocabulary is extremely beneficial. All use cases can draw advantages from such a feature, since it allows to decouple inter-module communication. The MASCARET framework theoretically would support this by means of the string-based access to the signal/slot mechanism, however, the lack of said vocabulary prohibits this feature.

Similar to uniform naming schemes, independence from underlying types is a required feature for the replacement use case 1.1. In the example of rendering module replacement this becomes apparent by the fact that different rendering modules apply different coordinate representations (left-handed vs. right-handed representation). Thus, even in the most unlikely case that two different modules use the same data types, a conversion between before-mentioned representations can be necessary. The same situation applies for sensor modules (use case 1.2) that provide spatial information.

Besides choosing an architecture (cf. section 2.3.2) for the IVE framework to be developed, a formalism to represent knowledge about the framework and VEs has to be chosen. The next section provides a brief overview of possible options for this.

2.4 Knowledge Representation

In order to utilize knowledge about the VE and the system itself, some form of knowledge representation is required. This could be achieved by means of internal data structures that contain knowledge about the current simulation state. A more appropriate approach, however, is to use an external data format the contents of which are loaded and then represented internally. In both cases an underlying model has to be selected.

The following sections will discuss some of the possible forms of representation and their use in the context of software engineering and IVEs. Due to the desire to make represented knowledge accessible at every stage of the IVE development process, the work focuses on symbol-based representations, whereas other approaches, for example, neural networks and support vector machines, are not considered directly.

Such methods would be integrated in the form of a simulation module, which performs the required calculations internally. For example, a neural network that perceives its input from observable simulation aspects (which, in turn, might be updated by the sensor modules mentioned use case 1.2) would internally process such data and add results to the simulation state. The latter can either occur in the form of raw numbers, in which case further interpretation by other modules is required to translate those numbers into a symbolic representation, or by directly publishing respective symbols.

It has to be noted that the list of discussed methods is far from being complete. For more comprehensive lists regarding the field of software reuse the reader is referred to related surveys, e.g., Frakes and Gandel (1990) or A. Mili, Mili, and Mittermeir (1998). In the more recent field of IVEs no comprehensive survey regarding the used form of knowledge representation exists. However, the majority of IVE applications is somewhat related to the field of intelligent virtual agents, wherefore the respective literature (e.g., Wooldridge, 2009) can be consulted to obtain an overview of applicable forms of representation. A more general introduction to different forms of knowledge representation can be obtained from the relevant literature, e.g., Russell and Norvig (2010).

2.4.1 Forms of Knowledge Representation

The following sections will briefly introduce two types of knowledge representations: structural representations and logical ones. While the former provide a comprehensible format, the latter provide a formal basis for the representation of knowledge.

Structural Representations

Different approaches to structure information about entities and relations between them exist. These include object centered representations, like *frames*, which essentially consist of a collection of *slots* that can be filled with values. Each such slot is assigned a symbol, which provides the assigned value with meaning. Relations, in this model, are expressed by inserting a reference to a frame into a slot of another one.

A similar approach, which allows for comprehensible visualization, is taken by *semantic networks*. Instead of including all information about the described entity inside a single object, a semantic network constitutes a graph. Its vertices represent concepts, while its edges represent the relation between those concepts.

Semantic networks have, for example, been used to represent knowledge about software components in the context of component retrieval (A. Mili et al., 1998). In the context of Intelligent Virtual Environments semantic networks have been used, e.g., by Peters and Shrobe (2003), Latoschik and Schilling (2003) as well as Lugrin and Cavazza (2007) to represent knowledge about the application and its state.

While semantic networks can easily be visualized and hence are comprehensible for humans, the absence of a widely accepted formalism to exchange their content complicates their distribution and reuse. The same holds true for other forms of structural representation, like the above-mentioned concept of frames. Moreover, due to the lack of a formal basis, specialized mechanisms are required to infer information from the represented knowledge.

Logical Representations

In order to avoid such a lack of a formal basis a logical representation can be applied. An example for such a representation is the so-called *propositional calculus*, which allows for the application of inference rules to infer new propositions from given ones. In this context, commonly the example involving the implication 'if it is raining, the street is wet' and the assertion 'it is raining', resulting in the inference 'the street is wet', is given.

The expressivity of propositional logic, however, is limited, because it does neither include the use of quantifiers (i.e. 'for all' ($\forall$) and 'there exists' ($\exists$)) nor the definition of predicates that represent statements about propositions. These features are introduced with First-Order Logic (FOL), which therefore allows to formulate more expressive statements. For example, a statement like 'everything gets wet when it rains' can be expressed:

$$\forall x (rainOn(x) \rightarrow isWet(x))$$

. Second-order logic (as well as higher-order logics) does provide the possibility of quantifying relations, or more generally, to use predicates to represent statements about other predicates.

High expressivity is a desirable feature, but a Knowledge Base (KB) expressed in FOL is already undecidable (more specifically, semidecidable) when predicates with two or more

Symbol	Description Logic Features
	Basic Language
$\mathcal{AL}$	atomic negation, concept intersection, universal restrictions, and limited existential quantification
$\mathcal{EL}$	concept intersection, existential restrictions (of full existential quantification)
$\mathcal{S}$	same as $\mathcal{ALC}$ with transitive roles
	Extensions
$+$	transitive roles
$\mathcal{C}$	complement of roles
$\mathcal{E}$	full existential quantification
$\mathcal{F}$	functional roles
$\mathcal{H}$	role hierarchy
$\mathcal{I}$	inverse roles
$\mathcal{O}$	nominals
$\mathcal{Q}$	qualified number restrictions
$\mathcal{R}$	limited complex role inclusion axioms, reflexivity, irreflexivity, and role disjointness

Table 2.3: List of Description Logic expressivity identifiers (cf. Baader, Calvanese, McGuinness, Nardi, & Patel-Schneider, 2004).

arguments are used. Consequently, formulas that cannot be proved to be correct within finite time may exist in such a KB. In order to avoid this problem, the field of Description Logics investigates (mostly) decidable logics (most of which are fragments of FOL) that are appropriate for knowledge representation.

Description Logics (DLs) (Baader, Calvanese, McGuinness, Nardi, & Patel-Schneider, 2004) provide a formal logic-based framework for semantic knowledge representations. Through this framework the expressivity of a formalism can be classified and its reasoning complexity be categorized.

In description logics usually two parts of the represented knowledge are distinguished: terminological knowledge (the Terminological Box (TBox)) and assertional knowledge (the Assertional Box (ABox)). Furthermore, DLs are categorized according to their expressivity. A particular DL is categorized depending on the concepts it provides to express certain facts. The performance of a reasoning module operating on a certain KB is not necessarily determined by the expressivity of the underlying DL but rather by the set of its features that are actually used. However, restricting the expressivity of a language is a common means to determine lower and upper bounds for the computational properties (if known for the respective DL family). For example, concept satisfiability for the DL $\mathcal{ALCQO}$ (with acyclic TBoxes) is known to be decidable in PSpace (Baader, Miličić, Lutz, Sattler, & Wolter, 2005), whereas it is ExpTime-hard for $\mathcal{SHIF}$ (Tobies, 2001), the DL that underlies OWL-Lite. The symbols that are commonly used to specify the features of a DL are explained in table 2.3.

Two further characteristics of DLs are the so-called Open World Assumption (OWA) as well as the absence of the Unique Name Assumption (UNA). The former leads to the circumstance that facts that are not explicitly asserted to be false will not be assumed to be so, whereas the absence of the unique name assumption implies that two individuals with different names can be inferred to be equivalent. The implications of these characteristics will be discussed in section 3.2.6 in the next chapter.

In the area of software reuse, LaSSIE (Devanbu, Brachman, Selfridge, & Ballard, 1991) is an early system that applied Description Logics to facilitate semantic retrieval of software components. The application of description logics in knowledge-based software engineering is discussed by Devanbu and Jones (1997).

Although providing a basis for representing shareable knowledge about different concepts, DLs themselves were often stored using proprietary formats. In the area of multi-agent systems this observation led to the development of common formats to allow for interoperability (Hendler, 2007). Based on the thus created *DARPA Agent Markup Language* (DAML) and its successors large repositories of ontologies were created.

2.4.2 Ontologies

Although no single, commonly agreed upon definition exists, an often cited definition by Gruber states that "an ontology is an explicit specification of a conceptualization" (Gruber, 1993, p. 199). More specifically, he states that "a specification of a representational vocabulary for a shared domain of discourse – definitions of classes, relations, functions, and other objects – is called an ontology" (Gruber, 1993, p. 199).

In other words, an ontology provides the set of symbols that represent the concepts in a certain domain and furthermore does specify relations between these concepts (in turn, using the symbols that are specified in the ontology). In this regard, an ontology can be considered to be self-contained. This way, the problem of symbol grounding (Harnad, 1990) is addressed, which regards the issue that the meaning of a certain symbol is not encoded by the symbol itself (the symbol rather is a representative for a certain concept).

Besides applications in other fields, ontologies have been considered in the context of software engineering. For example, Sugumaran and Storey address their advantages by stating that "ontologies aim at capturing domain knowledge in a generic way to provide a commonly agreed understanding of a domain that may be reused and shared across applications and groups" (Sugumaran & Storey, 2003, p. 12). On a related note, Happel and Seedorf (2006) provide an overview of applications of ontologies in the area of software engineering, and Oberle et al. (2006) discuss the use of ontologies for modularization of large software systems. Similarly, the application of ontologies and reasoning in enterprise service ecosystems is addressed by Oberle (2014).

In the context of virtual environments, ontologies have often been applied to represent knowledge about the environment's contents. For example, Coninx et al. (2006) utilize ontologies for conceptual modeling. Their VR-DeMo[4] project aims at facilitating the process of creating virtual environments by the use of domain ontologies. Similarly, Otto (2005a) applies the Resource Description Framework (RDF, Manola & Miller, 2004) to describe the contents of semantic virtual environments.

---

[4] Virtual Reality: Conceptual Descriptions and Models for the Realization of Virtual Environments

Regarding virtual agents, Huhns and Singh (1997) suggest the application of ontologies to allow for communication between agents that do share knowledge only in parts. In their example they think of two virtual agents that communicate about a flight on a certain type of aircraft. If both agents share the concept of an airplane but only the speaker knows about the concept of the particular aircraft, the airplane concept can be used to provide a common ground for this communication.

Web Ontology Language

The Web Ontology Language (OWL, W3C OWL Working Group, 2009) is the de facto standard for specifications of ontologies in the context of the Semantic Web. It is based on RDF, which can be used to express information about arbitrary resources. The latter can be any thinkable object, be it real, virtual, or possibly only a concept. In OWL resources are identified by International Resource Identifiers (IRIs).

Owed to the language's origins, OWL ontologies are highly modular and can be spread over multiple files. This—and the fact that it is formally based on a description logic—makes it a perfect candidate for knowledge representation in reusable IVEs.

Several publications address the utilization of OWL ontologies in multiple contexts. For example, efforts have been made to represent ontologies of services (Martin et al., 2004; Ferrario et al., 2011), creating plans using such service descriptions (Ziaka, Vrakas, & Bassiliades, 2011), and supporting natural language queries to find components in an integrated development environment (Würsch, Ghezzi, Reif, & Gall, 2010). Happel, Korthaus, Seedorf, and Tomczyk (2006) present a system that allows for querying background knowledge of software artifacts.

OWL ontologies also have been used in the context of VR applications: Metral, Falquet, and Cutting-Decelle (2009) present an approach to enrich 3D city models. Similarly, Kalogerakis, Christodoulakis, and Moumoutzis (2006) use OWL ontologies to represent information about visual content. Moreover, the ISReal platform (cf. section 2.3.4) uses OWL to store high-level information on semantic objects. Finally, approaches to bridge UML, as used by the MASCARET framework (cf. section 2.3.4), with OWL exist (Frankel, Hayes, Kendall, & McGuinness, 2004).

OWL profiles   In order to restrict the expressivity of the DL that underlies an ontology, three languages profiles have been specified for OWL 2 (Motik et al., 2012). Each of the profiles puts different restrictions on the designer of an eventual ontology. A detailed introduction into these language profiles is given by Krötzsch (2012).

It is important to mention that the choice of a certain profile does not have to be specified explicitly but results from the used language elements. In combination with the fact that OWL allows for spreading a knowledge base over multiple files this circumstance is highly beneficial: by interlinking files that comply with a certain profile, the characteristics of the profile are maintained. However, if higher expressivity is required for a particular application, an additional file that contains language elements that are disallowed by the profile can still be added. This way, the content of the original ontology can be (re-)used in the more complex one without modification and, hence, remains compatible to preexisting applications.

2.4.3 Action Representation

Although this work is not primarily concerned with the integration of intelligent virtual agents, the aspect of action planning is related. If an action is rather interpreted as a part of executable program code than as an operation executed by a virtual agent, the initially addressed issue of component retrieval in reusable software becomes applicable. The means that are provided by an IVE framework that applies a method similar to semantic reflection could also allow for querying semantically annotated software methods. In combination with facilities known from the planning area automatic problem solving on a low level could be achieved. Common approaches to the representation of actions are largely based on the specification of preconditions and (side) effects of such action (e.g., Fikes and Nilsson (1971) or Badler et al. (2000)).

Regarding action planning in IVEs, Kallmann (2001) introduced the concept of smart objects. Such an object is associated with a machinable description of the way it is intended to be used. Abaci, Ciger, and Thalmann (2005) build on these results by adding above mentioned planning facilities. On a related note, Lugrin and Cavazza (2007) apply a KRL to represent actions and common sense knowledge in order to simulate physical behavior of objects in an IVE.

A common language to specify planning problems is the Planning Domain Definition Language (PDDL, McDermott et al., 1998). Since different implementations of planning modules do support problems specified in the PDDL, the utilization of this representation is desirable.

McDermott and Dou (2002) present Web-PDDL, an extension which allows to combine RDF documents with PDDL and thus bridges the gap between ontology specifications and plan descriptions. Similar to the intended approach of automatic combination of software methods, Klusch, Gerber, and Schmidt (2005) present a combination of OWL-S (Martin et al., 2004) with a service composition planner for planning in combination with Semantic Web services. This is very similar to the intended idea of planning with services (i.e. software methods) that are described in an ontology and hence suggests its feasibility.

The beneficial aspect of focusing on the representations of actions for reusability is also addressed by Soto and Allongue (2002). They provide a way to create reusable virtual entities by taking an alternative point of view: they regard an *action* as the main concept of virtual worlds. By separating behaviors of entities and the virtual world from reactions to these behaviors locality regarding an action is created. This way, entities can be reused in different virtual environments with diverse characteristics (i.e. different reactions on behaviors).

2.4.4 Knowledge Representation Layers

The term *Knowledge Representation Layer* (KRL, Cavazza & Palmer, 2000) denotes the knowledge representation that is integrated into an IRIS application. A KRL commonly contains high-level semantic descriptions of the concepts that are applicable in the application's domain. Its main purpose is to integrate AI methods and to allow for alternative forms of access to the application state, e.g., natural language interfaces.

Aspects of KRLs

Obviously, a Knowledge Representation Layer, or more generally a Knowledge Base that is utilized by arbitrary components of an IRIS framework, necessarily has to be synchronized with the application's state. This synchronization can occur not only at different levels of abstraction but also at different frequencies.

Another aspect that has to be taken into account is the interface that is provided to access the KRL. The respective implementation is highly dependent on the required level of abstraction, since a low level of abstraction requires low level access to the architecture elements of the framework. In the most invasive case, the Knowledge Representation Layer is directly connected to the elements of the framework. This implicates high coupling and, in addition, the integration of such kind of layer requires access to the complete code of the framework. The content of such a low-level KRL would include entities, attributes, relations, and concepts (Latoschik, Biermann, & Wachsmuth, 2005).

For different reasons, this low level access often cannot be achieved. The most obvious limitation arises with the utilization of a closed source framework. In that case, the missing access to program code that is required in order to introduce the necessary modifications renders low level coupling impossible.

Yet, even if access to all program code and the possibility of introducing changes is given, the internal structure of the framework might hinder respective access. If the KRL should reflect all aspects of the application state, it has to be integrated into the application's update loop. This means that each update to the internal state has to be interceptable by the respective implementation.

Alternatively, the KRL could be static, i.e. it could couple entities with concepts that are not updated at all. This allows to request information about the entities and their relations among each other, but does not permit to react to changes other than insertion and deletion of entities. This approach can be extended by enabling updates of the Knowledge Representation Layer through changes that are initiated by the application. While this allows a developer to integrate the KRL at the desired abstraction level, it also involves the manual specification of both content and frequency of updates. Since the latter are specified on the application level, they do not require low level access to the framework's internals. However, it requires a highly application dependent coupling of the KRL, thereby reducing the opportunity to reuse.

Disregarding the particular situation, the frequency with which synchronization occurs is relevant for performance considerations. While the integration of every single state update into the KRL may not be critical regarding performance itself, possibly triggered computations might cause severe problems. For example, calculating the implications of a single position update for the spatial relations that are possibly stored in a Knowledge Representation Layer might be quite expensive. If such update occurs at the same rate that, e.g., a physics engine updates its internal representation, a rule engine or reasoning module will most certainly not keep up calculating all implications. However, low level information might be required for certain inferences, wherefore a framework should at least be capable of providing such information to the KRL.

The most common approach to the integration of a KRL is to create a layer that wraps a complete existing framework. This can, for example, be used to represent high-level information about the content of the IVE at runtime (Cavazza, Hartley, Lugrin, & Le Bras, 2004;

Lugrin & Cavazza, 2007). Other applications of this approach include querying information about the semantics of objects (Chevaillier et al., 2012; Kapahnke et al., 2010), implementation of multimodal interfaces (Latoschik, 2005), or planning (Abaci et al., 2005). Kleinermann, De Troyer, Creelle, and Pellens (2008) present an approach that even allows to add semantics to existing VEs. Commonly, external formats are used to describe the contents of a virtual environment, for example, in the context of conceptual (Coninx et al., 2006) or semantic modeling (Chevaillier et al., 2012).

2.5 Summary

The requirement for more software reuse in the context of VR framework development recently was reinforced in a panel discussion titled "why do we keep reinventing the wheel?" (Acevedo-Feliz, 2014) at the IEEE Virtual Reality 2014 conference. To provide a basis to meet this demand this chapter provided an overview of related work, which is summarized in the next sections.

Software Reuse

The review of terms that are related to software reusability (cf. section 2.2.1) revealed multiple important aspects for the development of reusable IRIS applications: maintainability, understandability, and modularity are non-functional requirements that have to be taken into account. The latter especially involves the concepts of low coupling and high cohesion, which were emphasized by multiple researchers in both the area of software engineering and the field of IRIS development.

Especially use case 1.1, which deals with the replacement of a rendering module from an existing application, benefits from these aspects. If the system is developed in a way that fosters low coupling, the number of interfacing points between the renderer and the system is reduced and thus is the amount of work necessary to replace that module.

Publications in the area of software reuse reveal that reuse on the one hand promises benefits like increased quality and productivity, but on the other hand multiple aspects inhibit its achievement (cf. section 2.2.2). These are related to a lack of commitment by the project management, misconceptions regarding requirements for a successful reuse program (e.g., using OOP is sufficient), a lack of careful planning of the whole reuse program, missing repositories of reusable components to support both storage and retrieval, a lack of interoperability between produced assets, and incomprehensible software interfaces. Consequently, a carefully planned framework that counteracts these inhibitors is required to facilitate software reuse for IRISs.

A survey of facets of software reuse (see section 2.2.3) indicated a black-box framework to be a desirable architecture. In this context, the software reuse process, as described by Kim and Stohr (1998), provides a structured categorization of steps that occur during the utilization of an eventual IRIS framework.

The reuse techniques that were considered in section 2.2.4 revealed a Component-Based Software Engineering approach in combination with OOP techniques to be promising. Misconceptions that involved the latter, however, were one of the reasons that resulted in reuse programs to fail, wherefore their adoption will be carefully examined in later chapters. Besides these composition based techniques, findings by Krueger (1992) suggest that the application of generative techniques is appropriate as well. On a related note, the area of domain engineering bears resemblance to the pursued goal of integrating a KRL into an eventual framework, thereby allowing for utilization of domain knowledge at runtime.

Finally, it was observed that most of the methods to measure reusability of software require the software to exist in advance (cf. section 2.2.5) and consequently cannot be applied to a framework that is intended to support the development of such software. However, they can serve as design guidelines, suggesting that such framework should foster low coupling and high cohesion, facilitate customizability of components, provide support for searching for components, reduce the complexity of using them, ease upgrading to newer versions, be portable, modular, well-documented, and mature.

IRIS Frameworks

Publications in the field of VE development reveal that software reuse still is in its infancy in this field: due to incompatibility, tools are not shared between different groups of developers and a lack of standardizations makes most programmers to choose building over reusing (cf. section 2.3.1). The introductorily mentioned realtime constraints make this situation even more difficult, since they encourage close coupling. In this regard, shared memory access and the application of related synchronization mechanisms complicate the creation of reusable black-box components.

In the context of RISs frameworks developers assume one or more of three main roles: framework developers, simulation module developers, and application developers. A framework that aims for decoupling modules has to accommodate this categorization, since it prescribes a natural separation of concerns. More precisely, it has to facilitate the development of a simulation module independently from other modules and eventual applications. This categorization is in line with the different steps of the software reuse process, which involve the creation of reusable resources (by modules developers) as well as consuming them (performed by application developers).

For instance, the development of a reasoning module that shall be used in the context of use case 1.3 could neglect the existence of possible further AI modules and instead be implemented to retrieve information from a globally represented simulation state as well as to update that state with results from its inference mechanisms. In that case, no other dependencies than the existence of such global simulation state arise and modules inevitably reveal low coupling among each other.

Reviewing architectures that are commonly adopted by VE frameworks (cf. section 2.3.2), each was found to have advantages and disadvantages. In the end, an approach that subsumes the presented ones and thus allows to rebuild the existing solutions is desirable. Especially supporting both an entity model and an event system was found to be promising. At this point, a message-based architecture is beneficial, since it inherently supports the implementation of event systems and facilitates decoupling.

Existing frameworks in the area of IVE development (cf. section 2.3.4) reveal further aspects that are beneficial for decoupling individual elements and thus for their reuse. For example, the representation of application knowledge in external formats supports semantic modeling (which is related to domain engineering in the field of software engineering). Furthermore, it allows for reuse of existing software modules that have been developed in the area of AI.

Regarding the exchange of a module the structure of the REVE framework, which was discussed in section 2.3.4, showed to be reasonable: its developers found that partitioning simulated entities into so-called item aspects allowed to easily integrate further modules, which is very similar to use case 1.2. In their case a physics engine was integrated into an existing application.

The actor model, which was integrated into the SCIVE framework (cf. section 2.3.4) was reported to foster decoupling and concurrency. Since this model restricts communication between actors (e.g., simulation modules) to messages, it fits the above-mentioned intention to adopt a message-based architecture.

Knowledge Representation

Among the different forms of computerized knowledge representation logic-based ones are most adequate for the creation of reusable IRISs, due to their formal basis. Here, Description Logics provide a means to choose computational complexity over expressivity. Since it is rather complex to specify knowledge by means of a DL, a more comprehensive form of representation, which ideally supports a developer with different tools, is required to permit non-experts to edit knowledge bases.

In this regard, the Web Ontology Language (OWL), which is based on such a DL, is a reasonable choice. It inherently supports creation and sharing of ontological knowledge, since it was developed in the context of the Semantic Web. Multiple tools for editing and processing OWL ontologies, such as the protégé editor (Stanford Center for Biomedical Informatics Research, 2015), exist. Choosing from the existing language profiles, optimized software tools can be utilized and thus efficient reasoning be ensured. Consequently, OWL is beneficial for the creation of reusable knowledge bases and will be utilized in this work.

In the context of IRISs OWL ontologies provide a means to establish a KRL that can be accessed by different simulation modules. For instance, in the situation of use case 1.3, where multiple AI modules are required to interact, the utilization of externally specified OWL ontologies allows to decouple such modules from the actual application (and from each other). More specifically, the vocabulary that is established by an ontology provides different AI modules with a common ground for communication and knowledge exchange. Apparently, the content of such ontologies has to be linked with the simulation state to integrate ontology updates into the simulation state (and vice versa). This issue is addressed by the concept of semantic reflection (cf. section 2.3.4), which thus is relevant for an eventual framework.

Implications for IRIS Framework Design

In summary, a framework has to provide understandable, well-conceived software interfaces, which are used by both simulation module developers and application developers. Ideally, an interface that is appropriate for all types of simulation modules has to be created.

Moreover, a framework should foster the creation and use of decoupled black-box components, which can concurrently perform simulations. This is facilitated by the adoption of the actor model, which restricts the communication of concurrent threads of computation to the use of messages. Furthermore, substituting direct inter-module communication to performing and observing updates of a centralized simulation state fosters decoupling. Aiming for a single interface, which can be used by common RIS modules and AI modules that rely on symbolic representations, the adoption of semantic reflection and the integration of a KRL on a core level is desirable.

In order to connect such a KRL (that reflects the internal state of an IRIS) with an external OWL ontology, the next chapter will develop a knowledge representation model for IRIS applications with arbitrary scope.

Chapter 3

A Knowledge Representation Model for Intelligent Realtime Interactive Systems

The goal of various metadata proposals is to make those mental connections explicit by tagging the data with more signs. Those metalevel signs themselves have further interconnections, which can be tagged with metametalevel signs. But meaningless data cannot acquire meaning by being tagged with meaningless metadata. The ultimate source of meaning is the physical world and the agents who use signs to represent entities in the world and their intentions concerning them.

Ontology, Metadata, and Semiotics
John F. Sowa (2000)

3.1 Semantics

The integration of a semantic layer into a RIS framework often is assumed to be sufficiently covered by the annotation of architecture elements with meaningful symbols. In this context, the above-quoted statement by John F. Sowa is highly relevant; although such signs (and symbols) may carry meaning for a person who understands the language they originate from, an application cannot draw meaning from such symbols, per se.

It is the entirety of entities, their properties, and relations between them, which inherently bears meaning. The notion of the concept that is represented by a certain symbol highly depends on the person interpreting the symbol. More precisely, a person who does not know a particular symbol at all can impossibly have a notion of the associated object. If, however, that person is given more details regarding the denoted object, he or she can probably infer the meaning of the given symbol. This is facilitated by the person's knowledge on related concepts, their properties, and their relations to each other.

Extending on this basic knowledge and abilities, more complex elements, processes, and actions become graspable. Obviously, a concept can be recognized as a composition of other concepts. Moreover, a concept can be of use without being fully specified. For example, a car can be specified as the composition of four wheels and a chassis. Concepts often are hierarchically structured; e.g., a cat is a mammal, wherefore it also is an animal. Furthermore, concepts and relations are mutually dependent: a concept stays meaningless without relations to other concepts, and a relation cannot exist without connecting two (or more) concepts.

In human conversations the placement of a concept in the hierarchies is assumed to be known, wherefore use of the associated symbol in itself creates a level of abstraction (for those who know the symbol's meaning). This allows to reference an object by a symbol that is used for a more general concept, e.g., saying "Look at the animal!" when referencing a cat. In the computing context, this is partially adopted by classes and their hierarchies in object-oriented programming languages.

Similarly, objects can be identified by stating some of the relations they are involved in. For example, the cat from above could be referenced as "the thing with paws." Obviously, if more similar objects are around, a description has to be more specific in order to prevent ambiguous references. This concept is similar to the *pattern matching* technique that is commonly found in functional programming languages.

While objects represent the static elements in the world, actions and processes add dynamics to these elements. In this context, a process is a sequence of actions over a certain amount of time. An action, in turn, modifies the current state and thereby creates a subsequent state. Finally, a state is defined by the contained objects and their relations. Building thereon, an action can be defined by its preconditions (requirements concerning the current state) and effects (differences between the current and the subsequent state).

Similar to the abstraction introduced by a symbol that denotes a certain concept, the symbol associated with a certain process allows a person to identify the preconditions and effects of the associated process. Moreover, a certain action can be inferred from its effects, even if they only are specified in part.

3.2 Semantics of IRIS Frameworks

The abilities mentioned in the previous section allow humans to adapt to unknown situations and deal with unfamiliar objects. Some of those mechanisms, like concept hierarchies, are integrated into programming languages, not least because they match the human view of the world. However, more complex inference mechanisms are usually added on top of an existing application. Unless features like reflection are provided by the programming language in use, these inference mechanisms do only have restricted access to the information that is encoded in the program code. This is especially problematic when parts of this information are lost during the translation into machine code. For example, the semantics that a developer encoded in variable names usually is not reflected at runtime.

3.2.1 Benefits of Integrated Semantics

Concerning the reusability of an application, inference and abstraction mechanisms, like those mentioned before, can be highly beneficial in many regards.

For example, the rigid structure prescribed by the class hierarchy known from object-oriented languages can be softened. While such structures allow for static type-checking, the reconfiguration of objects at run-time is not supported. With integrated semantics, objects that have certain properties could be attributed to a certain class according to their sets of properties. Matching such objects against a class description instead of performing type-checking would allow to dynamically determine its class affiliation. In this way, an object can be inferred to be an instance of a class that it is hierarchically independent of, if the object fits the requirements that are defined by the former class. It even would be possible to define such classes after the instance was created, allowing for reuse of objects in customized contexts.

Additionally, a property-based classification would allow to specify the parameters of functions for objects without knowing their specific implementation. This approach is not restricted to data types but can involve more complex specifications. For example, a parameter could be required to bear certain relations to other objects (as opposed to having a certain type). The application of inference mechanisms during the parameter matching phase would furthermore permit to pass parameters that are no immediately obvious match for the requirements but can be inferred to be.

This approach bears resemblance to so-called duck typing. With that technique it is simply assumed that a given object supports the desired operations (i.e. method invocations and access to properties), otherwise an exception is thrown. A semantics-based approach is situated in between duck typing and dynamic typing: it allows to break out from strict syntax checks but retains the possibility to check for required semantic characteristics. Some of such checks could even be implemented in the form of static typing, depending on the features that are provided by the programming language in use (cf. section 4.2.2).

With this technique, existing applications can be extended more easily without knowing the exact internals, as long as a common ground for symbols and concepts does exist. Thus, this approach significantly extends the semantic reflection paradigm (cf. section 2.3.4), where central programming primitives are accessed by means of semantic descriptions that reflect dynamically changing aspects of these primitives. The specifics of an implementation of this approach will be discussed in chapter 4.

Concerning virtual environments, access on a semantic level can be achieved: users of an application could request entities and actions by specifying desired properties and effects. This would not only work for users but especially for programmers, since the features would be available at development time. Hence, a rather description based access (as opposed to a reference based one) can be implemented, allowing for more flexible interaction.

For modern intelligent user interfaces, which may involve voice commands and similar interaction, the association of symbols with objects and functions allows to thin out the layer that provides the required mapping. For example, assume the function create, which visualizes an object, is accessible using the symbol CREATE. Furthermore, if objects are also accessible by means of symbols, the implementation of voice commands like "Create a box!" would be rather easy. Of course, this does not directly affect the natural language processing stage—although a feedback regarding available concepts could be beneficial for the improvement of its results—but utilizing the output of that stage would be simplified a lot.

3.2.2 Aspects and Requirements

As stated initially, representing semantics and inferring new facts requires a KB that contains relations between known individuals and concepts. Thus, it is not sufficient to simply annotate some of the simulated entities with symbols. In order to integrate the information that is necessary to facilitate the above-mentioned features, a framework is required to support annotating *any* instantiated entity and property. Similarly, the possibility of defining relations between these elements is mandatory.

The following paragraphs survey the aspects that have to be addressed in this context. Afterwards, a list of arising requirements is created, which has to be considered for the creation of an IRIS framework.

Form of Representation   As mentioned in section 2.4.4, a knowledge representation is commonly integrated into IRIS applications in the form of a dedicated layer or module that can be accessed by the simulation modules that depend on it.

In this context, the way in which information will be used is highly relevant for choosing an adequate form of representation: if later usage is restricted to annotating objects, a plain text representation might be sufficient. If, however, more complex operations like inferring new facts based on the existing knowledge are required—as it is the case with most IRISs—a more structured representation is necessary. Thus, the form of representation has to be chosen carefully to not impose restrictions from the beginning.

Maintenance   The creation and maintenance of the vast amount of entries in the corresponding knowledge base often involves a great deal of work (Neches et al., 1991). In order to facilitate this task, such knowledge bases often contain domain specific knowledge only, (partially) covering the particular application domain. The creation is usually performed by knowledge engineers and domain experts, who model the contents of the knowledge base which underlies the respective application.

Since a knowledge engineer is not necessarily involved with application programming, remodeling may be tedious and costly: the updates have to be coordinated between module developers, carefully integrated, and the results have to be tested. Especially custom-made solutions are prone to such issues, because there is little chance to be able to reuse results from other projects.

In this context, an external form of representation, like OWL, is desirable. The files that contain the formalized knowledge can serve as an interface and thus allow knowledge engineers to perform their tasks independently from programmers and application developers.

Reuse   The amount of work that is required to systematically integrate the desired information into a KRL is easily underestimated. This is not only owed to the requirement of consistency of the knowledge base, but also to the mere amount of information to be added. In order to reduce efforts, reuse is a desirable approach in the area of semantic modeling, too. This way, a close connection to the topic of domain engineering (cf. section 2.2.4) arises.

Indisputably, the design and maintenance of a knowledge base is a complex and demanding task. Nevertheless, its contents can be reused, if appropriate standards are set and maintained. For example, in the context of the Semantic Web, ontologies are interlinked in order to avoid the need for remodeling of content.

While the application of Semantic Web technologies is a reasonable starting point to create reusable KRLs, the connection to the application, and especially its state, remains an open question. This is mainly due to the fact that there is no standard approach to incorporate a knowledge base into an IRIS framework. As a result, the contents of the applied tailored knowledge bases are not reusable.

Standards As mentioned before, the interpretation of a particular symbol may vary, depending on the person perceiving it. The related lack of a standard for the structure of ontology contents is a problem that is similarly known in the field of software engineering: regarding software development, this can result in difficulties when variable and function identifiers are misinterpreted and possibly misused (Garlan et al., 1995).

In software companies this commonly leads to the introduction of coding conventions to limit the variety of coding styles. Ambiguity of symbols may be negligible within a small development team, but regarding reuse among most different groups of developers it needs to be possible to specify synonyms and translations for symbols.

The intent to create a standard KB for all kinds of applications is far beyond the scope of this work and can impossibly be achieved by a single person (a related project, the *Cyc* ontology (Lenat, Guha, Pittman, Pratt, & Shepherd, 1990; Matuszek, Cabral, Witbrock, & DeOliveira, 2006), which is addressing common sense knowledge, is being developed since 1984). In contrast, this thesis aims at providing means to develop such a standard KB incrementally.

Expressivity Most of the time, the decidability of queries is more limited, the more expressive the representation becomes. Moreover, it is not desirable to simply choose the most powerful representation, since this might prevent later usage due to performance requirements that cannot be met. On the other hand, it might be desirable or even required to permit to specify knowledge in a more expressive way, trading performance for simplicity. Different approaches to this issue do exist and it has to be carefully evaluated which one promises to be the right choice.

Understandability The more complex the chosen representation is, the higher is the probability that it is not accepted by users. This issue is largely related to the inherent complexity of the chosen format.

For example, a developer will probably prefer to write program code or even use natural language instead of expressing information using a DL. In addition, the way it is presented to the user plays an important role (think of reading plain HTML code as opposed to viewing a rendered website). Consequently, the understandability of the used representation as well as preexisting tools and support for the integration into an application are a major decision criterion.

Nature of Integration The integration of a KRL can be achieved in different ways. One possible solution is to add the knowledge representation on top of a software system's functionality (cf. Lugrin & Cavazza, 2007; Nesbigall et al., 2011). This is less invasive, since it does not require to modify the internals of possibly preexisting software. However, it requires to establish and maintain an independent knowledge base, which contains more abstract information and is fed from the application state. This is problematic for different reasons.

Most importantly, it has to be ensured that the knowledge representation always is synchronized with the system state. This entails some risks regarding reusability and maintainability. For one thing, the represented knowledge is defined twice; explicitly in the KRL and implicitly in the software itself. This duplication of data possibly increases the incomprehensibility of the software and complicates its maintenance.

This issue cannot be avoided completely due to the different forms of representation, which are used by different modules (e.g., an AI module and a 3D renderer). Yet, it is desirable to implement an update mechanism that is as transparent as possible.

Since the knowledge representation is added subsequently, it tends to constitute a loosely coupled, monolithic component on its own. Consequently, knowledge that is related to a certain simulation module is captured by this application specific component. This way, reusability of the whole, possibly modular system is decreased. In addition, any change to the system would require an adaption of the KRL, which is a bad design regarding maintainability. Finally, it can be troublesome to grant a subsequently added KRL access to certain aspects of the system state.

As opposed to adding the knowledge representation on top of a system, the other extreme on the scale of knowledge integration depth is to a priori represent all parts of the software, starting with variables, functions, classes, et cetera. Related achievements are indicated by Latoschik and Fröhlich (2007a) in the context of the SCIVE framework. Their implementation has never extended beyond a prototypical state, though. While this approach obviates the need for data duplication and multiple forms of representation, it creates higher amounts of work during the initial development process.

Moreover, such a deep integration requires custom-made tools and languages, which can operate on this kind of internal KRL. This complicates the utilization of external software libraries, tools, and existing knowledge bases and thus impedes reuse. If this approach is chosen, the possibility to interlink the internal representation with an external one, which can be processed by external modules and tools, is necessary to allow for its reuse.

In addition, the contents of the KRL have to be specified on the program code level. If only a subset of the possibly available information should be inserted into in the KRL, a change to KRL would require to adapt the internals of the simulation modules. Alternatively, all of the available information could be inserted, which easily can result in a KB of enormous size. Such a knowledge base can be useful for offline computations. For example, it could be used to support developers when searching for reusable components. Run-time access to such detailed information, however, might become too inefficient and thus renders it useless for IRIS applications.

Resulting Requirements

Based on the above-mentioned aspects, the following set of requirements for the KRL to be integrated into a VRs framework is defined. It is desirable to develop an approach that

R1 facilitates and maintains modularity. In this context, it is desirable to facilitate semantic augmentation of existing assets.

R2 is transparent in the way that extensions to an application do not necessitate manual modifications to the knowledge representation.

R3 facilitates reuse and individual modification of stored knowledge. In this context, the adoption of an external storage format is desirable.

R4 is scalable, i.e. content and complexity of the knowledge base can easily be adapted to an application's needs.

R5 avoids duplication of information.

R6 is comprehensible and thus minimizes additional work and required knowledge when used. This especially includes availability of tools for viewing and editing.

With these requirements in mind, the following sections systematically review the conceptual elements of IRISs and develop a universal model for the representation of architecture elements as well as simulated content. Said review begins with the selection of an appropriate level of integration into an IRIS framework.

3.2.3 Level of Integration

In order to meet the requirements specified in the previous section, the following observations can be made: the approach has to couple information to single architecture elements, since it shall maintain modularity (R1). In addition, it has to be integrated into the programming environment, since information should be interlinked with program code. This way, a modification to an existing application would inherently result in an update of the KRL (R2).

Furthermore, the approach has to have an add-in or wrapping nature, since it shall be usable with preexisting software (R1). Ideally, each developer should be able to define module-specific information independent from other parts of the application, wherefore a layered approach is desirable (R3). The negative effects on the application's performance must be as low as possible, especially when the represented knowledge is not accessed (R4 and R5). Moreover, information should be available at compile-time as well as at run-time in order to facilitate retrieval of assets and the integration of AI methods, the latter of which is a major goal of this work. Finally, the approach also should involve as few additional concepts as possible (R6), which has to be taken into account when the elements that shall be represented are defined (cf. section 3.2.4).

Assuming that no restrictions regarding the integration exist, every type, variable, and function could be semantically annotated. While this approach does grant the maximum amount of information, its implementation would require enormous efforts. It also would require full access to program code, which usually is unfeasible in an environment of (black-box) reuse. Moreover, it is contrary to the desire that a wrapper-based approach should be applied. Thus, it would require programmers to deal with the knowledge representation, which rather is a knowledge engineer's task. A large amount of the information that would be added to the KRL in this way would be unused, since it involves elements that are hidden behind software interfaces and not accessible by the IRIS application. Alternatively, only a manually selected subset of these types and functions could be linked to the KRL, thereby reducing the required amount of work.

The approach that is commonly applied to integrate a KRL into an application (besides using callbacks where possible) involves synchronizing the KRL by accessing the simulation state in a polling manner. As an alternative to this, all updates that are performed by each simulation component could be intercepted in order to minimize the risk of missing valuable information on occurring changes.

The approach proposed in this work involves creating a semantic layer around existing software modules or, taking an alternative point of view, around the centralized application state. In this context, a component model is created, which channels state updates through a comprehensible software interface and thus allows to annotate them semantically. Thereby, the ideas introduced by the SCIVE framework, which was discussed in section 2.3.4, are extended. In order to capture all application state changes, communication between the application and components as well as between different components may occur only through this layer.

To specify the basic elements, different aspects of an IRIS application have to be taken into account. These do especially involve the represented content, participating modules, and the application itself.

3.2.4 Representable Elements

The process of creating a KRL often includes gathering domain specific knowledge and storing it using an adequate form of representation. However, due to the range of possible applications, there is no single domain which can be determined for an IRIS, per se. Therefore, a more abstract approach is required. The following elementary observations regarding VE applications help to pinpoint the necessary basic elements.

Regardless of the eventual purpose of an application, each program run can be interpreted as the transition from a start state into an end state. In between these two states, there is a countably infinite number of further states which can possibly be entered.

Transitions, in this context, are discrete events, one of which can occur at a time. A single transition does modify exactly one aspect of the application state. Essentially, such a modification to the application state is represented by a single value update in the computer memory. Two transitions are said to be *dependent* regarding a certain state, when the two resulting states are in conflict, i.e. when the simultaneous execution of the associated value updates would create an invalid state.

It has to be stressed that the term application state does not necessarily denote the contents of the computer memory and registers (although it could) but rather an abstract representation of the application's state.

The assumption that only one transition occurs at a time might be questionable in the context of current multi-core or multi-processor setups. However, since the hardware in use is assumed to run at a certain clock speed, a higher (virtual) clock which covers all real clocks can be constructed. Then any two concurrent, independent transitions can be assumed to occur in an arbitrary order between two of these virtual clocks. Assuming that two dependent transitions never occur at a time, a serialization of transitions exists that meets the questioned assertion.

In the case that two dependent transitions occur concurrently, the resulting state would be invalid. This issue is independent of the presented transition-based perspective but rather an inherent aspect of concurrent programming. Consequently, it has to be prevented by software developers with any means at hand and thus will not be discussed any further. A formalism to represent the ordering of events, which can be applied to analyze concurrent processes and possibly arising inconsistencies, is presented by Lamport (1978).

This considerations result in the observation that the utilization of states and events is sufficient to describe an IRIS application. In order to find a uniform representation, the basic elements of an IRIS application have to be examined. In this context, the introductorily mentioned classification of objects into entities, properties, and relations among them constitutes the basis for the semantic facet of the sought representation.

Content Representation

As mentioned before, not only an IRIS but every application simulates some kind of virtual environment. Since being simulated, each of those environments inevitably contains virtual aspects. But, due to its interactive nature, at least the user of an application and the used input devices introduce a real aspect. Consequently, each IRIS application always combines virtual and real aspects.

Regarding objects residing in virtual environments, the adoption of an entity centered model is a common approach (cf. section 2.3.2). Yet, it is less common to treat the user, input devices, and especially simulation components in the same way. However, nothing prevents from adopting this kind of representation, since all of those objects can be defined by means of an associated state representation. For input devices, for example, this could be the state of buttons or a tracking-target's position, for simulation components it would be the respective component's configuration.

State Values, Semantic Values and Relations   In search of a common ground for all of the represented objects, the concepts of semantic values and state values are proposed. They provide the basis for a semantic, uniform interface between simulation modules and the application state. As indicated, their definitions involve the introduced concepts of properties, relations, and entities.

Definition 3.1. The combination of a property with a link to the representation of its semantics is called a *semantic value*. It comprises a value, the associated data type, and said link to its semantics.

Such a semantic value can be considered as a unary relation. A relation, in this regard, is defined as follows:

Definition 3.2. A semantic value that contains an n-tuple of (references to) semantic values is called a *relation*.

The only difference between semantic values and relations is the type of values they can assume: while a semantic value can have a value of arbitrary data type, relations are limited to hold tuples of semantic values. This distinction ensures that no meaningless value can be related to a semantic value or even exist in this representation.

The possibility to link a value to its semantics provides the basis for semantic augmentation of any static element of a program. This way, the goal to create a model that allows for semantics-based representation of IVEs contents is supported by the concept of semantic values.

Definition 3.3. A semantic value that represents one particular characteristic of the simulation state is called a *state value*. Characteristics, in this case, are atomic properties of entities as well as relations between them.

Conceptually, a state value is immutable and has a fixed data type. However, an implementation will employ so called *state variables* that can assume such state values. For a description concerning the implementation of this concept refer to section 5.2.5.

The range of data types, which may be accepted by state values that are not relations, is only restricted in that it must not comprise container types (i.e. tuples, lists, sets, etc.). Each semantic value that is related to a state value, by being part of the simulation state, is a state value and thus underlies the same rules. This restriction is made to prevent the insertion of possibly meaningless values in such containers. Instead, the presented model introduces a specific type to represent such containers, called entities, which provide a single interface to the application state (cf. definition 3.4).

With the introduced abstractions each application state n is defined by the set of all present state values:

$$State_n = \bigcup_{i \in I_n} StateValue_i \quad \text{where} \quad StateValue_i \in S \tag{3.1}$$

The set I_n in equation 3.1 depicts the index set that contains the indices of all state values belonging to a given state n. Every state value $StateValue_i$ is an element of the set S of all possible state values.

To avoid misunderstandings it has to be clarified that only the aspects that are relevant to the simulation state are addressed by state values. Internal variables of simulation modules, temporary variables inside functions, or similar elements are not in the domain of state values. This does neither mean that such variables are not related to the simulation state (they most certainly are) nor that they may not be represented by semantic values. But they are not part of the interface that simulation modules use to communicate with one another and thus not represented by state values.

Entities   Although the entire application state could be represented by state values only, this representation would be far from being comprehensible. The vast number of state values would require enormous efforts regarding structured storage and retrieval. Without any prescribed way of accessing values, applications would end up incomprehensible and thus unmaintainable. Hence, a layer of abstraction is created by the introduction of entities.

Definition 3.4. An *entity* is the set of all state values that belong to the concept that is represented by that entity.

$$Entity_n^k = \bigcup_{j \in J_n^k} StateValue_j \quad \text{where} \quad \dot{\bigcup_l} J_n^l = I_n \tag{3.2}$$

For example, the position and rotation as well as the graphical representation of a sphere-shaped object could be stored in state values, which (partially) constitute the entity that represents a virtual ball.

Equation 3.2 describes an entity k as part of the state n: It is the union of all state values that belong to the subset J_n^k of the index set I_n (which is defined in the same way as in equation 3.1). Moreover, the disjoint union of all sets J_n^l constitutes the set I_n, whereby a further restriction on state values is added: every state value must belong to exactly one entity, wherefore an entity always is a container for state values.

The above-mentioned restriction implies that every object inside an application, which shall be accessible by means of the sought-after interface, must be represented by an entity, since the entire state is represented by means of state values. It furthermore leads to the fact that every aspect of the application state can be accessed through the entity which the element belongs to.

Note that an entity cannot be directly represented by a state value, since this would contradict the rule that state values may not contain collections of further state values. This is reasonable, since the entity itself is a structuring element and therefore not an actual element of the simulation state. However, entities can be represented by a state value that contains an identifying reference. Consequently, the only way to link two entities is by representing them as such references, creating two relations that provide a meaningful connection between the associated state values and asserting one of them to each of the entities. For example, a HASPART(ENTITY2) relation could be asserted to the entity ENTITY1 and a PARTOF(ENTITY1) relation to the entity ENTITY2.

Similarly, the concept of composition of semantic values is represented by the utilization of relations, using a dedicated HASPROPERTY relation. The assertion of each state value that does not represent a relation will thus be interpreted as an instance of a relation between an entity and that state value. A later implementation, however, will conveniently allow for direct access to state values via the related entities. Observably, an entity is defined by the set of relations it takes part in.

In summary, three elements are introduced to form the basis for further concepts: the entity class, the set of relations, as well as the set of semantic values (which includes state values). This structure is very similar to that of ontologies that are used in the field of AI, wherefore each object could easily be linked to a concept in an ontology that specifies relations between those objects.

Events When representing the complete simulation state by means of state values, a way to represent changes to the simulation state (i.e. state transitions) is required. A state transition conceptually specifies a single modification of the application state. More precisely, it represents the addition, update, or removal of a state value.

Regarding the application state n, an event i can thus be represented as the two sets Add_i and $Remove_i$ of added and removed state values:

$$Event_n^i = \{Add_i \notin I_n, \; Remove_i \subset I_n\} \tag{3.3}$$

Since state values are immutable, value updates can conceptually be regarded as removing and instantly (re-)adding a state value. Given a certain state n, the observation of an event will result in the transition into a subsequent state $n + 1$:

$$State_{n+1} = State_n \circ Event_n^i = State_n \setminus Remove_i \cup Add_i \tag{3.4}$$

Because each event—as long as it is not ignored—eventually ends in the manipulation of the world state, events are not limited to indicate state changes: it is also convenient to represent other occurrences, like the application of a physical impulse to an object or the collision of two objects, by means of events. For this purpose, events may carry additional payload in the form of semantic values (cf. figure 3.1). A collision event, for instance, may incorporate the colliding entities.

Events can be emitted and received by any active element of the architecture and usually represent a certain occurrence that was detected by a simulation module. Similar to concepts,

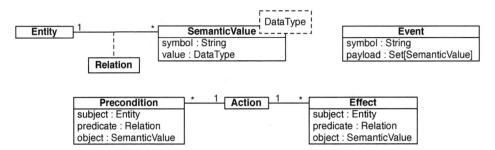

Figure 3.1: The seven basic elements of the approach. Static elements are represented by means of entities, which are linked to state values by means of relations (left). Change is indicated by events (right) that can be triggered by actions, which are described by means of preconditions and effects (bottom).

an event provides a link to the representation of its semantics. By the observation of all such events (i.e. by observing all changes to the simulation state) a homogeneous interface is created. This interface connects the application to the utilized simulation modules in the same way it connects those modules among another.

In contrast to state values, events do represent incidents that do not have an associated duration but occur at a certain point in time. For example, the update of a state value occurs instantly, wherefore it is represented as an event. As opposed to this, the fact that an object has a certain state (e.g., ENABLED) is represented by state values.

The utilization of state variables and events is redundant: If each simulation module (including the application logic) would observe all events, no centralized representation of the simulation state would be necessary. Yet, in this case each module would have to maintain its own representation of the current state. If, in contrast, each simulation module would observe all state variables, it could detect all effects of the state change events, update its internal representation, and react accordingly.

The advantages of a purely state variable based approach include the fact a module does not have to maintain a representation on its own. This relieves the module of having to store every aspect of the simulation in order to be able to access it later. Since such access may never occur for certain simulation aspects, a lot of potential overhead is removed, if they are stored globally. Moreover does this approach allow to store and load states, which would have to be recreated by re-emitting and processing every event.

On the downside, inferring semantics from the occurring value updates is a complex task, which is simplified a lot by processing an event that semantically describes the indicated occurrence. Furthermore, the utilization of event-callbacks does promise higher performance than the observation of the simulation state, which requires manual reaction to inferred events. In this regard, the simulation state would also have to be more comprehensive, since each aspect that is indicated by a certain event would have to be reflected by a state value.

However, the pure, unstructured handling of events would result in unmaintainable, incomprehensible applications. As a result, both interfaces have to be provided, allowing a developer to choose the most appropriate one for each purpose individually.

Actions   In the same way that ontologies are useful to represent the semantics of static elements of an application, methods from the field of automated planning are useful to represent dynamic aspects (i.e. functions in the program code that modify the static content). Common representations of actions take the preconditions and effects of these aspects into account (see section 2.4.3). This view can be mapped onto the concept of functions in program code by regarding their parameters as preconditions. Similarly, a return value as well as a function's side-effects can be viewed as its effects.

Ontologies and action representation fit together well, as the latter is built upon the first (cf. figure 3.1). This way, decoupling static scene content from the applied software functions is facilitated. Given a repository of methods that are sufficiently described, an application that implements this approach can reuse functions from the repository without necessitating further adaption. In this context, a description-based approach facilitates automatic look-ups from such repositories.

In summary, the basic elements to describe an IRIS application include: *Semantic values* and *relations*, that are used to specify instances of the structuring element, which will be called an *entity*. These three elements can further be used to define *preconditions* and *effects* of *actions*, which perform a modification of the current application state. Such modifications are represented by *events*.

Simulation Module Representation

The discussed seven basic elements can theoretically be used to describe an application and its internals completely. However, in their plain form they are too unspecific and therefore require further considerations to be of help in the software engineering context.

An additional layer that is found in IRIS applications has to be examined to address this issue: each application is composed of multiple simulation modules, which according to their intended nature will be called *simulation components*, or *components* for short. These terms are based on the definitions of software components by Councill and Heineman (2001), which were quoted in section 1.4. Commonly, each of these simulation components is responsible for a certain simulation aspect. For example, a physics engine is concerned with the simulation of all physics related processes, whereas a visual rendering component visualizes the current application state.

Simulation modules usually perform highly specific computations, wherefore they require purpose-built representations of the simulation state. These representations often do not include all of the information that is available for a certain simulated entity. For example, a visual rendering engine most certainly does not require knowledge about the mass of an object, whereas the physics engine will be highly dependent on this information. If, however, the visual rendering component would for any reason have to request the mass of the object this needs to be feasible, too.

Apparently, the required information depends on the modules in use and even might vary between two components that are responsible for the same simulation aspect. In order to avoid duplication of data at this point (requirement R5) the concept of *aspects* is introduced. An aspect is similar to a view in database theory as it represents a partial set of properties of a certain entity.

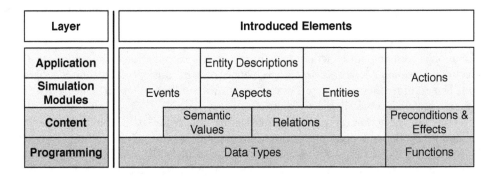

Layer	Introduced Elements			
Application		Entity Descriptions		Actions
Simulation Modules	Events	Aspects	Entities	
Content		Semantic Values	Relations	Preconditions & Effects
Programming		Data Types		Functions

Figure 3.2: The application layers, which reflect the categorization of developers from section 2.3.1, and associated elements. The elements on higher layers provide access to those at lower layers.

As the term suggests, it is intended to subsume the state values that are required by a certain simulation module to be able to simulate the corresponding aspect. Therefore, it matches definition 1.4 (simulation aspect). It is worth mentioning that the properties of two aspects do not have to be mutually exclusive. For example, the position of an object is most certainly required by both a visual rendering and a physical simulation module.

In order to maximize reusability of single parts of an application, simulation modules should be as independent from each other as possible. Using aspects to specify the properties of an entity allows to completely reduce the coupling of simulation components to the agreement on the access to the state variables of simulated entities and support for a specified set of events.

Since a simulation component can be viewed as an entity itself, the associated state variables can be used to form its interface. Thus, no further concepts have to be defined. Most of the elements of the component-entity's interface are specifically tailored for the respective component. However, the component type, a component name, and the update frequency are shared by each component.

In addition to the previously defined elements, the component level thus adds the concept of *aspects* to the set of elements to be represented.

Application Level Representation

On the application level entities are instantiated and components are composed to form a complete system. Building on the concepts that were introduced in the lower layers, an *entity description* is composed by combining multiple aspects. Such a description specifies the properties of an entity as well as the relations in which it will take part.

Since a component is regarded as an entity, its instantiation is performed in the same way as the instantiation of entities. Hence, no additional concepts regarding components are required. Similarly, an application can be interpreted as a further component that creates entities (and possibly modifies them in a certain way).

3.2.5 Summary

Figure 3.2 provides an overview of the discussed layers and the elements to be represented in a knowledge representation. This set of elements is sufficient to represent the state of an application as well as updates to it. Every simulation module is added a wrapping layer, which will be called a *module adapter*. Its task is to update the simulation state which is represented by the elements of the content layer. In the same way, a module's internal representation can be updated by observing value changes in the KRL. Briefly speaking, a module adapter turns a simulation module into a simulation component. Finally, an application can orchestrate the creation and maintenance of elements from the lower layers.

With this approach the initially stated requirements are addressed as follows:

R1 The structure of the development process of IRIS applications is taken into account. In doing so, especially the different roles of developers are considered. As a result, preexisting simulation modules are provided with individual adapters, wherefore their modularity is maintained.

R2 Following the proposed approach, the simulation state is inherently augmented with semantic information that is attached to semantic values, relations, state values, and events. If a way to inherently add semantic links to semantic values can be found, extensions to an application do not necessitate manual modifications of the knowledge representation but the KRL is updated automatically. This issue will be addressed in section 3.3.

R3 & R4 The added semantic layer only consists of links to semantic representations, which can be of arbitrary complexity. In simple cases the link is a symbol, in more complex cases it can relate an architecture element to a highly elaborated ontology.

R5 The approach does not duplicate information: depending on the particular implementation of semantic values, existing values can be wrapped and only the link to the semantic representation is added.

R6 Only few concepts were introduced for the approach, wherefore it bears potential to be easy to understand.

In order to facilitate the utilization of existing tools for editing the knowledge base, a formal basis for the model has to be detected. While chapter 4 discusses the software implementation of this model, the following sections will be concerned with the choice of an adequate knowledge representation and its interface to eventual applications.

3.2.6 Adopting the Web Ontology Language

The *Web Ontology Language* (OWL) is the de facto standard for specifications of ontologies in the Semantic Web. Characteristics like the possibility of modular organization of ontology files and the existence of language profiles that allow for efficient reasoning make it a perfect fit for the representation of ontologies in the IRIS context.

Large ontologies are available in the Semantic Web, which can be incorporated into applications in order to benefit from previous knowledge engineering efforts. Moreover, its wide prevalence resulted in a huge amount of tools that are available for multiple purposes, e.g, editors, reasoning software, data bases, etc. This is in compliance with requirement R6.

An OWL ontology corresponds to a certain DL, depending on the fragment of OWL that is used. Consequently, the restrictions that apply for the respective DL do also apply for the OWL ontology. The following section addresses the implications that arise in this context. The OWL examples that are presented in this chapter use OWL functional-style syntax. Essential ontology contents that are used in this work are listed in appendix A.

Description Logics

DLs provide a formal logic-based framework for semantic knowledge representations. By means of this framework the expressivity of a formalism can be classified and its reasoning complexity can be categorized. In the following sections, the terms concept, role, and individual from the field of description logics will be used to identify classes, relations, and objects, respectively.

As mentioned in section 2.4.1, DLs adopt the *Open World Assumption* (OWA) but do not make the *Unique Name Assumption* (UNA), wherefore some implications have to be taken into account. In general, the OWA implies that a fact that is not explicitly asserted to be false rather will be regarded to be unknown than to be false. As a consequence, checking whether or not an individual is an instance of a concept that contains a negated role assertion does require this fact to be provable with the contents of the knowledge base. For example, suppose that the concept STATICOBJECT is defined to be equivalent to the class of individuals that are not instances of the concept MOVABLEOBJECT. Then an individual that is not an instance of either concept is not inferred to be a STATICOBJECT, because it still could be a MOVABLEOBJECT. Accordingly, the classification of individuals according to the absence of a certain characteristic is not possible.

While this at first seems to be an issue, the adoption of its counterpart, the *Closed World Assumption* (CWA), would create a different problem: with the CWA an individual that is not explicitly stated to have a certain property is assumed not to have it. In consequence, extending a CWA knowledge base—which is highly desirable regarding reusability—can lead to inconsistencies. For instance, suppose that the KB contains the statement that every individual is either big or small. If later any individual would be added without specifying if it was either big or small, the KB would become inconsistent. This is because it is assumed to be neither big nor small, which is in conflict with the assertion that every individual must be one of the two.

Similarly, the UNA could cause problems when knowledge bases are extended or combined. With this assumption a certain object must be identified by exactly one symbol. This would require each developer who wants to extend a knowledge base to exactly know about its internals. In this context, the combination of two knowledge bases would most certainly require re-engineering to ensure that the UNA is maintained.

Aiming for an extensible, layered approach, both the open world assumption and the absence of the unique name assumption are hence a reasonable choice. A further aspect, which is important in the context of reasoning performance, is the required expressivity.

Depending on the combination of used features, the computational complexity regarding reasoning processes increases according to the expressivity of the description logic in use. In the same way, it affects the decidability of queries against the knowledge base. Using too many language features to achieve higher expressivity thus could result in undecidability of the KB (i.e. a reasoner cannot be guaranteed to infer all facts in a finite amount of time).

Although the utilization of a certain set of language features does not necessarily imply that a particular KB is undecidable, the mere possibility is undesirable and should be avoided. Hence, the following section discusses the features that are required to represent the elements that were determined before.

Description Logic Features

In the previous sections, nine elements were detected: semantic values, events, relations, entities, aspects, actions, preconditions, effects, and entity descriptions. Out of these, semantic values and events are the most easy to represent: the IRI of an ontology concept will be used as a link for an associated semantic value. Instances of the semantic value are represented by individuals of that concept. If required, the value of a semantic value is associated to the respective individual by a HASVALUE role. Similarly, events are composed of a concept and related to semantic values by a HASPROPERTY role.

Role Characteristics   Relations can be more complex to represent than plain properties. A relation is represented by a role, which may have multiple of the characteristics listed in table 3.1. The values listed in the column 'relevance' reflect the chance that the characteristic is required for the design of an IVE. Transitivity and symmetry are regarded to have high relevance, since they are required to model essential relations like PARTOF, HASPART, and CLOSETO. Similarly, asymmetric roles and the possibility to specify inverse roles are commonly used, e.g., in the context of comparisons (BIGGERTHAN, LEFTOF, etc.).

Disjoint roles, functional roles, and inverse functional roles are less often required, since the potentially inferred knowledge is rather beneficial for consistency checks than for content modeling. The utilization of functional roles allows to emulate the UNA for individuals by assigning distinct identifiers to each of them, which is desirable in the context of cardinality restrictions (see below). Inverse functional roles allow to specify equivalent individuals by relating two of them to an identifying individual. Although their relevance is categorized as medium, their utilization is still desirable.

The remaining characteristics, reflexivity and irreflexivity, make the respective role relate every individual to itself. This is valuable when assertions about individuals are queried, e.g., to retrieve all objects that are close to an object or not left of an object, which in both cases should return at least the object itself.

As opposed to applying a reasoning module, every characteristic can be reproduced by programmatically inserting the resulting assertions (cf. column programmatic solution in table 3.1). Hence, if a chosen DL does not support some of the required characteristics, the IRIS application can compensate for this. In this regard, transitivity is a problematic characteristic, since it possibly requires to update all individuals that are related by the transitive role that was altered. Consequently, at least transitivity should be supported by the chosen DL.

characteristic	example	relevance	programmatic solution	notes
transitive	$partOf(i_1, i_2) \land partOf(i_2, i_3)$ $\implies partOf(i_1, i_3)$	high	traverse property chain and update affected individuals	programmatic solution possibly complex
symmetric	$closeTo(i_1, i_2)$ $\implies closeTo(i_2, i_1)$	high	assert reverse role	
asymmetric	$leftOf(i_1, i_2)$ $\implies \neg leftOf(i_2, i_1)$	high	assert negated role	
inverse roles	$hasPart(i_1, i_2)$ $\implies partOf(i_2, i_1)$	high	assert inverse role	
functional	$isAt(i, loc_1) \land isAt(i, loc_2)$ $\implies loc_1 = loc_2$	medium	check for same roles and assert equivalence of values accordingly	allows to emulate UNA using dedicated identifiers
inverse functional	$hasID(i_1, id) \land hasID(i_2, id)$ $\implies i_1 = i_2$	medium	check for equivalent ids and assert equivalence of individuals accordingly	allows to specify equivalent individuals using dedicated identifiers
disjoint roles	$leftOf(i_1, i_2)$ $\implies \neg rightOf(i_1, i_2)$	medium	assert negated disjoint role	
reflexive	$\forall i : closeTo(i, i)$	medium	assert role on individual creation	
irreflexive	$\forall i : \neg leftOf(i, i)$	medium	assert role on individual creation	

Table 3.1: Available characteristics for DL roles in OWL including examples that show their effects. The entries in the column 'relevance' provide an estimation for the number of situations in which the respective characteristic is useful. The column 'programmatic solution' provides a possible alternative to achieve the resulting changes to the KB by an IRIS framework.

Definition of Concepts   In order to describe a certain part of an entity, especially in the context of aspects, further concepts have to be supported by the chosen description logic. First of all, concept intersection is required in order to create more specific concepts from existing ones. In this context, the feature of full existential quantification is necessary in order to specify a concept based on the roles it is involved in. For instance, it could be necessary to state that the class of tables contains all elements that are a piece of furniture and that have legs.

At run-time it may become desirable to use concept definitions that involve existential quantification to an individual or literal. This way, for example, the class of all objects that are red can be defined.

The remaining features are concerned with cardinality restrictions. These split up into the two groups of unqualified and qualified cardinality restrictions. While the former specify cardinality restrictions on roles only, the latter also restrict the types which the role may involve. This is required, for example, if a car shall be defined to be any object that has four wheels (as opposed to having four arbitrary individuals). Since such definitions relate to entity descriptions, this feature is possibly required in the application layer.

3.3 A Reusable Knowledge Representation Model

To enable sharing the representation among different applications the previously mentioned architecture elements have to be represented in a uniform way. Aiming for efficient handling of the knowledge base's contents, the represented elements have to be carefully examined to determine the required minimal expressivity of the underlying DL.

The following sections investigate restrictions regarding the DL for each of the previously identified architecture elements.

3.3.1 Relation Descriptions

In common RIS frameworks the concept of relations is not explicitly supported. For instance, a part-of relation would be represented by aggregating entities, an is-at relation would be stored in a dedicated variable, and a close-to relation might be realized by invoking a function that performs a distance check. This results in huge efforts, and often characteristics like transitivity have to be implemented manually.

In contrast, relations are inherently supported by description logics. As discussed above, transitive relations are required to specify relations like PARTOF. In the context of an integrated knowledge layer, the direct support for further characteristics is optional, since these can be maintained programmatically (see section 3.2.6). Consequently, the expressivity of the DL in use varies between that of the DLs $\mathcal{EL}+$ and $\mathcal{ELRIF}+$ (cf. table 2.3 on page 46).

A problem commonly faced by a knowledge engineer who is using OWL is the fact that no assertions about roles can be made. For example, it is not possible to state that a WILLWIN role has a probability of 50%. Whereas in RDF statements can be reified to address this issue, in OWL 2 the support for annotation properties was introduced. These allow to add structured information to any element in the ontology, but are not handled by reasoning modules, wherefore they have no effect on reasoning efficiency.

The feature of annotations will be used especially in cases when no reasoning facilities are required but more information is necessary to connect the ontology with an application. In order to link a relation data type with the associated role in the ontology the following approach can be adopted: for every role that shall be reflected a concept is created, which is linked to that role by means of a HASPREDICATE annotation. To use these relation concepts, the associated individuals are linked to others via the roles HASSUBJECT and HASOBJECT. The concept is furthermore asserted to be a subconcept of the SEMANTICVALUE concept, which will be introduced in the next section.

Required DL features

The expressivity of the underlying DL is highly dependent on the utilized characteristics of roles. As discussed above, this results in an expressivity requirement of at least $\mathcal{EL}+$ and at most $\mathcal{ELRIF}+$.

3.3.2 Value Descriptions

From the application developer's point of view the most basic element is a single property. In programming languages plain variables are commonly used to represent these, whereas in the proposed approach semantic values are applied for this purpose. In both cases a value is defined that is accessed by different simulation modules to access an entity's current state.

As mentioned before, a semantic value stores data that is represented by means of single a data type. Regarding modular IRIS applications this is a rather problematic representation, since different simulation modules will most certainly use different data types to store a particular property. The discussion of implications related to required data conversion mechanisms is deferred to chapter 4, whereas the fact that multiple representations may exist for the same concept is addressed below.

There are two aspects to this problem: on the one hand, multiple data types have to be linked to a certain concept. On the other hand, a specific data type can solely be asserted by the developers of the simulation component in question. In fact, the developers of a simulation component should be the only ones who are concerned with its internal data representation in order to maintain modularity (requirement R1). As a result, each component has to be accompanied by at least one ontology file that imports the ontology that establishes a common ground for the definition of properties and concepts related to the simulation module's domain.

Figure 3.3 exemplifies the modular description of semantic values. All elements that are not inside of a rectangle with a dashed outline are associated to the *core ontology*. This ontology contains only TBox content and defines the concepts and relations required to specify semantic values. All core ontology concepts are visualized with a solid red outline. Since all relations originate from the core ontology, no specific coloring is used for them.

If all components make use of the same data types, the use of the *Basic Types* ontology, which is depicted in the center, is sufficient to define the available semantic values. For this purpose, a subconcept of the core ontology concept VALUEDESCRIPTION as well as an associated individual is created for each semantic value type. This individual is assigned the respective data type and possibly further relations.

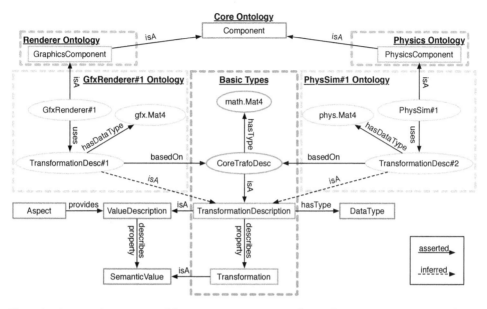

Figure 3.3: An exemplary structure of the semantic representation of a transformation property across different ontologies. The ISA relation is used to depict both instance and subclass relations. Component ontologies (dashed oranges outlines) use concepts from the basic types ontology (dashed red outline) and the core ontology (outside dashed frames). Rectangles represent concepts, whereas ellipses represent individuals.

Adding Descriptions

As soon as further components that use different data types are added to an application, their ontologies are imported by the final application ontology. At this point, there are two possible situations: either a concept is already defined in the basic types ontology and is reused by an imported ontology or a completely new concept needs to be added.

Using existing concepts The orange colored rectangles in figure 3.3 exemplify the additional definition of descriptions for the TRANSFORMATION property: GRAPHICSRENDERER#1 is asserted to be a graphics component that uses a different data type for the TRANSFORMATION property TRANSFORMATIONDESC#1. Since this data type is specified to be BASEDON the core transformation type, it can be inferred to be a value description for the transformation concept. In the same way, a third data type can be associated with the transformation concept for a possible physics engine (see right side of figure 3.3). Note that the only links to external ontologies are created by the subclass definition for the components and the BASEDON relations for value descriptions.

Adding new concepts Although this approach does allow for highly modular property specifications, it only is feasible as long as the described property is defined in the basic types ontology. However, this cannot be assured, since a highly specialized component may introduce new properties that have not been anticipated. This does become a major issue, if

```
EquivalentClasses (
    :ValueDescription
    ObjectSomeValuesFrom ( :describes :SemanticValue )
)

SubClassOf (
    :ValidValueDescription :ValueDescription
)

SubClassOf (
    ObjectSomeValuesFrom (:basedOn :ValueDescription)
    :ValidValueDescription
)
```

Listing 3.1: Definition of the ValueDescription concept. Invalid descriptions can be detected by investigating the individuals that are ValueDescriptions but not ValidValueDescriptions.

two such components address the same concept and that concept is not represented in the basic types ontology (but in each of the component ontologies). In this case, a link between the two definitions of the concept has to be created in the ontology that imports the associated components' ontologies manually. Alternatively, the basic types ontology could be extended by the new value description.

Detecting ill-defined Value Descriptions

The class of such problematic descriptions can be detected by listing all value descriptions that are not based on another value description and do not originate from that basic types ontology. Due to the OWA, this requires some efforts: a class VALIDVALUEDESCRIPTION is defined, which is a subclass of the VALUEDESCRIPTION class and subsumes all value descriptions that are based on another description. Furthermore, the VALUEDESCRIPTION is specified to subsume all descriptions that participate in a DESCRIBES role.

All individuals that are value descriptions but are not valid value descriptions have to be manually adjusted by either basing them on another value description or adding them to the class of valid descriptions. This task has to be performed by the developer who combines the respective component ontologies. The manual adjustment should be stored in an additional ontology file, which can be imported into all applications using the same combination of modules to facilitate reuse by other developers.

Required DL features

Regarding the features of the underlying description logic, the definition of value descriptions requires concept intersection and full existential quantification. Both is owed to the definition of concept equivalences that use existential quantification, as exemplified in listing 3.1. This could be avoided, if all class assertions are ensured to be specified manually. Since this would complicate the definition and maintenance of value descriptions, whereas no significant reduction in reasoning complexity is gained, these features are kept. Since no restrictions are imposed on the used relations, the minimum expressivity of the DL used for value descriptions is equivalent to that of an $\mathcal{EL}$ description logic.

3.3.3 Aspects and Entity Descriptions

In most RIS frameworks, entities are specified by means of an OOP approach, i.e. in the form of classes. The entities then either form a hierarchy and inherit characteristics or are composed of small building blocks that indirectly specify their properties (cf. section 2.3.2).

By building on the concepts of semantic values and relations it is possible to represent entity descriptions and the aspects they are composed of. The required concepts are introduced using the example of a virtual ball entity. Figure 3.4 depicts the information required to instantiate and simulate such an entity. In the given example a physics engine as well as a 3D rendering module are said to be sufficient for the simulation.

First of all, the ball entity itself has to be represented, wherefore the concept BALL is created. It can either be added to the Basic Types ontology or the application ontology, depending on whether it shall be available to other applications or not. The role DESCRIBESPROPERTY sets up a relation to the BALLDESCRIPTION concept, which originates from the entity description layer. A code transformation mechanism can then use the ENTITYDESCRIPTION concept as an entry point to transform entity descriptions into program code (cf. section 3.4.2).

Describing Entities

In order to represent the structure of the ball entity, two relations are required: HASASPECT and HASPROPERTY. By means of these relations, entity descriptions and aspects can be defined. In the given example, one aspect for each of the two involved components is defined. Both share the sphere aspect, wherefore an eventual ball entity will contain a position and a radius property. This exemplifies the fact that multiply defined properties are merged into one coherent description. The PHYSICALSPHERE aspect is derived from a general PHYSICALASPECT, which adds the mass property. Similarly, the GRAPHICALSPHERE aspect adds a color property.

The depicted concepts are represented by means of terminological knowledge only. An eventual component is meant to provide the associated individuals, for example, individuals representing specific aspects. As visualized in figure 3.4, entity descriptions can be defined independently of such specific aspects and therefore are independent from the respective component: it is sufficient to specify the concept that is associated with a certain aspect individual, wherefore a component can be exchanged by a compatible other component, i.e. a component that provides aspects that are compatible to those of the original one.

If it is sufficient to specify the presence of properties, the introduced ontology structure is adequate to represent entities. In this case, the expressivity of the underlying DL remains expressively equivalent to $\mathcal{EL}$. In other cases, however, the structure has to be extended.

For example, the explicit assertion of a qualified number of properties to one entity can be required. This usually is the case for PARTOF relations, e.g., in the case that a car shall be specified to have four wheels. This does add the requirement of cardinality restrictions, thus the expressivity would be equivalent to that of an $\mathcal{ELQ}$ DL.

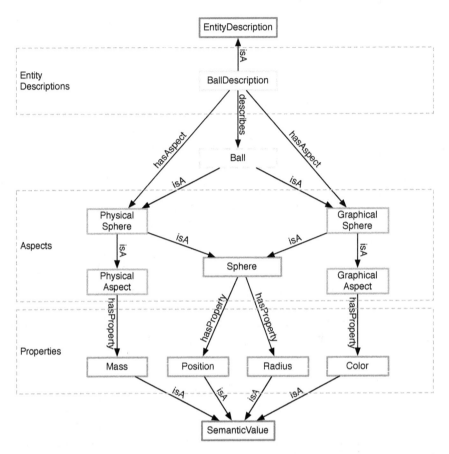

Figure 3.4: An exemplary structure of the semantic representation of a virtual ball entity. In addition to the red (core ontologies) and orange (component ontologies) elements, yellow outlined concepts are asserted in the application ontology.

Reasoning with Cardinality Restrictions

If a reasoner shall process such an ontology, two aspects have to be taken into account. The absence of the unique name assumption as well as the open world assumption requires that individuals are explicitly specified to be distinct. In the example of the car that is meant to have four wheels, the wheel individuals can be explicitly specified to be distinct. Alternatively, a functional data property that is used to assign distinct IDs to the wheels can be used. In addition, if other cardinality restrictions than minimum cardinality are to be used, the eventual car instance has to be specified to have no more than the assigned wheels. For this purpose, universal restrictions are required. Consequently, functional data properties and/or complex concept negation as well as nominals are required. The resulting DL would have the expressivity of an $\mathcal{ELFQ}$ (functional properties and minimum cardinality restrictions only) or a $\mathcal{SOQ}$ DL, respectively.

Splitting the ontology   Since reasoning for ontologies with this expressivity can become intractable, it is advisable to create ontology files that do only include the description of the respective entity. This allows for providing only relevant subsets of the ontology to a reasoning module, whereby reasoning performance can be improved. If cardinality restrictions are required for specification but not for reasoning, the OWL 2 feature of annotations is appropriate to specify a corresponding restriction.

Annotations

In other situations it may be desirable to distinguish between two properties of the same type without specifying additional concepts. For example, suppose that the front left wheel of a car shall be referenced explicitly. This requirement is dealt with by utilization of the above-mentioned annotations: an annotation property HASANNOTATION is introduced, which allows to assert an annotation to any value description. The range of values of the HASANNOTATION property is restricted to concepts and individuals that are defined in the ontology. This restriction is required to ensure consistent values for annotations. Annotations do not change the expressivity of the DL in use.

Required DL features

In consequence, if no cardinality restrictions are used, the expressivity of the DL remains equivalent to an $\mathcal{EL}$ DL. Otherwise, an $\mathcal{ELFQ}$ DL is sufficient, if only restrictions for lower cardinality bounds are required. In the remaining cases an $\mathcal{SOQ}$ DL is required.

3.3.4 Actions, Preconditions, and Effects

Commonly, actions are specified in the form of functions in the programming language. In order to invoke them dynamically, mechanisms like reflection have to be applied. In this context, the preconditions and effects of a function are inaccessible at runtime, thus complicating their selection and retrieval.

In order to overcome these limitations, the methods that are known from the planning area are applicable (cf. section 2.4.3). In this regard, preconditions and effects are the most complex elements to represent. This is due to the fact that these elements necessitate the representation of links between the parameters of an action and its preconditions and effects. For example, the moved entity in a PUTONACTION can be used in the description of an action's preconditions as well as in the description of its effects. In order to achieve this, an effect (or precondition, respectively) needs to address the same individuals that are parameters of the described action. Since effects and preconditions are represented equally, the next paragraphs will focus on the representation of effects. These considerations apply for preconditions in the same way, though.

To avoid creating an individual for the same effect for every action that is defined, the following approach is proposed: the roles HASPARAMETER, HASPRECONDITION, and HASEFFECT are introduced to specify the respective element of an ACTION. Each action is represented by an individual, which is associated with further individuals that represent its parameters. The action as well as its parameters are linked to further individuals which represent the action's preconditions and effects.

```
ObjectPropertyAssertion ( :hasParameter :putOnAction :putOn-object )

ObjectPropertyAssertion ( :subjectof-effect :putOn-object :isOn )

ObjectPropertyAssertion (
   :objectof-precondition :putOn-object :isCarrying
)


SubObjectPropertyOf (
   ObjectPropertyChain ( :hasParameter :objectof-effect ) :hasEffect
)
```

Listing 3.2: OWL code (functional syntax) showing the partial definition of an exemplary *putOn* action. Parameters of actions, such as the *putOn-object*, are linked to the respective precondition or effect.

Every effect and precondition is represented as a relation, wherefore it has an associated subject and an associated object. Since the effect individual is created only once, these associations are specified in the opposite direction: each parameter of the action is linked to the relation via the OBJECTOF-EFFECT or the SUBJECTOF-EFFECT role.

An exemplary definition of a 'putOn' action's parameter is shown in listing 3.2: the PUT-ONACTION action is asserted to have a parameter PUTON-OBJECT. This parameter is the subject of the ISON effect as well as the object of the ISCARRYING precondition. If a reasoning module is utilized, the HASEFFECT (and HASPRECONDITION) roles of an action can be inferred by means of property chains, like the one shown on the bottom of listing 3.2: an action that has a parameter that in turn is the object of a certain effect does have this exact effect.

The complete description of the putOnAction is visualized in figure 3.5. In addition to the effect specified in listing 3.2, two parameters that are used to specify (1) that the PUTON-OBJECT has to be carried by a PUTON-AGENT in advance and (2) the PUTON-TARGET (the location where the object shall be put). The depicted relations are specified in the same way as shown in the listing.

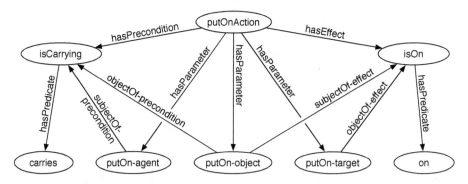

Figure 3.5: Representation of a putOn action. By centering the description around the action's parameters, these can be assigned to both preconditions and effects.

Linking Program Code

The link to program code is established using an additional IMPLEMENTEDBY role, which relates an action to a certain instance of program code. Since the approach is not restricted to a certain programming language, the values of this role are not fixed. Because these values are used by a code generation mechanism (see section 3.4.2), it is advised to provide the ontology that specifies the role and its instances with the respective code generator. In the case of the Java programming language, for example, values of the role could reflect the package structure of the application in order to locate a particular implementation. Finally, the HASRETURNVALUE role is supported to link an action to the property it returns.

Required DL features

The presented approach does not require specific DL features, hence the DL for the representation of actions is equivalent to an $\mathcal{EL}$ DL.

3.3.5 Events

Events are very similar to entities, since they can be associated with semantic values (their payload). Consequently, the HASPROPERTY relation, which has been introduced in the context of state value descriptions in section 3.3.2, can be used to specify their contents.

In order to allow for consistency checks regarding the provided and required events, the two roles PROVIDESEVENT and REQUIRESEVENT are introduced. Both relate an event to a component: the first states that the component is able to emit the respective event type, whereas the second specifies that the associated component requires other components to emit events of the given type. The PROVIDEDBY role states that a component does potentially emit the specified events, although it possibly never does. Nevertheless, in this way the highly beneficial possibility to detect incompatibilities before an application is developed is created.

Required DL features

Since no additional features are required, the underlying DL has to be as expressive as the one used for value descriptions ($\mathcal{EL}$).

3.3.6 Simulation Components

Simulation components have to specify the events they provide. Besides potential additional events and value descriptions, a component also has to provide information about the supported aspects. For this purpose, a PROVIDESASPECT role is applied. In addition, two further roles are introduced: PROVIDESPROPERTY and REQUIRESPROPERTY. The former is used to express that a component will provide all necessary information for the related aspect to instantiate a state value for the related property. The second states that this information has to be provided by another component to allow the former one to perform its computations. In order to allow to resolve conflicts, an OVERRIDESPROVIDE annotation is introduced, which can be used in a later application ontology to select among multiple PROVIDESPROPERTY specifications.

A component instance is identified by its COMPONENTTYPE and a COMPONENTNAME. The former is used to address all instances that share this type. This approach is useful for decoupling since aspects can be specified for a certain component type. In this way, the same aspects can be used for different instances of a particular type of component. Therefore, in use case 1.1 it would not be necessary to modify used entity descriptions when the rendering module is replaced.

The component's name is used to address a particular instance at runtime. For example, if multiple rendering components are present in an application, an aspect could be restricted to a certain rendering component instead of being broadcasted to all of them. Since this name has to be specified at the time an application is developed, it is not stored in the ontology.

Required DL features

As with events, no further requirements are specified, wherefore the underlying DL's expressivity remains equivalent to that of an $\mathcal{EL}$ DL.

3.3.7 Choosing an Adequate Representation

Having pointed out the potentially relevant DL features, this section aims at choosing the final set to be used. According to the previous sections, the different architecture elements require at least the following expressivity:

- *basic concepts*, including descriptions for components, events, relations, and semantic values: $\mathcal{EL}+$ if only transitive roles are used, up to $\mathcal{ELRIF}+$ if all role characteristics are applied.

- *actions*, including preconditions and effects: $\mathcal{EL}$

- *entity descriptions*:
    - without cardinality restrictions: $\mathcal{EL}$
    - with only minimum cardinality restrictions and functional properties: $\mathcal{ELFQ}$
    - with arbitrary cardinality restrictions: $\mathcal{SOQ}$

Since the final required expressivity cannot be determined, a flexibly adaptable formalism to represent knowledge is required. In the context of this work, the widely used Web Ontology Language was chosen for this purpose.

Adopting the Web Ontology Language

The web ontology language (in its second version) has three language profiles, which specify subsets of the language (cf. Motik et al., 2012; Krötzsch, 2012). By choosing one of those profiles the efficiency of reasoning is ensured to be higher than by using arbitrary language features. Different reasoning modules have been developed, which are optimized for processing ontologies that are formulated using a respective language profile.

Building on the observations from the previous sections, the profile to be selected has to support transitive roles. As the QL profile disallows this feature, it is ruled out from the start.

Concepts	Roles
Semantic Values	
SEMANTICVALUE, VALUEDESCRIPTION	DESCRIBESPROPERTY, BASEDON, HASANNOTATION, HAS-DATATYPE
Aspects	
ASPECT	PROVIDESPROPERTY, REQUIRESPROPERTY, OVERRIDESPROVIDE
Entities	
ENITITYDESCRIPTION	HASASPECT, HASPROPERTY, HASPART
Relations	
RELATION	HASSUBJECT, HASPREDICATE, HASOBJECT
Actions	
ACTION, PARAMETER	HASPARAMETER, HASPRECONDITION, HASEFFECT, SUBJECTOF-PRECONDITION, OBJECTOF-PRECONDITION, SUBJECTOF-EFFECT, OBJECTOF-EFFECT, HASRETURN-VALUE, IMPLEMENTEDBY
Components	
COMPONENT	SUPPORTSASPECT, REQUIRESASPECT
Events	
EVENT	PROVIDESEVENT, REQUIRESEVENT, HASPROPERTY
Application	
APPLICATION	USESCOMPONENT

Table 3.2: Overview of roles and concepts that are added to the ontology to describe the elements introduced in section 3.3. Definitions are provided in appendix A.

The OWL 2 RL language profile does not allow existential quantification to a class expression (owl:ObjectSomeValuesFrom) in superclass expressions. This is required, for example, to relate a value description individual to a certain property (e.g., 'describes some Color'). However, this can be avoided by specifying the reverse direction using a DESCRIBEDBY property. In this case, the concept that is related to a property has to be associated with the describing individual (e.g., 'describedBy colorDescription'). Since the RL profile allows to use all kinds of roles except for reflexive ones, the above-mentioned restriction can be considered negligible.

In contrast to the RL profile, the EL profile provides the required expressivity regarding the description of architecture elements. Apart from this, the missing features that might be required at an IRIS's runtime are inverse object properties, symmetric object properties and cardinality restrictions. The latter are supported by no OWL profile for values greater than one, wherefore this does not affect the choice of profile. As shown in table 3.1, the role characteristics that are not supported by the EL profile can be emulated. The necessity to do so can be signaled to an eventual IRIS application by adding an OWL annotation, which specifies the relation to have the desired characteristic.

Consequently, most of the mentioned elements can be used with both the OWL 2 EL and the OWL 2 RL profile. Table 3.2 overviews the elements and their properties that are finally represented in the ontology (appendix A contains their exact specifications). The RL profile is preferable to the EL profile, since it requires less implementation efforts and provides higher support for consistency checks. However, if external ontologies are imported by an application, a mixture of profiles can lead to incompatibility with both. Therefore, the implementation of the framework aspects should be compatible with both, thus allowing application developers to choose the most appropriate profile.

Ontology Partitioning

The fact that cardinality restrictions are not supported by the any OWL 2 profile is owed to their negative effect on computational complexity. Consequently, their use should be avoided if possible. Unfortunately, the information that is specified in this way often is required at runtime. For example, the possible assertion that the car entity from the previous examples has to have exactly four wheels will most certainly be required to check if a particular entity satisfies this requirement.

If this kind of instance checking shall be performed by a reasoning component, the utilized ontology should contain as few concepts as possible to ensure the highest possible efficiency. Thus, the TBox content has to be partitioned into multiple files, which contain only the concepts that are required for a certain instance check. However, this would require the reasoner to load or unload unnecessary concepts, which could reduce performance as well.

Alternatively, runtime instance checking that involves cardinality restrictions could be performed by the framework itself. For example, the reasoning component could be used to return a set of candidates from which a specialized implementation subsequently chooses those entities that meet the cardinality restrictions. Regardless of the chosen option, partitioning an ontology is a desirable approach, since it facilitates reusability of the knowledge base. Concepts that are contained in a certain ontology do not necessarily benefit all applications, hence a fine-grained selection of imported concepts is desirable.

Therefore, two heuristics for deciding on the form of partitioning are proposed:

1. Concepts that require different levels of expressivity should be defined in distinct OWL files. The content of these files has to be specified in such a way that files that specify concepts that require higher expressivity are based on those with lower expressivity. Then the former can import the contents of the latter. This way, the expressivity of the ontology can be decided on by removing the higher layers and maintaining the lower ones.

2. The partitioning should be performed in such a way that concepts that are self-contained reside in their own set of files. Nevertheless, these files can be based on other self-contained files. In the car example from above, wheels could be defined in an OWL file that imports basic concepts. Cars, in turn, would be defined in another file that imports the ontology specified for wheels.

Figure 3.6 provides an overview of this idea: Each rectangle represents an ontology file, which provides the concepts that are indicated by the rectangle's label. As shown, there are no dependencies between simulation components, actions, and entity descriptions.

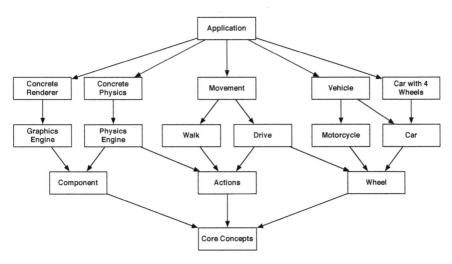

Figure 3.6: Exemplary import structure for different OWL files. Simulation component ontologies (left) are not dependent on specific definitions of actions (center) or entities (right). Associations, e.g., between a WALK concept and its actual implementation, can be inferred by matching preconditions and effects.

3.3.8 Summary

In this section, the knowledge representation model that constitutes the basis for reusable IRISs was presented. It provides a means to represent the basic elements from the previous section. Consequently, it addresses the initially stated requirements as described below.

R1 As indicated by the proposed partitioning of ontology files, the approach is highly modular and can be adapted to preexisting structures.

R2 The contents of an ontology are not affected by any changes to the application. Since all elements in the application are automatically linked to ontology concepts (cf. section 3.2.4), a developer does not even have to know about the underlying KRL.

R3 With OWL an external storage format was chosen that allows for modification of the stored knowledge without requiring changes to an underlying application.

R4 The compliance with the OWL 2 EL and RL language profiles ensures computational efficiency. In this context, an application is not limited to these profiles but can make use of the full expressivity of OWL 2 (at the cost of computational efficiency).

R5 Building on the concept of state values no data is duplicated but a link to the associated element in the ontology is added. In this way, no computational overhead (except for the creation of the link) is introduced by the approach.

R6 The utilization of human-readable identifiers allows for comprehensible specifications. In addition, multiple tools are available for editing OWL ontologies.

Considerations for an implementation   In order to keep computational complexity under control, the ontology should be partitioned according to the expressivity that is required
by the contained concepts as well as according to conceptual coherence. Moreover, each
component has to provide its own ontology files to maintain modularity.

Although the eventual expressivity of the DL that underlies the applications ontology
depends on the application itself, the minimum expressivity is equivalent to that of a $\mathcal{EL}+$
DL. Essentially, the proposed descriptions conform to restrictions defined by both the OWL
2 EL and the OWL 2 RL language profile.

The EL profile facilitates the creation of an ontology that is more general and, thus, allows
to infer more concepts, which would have to be specified manually using the RL profile. In
contrast, the RL profile allows for the utilization of nearly any of the role characteristics that
are available in OWL. For most aspects the computational complexities of both profiles are
identical.[5] Possible restrictions regarding the used profile can arise due to imported ontologies
or used reasoning modules. In the end it is up to the application developer to decide which
profile should be used.

3.4 Integration into an IRIS Framework

Having defined the elements that have to be represented as well as the formalism to do so, the
remaining task is to integrate the represented knowledge into an IRIS framework.

Besides the partitioning of ontology files described in the previous section, the question
how the modular architecture of a component based IRIS framework can be reflected by the
ontology file structure arises. The next section will address this issue by proposing a layered
approach.

3.4.1 A Layered Approach

As a result from the proposed model, the ontology is divided into multiple files according to
the expressivity of the underlying DL as well as to conceptual cohesion. In addition to this
partitioning, concepts that are only relevant for a certain set of simulation modules exist. For
example, the concept of gravity could be irrelevant for an application that does not include a
physics engine.

Thus, the following subdivision of ontology files is applied: each component is meant to
provide its own ontology files, which are based on a core ontology. This core ontology specifies
the concepts that were defined in the previous sections. The contents of the component
ontologies add component-specific knowledge, for example, information about aspects that
are supported by the component. An application then includes all the ontology files that are
provided by the components in use and can thus access the included concepts. Figure 3.7
visualizes the four main layers of the proposed ontology structure.

Building upon the core and component layer, two further layers are defined. The first one
specifies the configuration of the application in use. It contains initial values, parameters for
the components, and similar content.

---

[5] Complexities for OWL profiles are provided at `http://www.w3.org/TR/owl2-profiles/`.

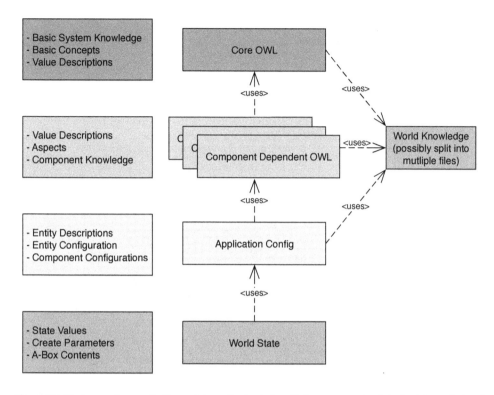

Figure 3.7: The layers of an application ontology. Content of multiple component ontologies is imported and thus becomes available to the application. The world state is not necessarily stored in OWL files.

The final layer represents the runtime information of the application. It contains the current application state, possibly including all information that is available to the running program. This layer is not necessarily stored in OWL files but could be maintained by a reasoning component at runtime. However, given a framework that allows for loading an application from such data, this layer could be used for hibernating an application or to implement similar functionality.

As indicated on the right side of figure 3.7, the first three layers may also include further common sense knowledge, possibly originating from external sources. At this point, the fact that OWL was especially designed for the Semantic Web is advantageous, since knowledge that is available on the Semantic Web can be (re-)used.

3.4.2 Integration into Program Code

Since OWL files are not inherently usable within program code, a transformation process has to be performed. This brings up the question which parts should be converted to program code. Obviously, all elements that describe static information can be transformed, especially including the set of symbols that will be used by an application. A list of the ontology content and associated program code elements is given by table 3.3.

OWL Individual	Transformed Element
General Elements	
\<role\>	`RelationDescription`
\<subClassOf BaseConcept\>	`GroundedSymbol`
Semantic Values	
VALUEDESCRIPTION	class name of `ValueDescription` subclass
BASEDON	base parameter of `ValueDescription`
DESCRIBESPROPERTY	semantics parameter of `ValueDescription`
HASDATATYPE	type parameter of `ValueDescription`
Relations	
RELATION	class name of `RelationDescription` subclass
HASPREDICATE	name of the relation
HASSUBJECT HASOBJECT	reference to left and right parameter of relation
Aspects	
ASPECT	aspectType and class name of `Aspect` subclass
PROVIDESPROPERTY	added to `providings` set of the `Aspect` subclass
REQUIRESPROPERTY	added to `requirings` set of the `Aspect` subclass
HASANNOTATION	annotation parameter for `ValueDescription`
Entities	
ENITITYDESCRIPTION	class name of `EntityDescription` subclass
HASASPECT	added to aspect list of `EntityDescription` subclass
HASPROPERTY	*none* (implicitly contained in the set of aspects)
Actions	
HASPARAMETER	named `Parameter` of the action template
HASPRECONDITION	reference to a `ParameterRelation`
HASEFFECT	reference to a `ParameterRelation`
HASRETURNVALUE	return value of the actions execute method
Components	
PROVIDESASPECT	*none*
Events	
EVENT	class name of `EventDescription` subclass
HASPROPERTY	named property of the event

Table 3.3: Overview of elements represented in the ontology that is associated with a framework that follows the presented approach.

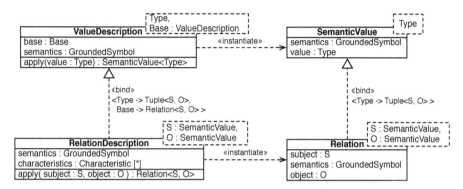

Figure 3.8: The `ValueDescription` and `RelationDescription` classes constitute factories for `SemanticValues` and `Relations`, respectively. For this purpose, the `apply` method has to be invoked with an appropriate value.

Code Generation

In order to avoid conflicts with imported files that contain additional knowledge, all transformed concepts have to be subconcepts of a designated concept or instances of these. Said concept constitutes the entry point for the transformation mechanism that generates program code. This allows to ignore knowledge that is imported from external ontologies. If this mechanism shall be disabled, the OWL THING concept can be defined to be that entry point.

Every subclass of the entry point is transformed into a `GroundedSymbol`, which basically is a data structure that provides a reference to concepts in the ontology. Due to the utilization of OWL ontologies, this reference is represented by an IRI.

The thus established link to an object's semantics is essential for the seamless integration between a KB and program code: the link is inherently available, but does neither affect computational complexity nor contain any further information itself, wherefore it facilitates modularity (R1) and transparency (R2), allows for reusing external ontologies (R3) and their adaption to an applications needs (R4), and avoids duplication of information (R5).

Other elements are mapped to classes and objects in the program code. For each architecture element (semantic values, relations, aspects, actions, entities, and events) an associated description class is specified in program code. The concepts that are specified in the ontology are transformed into a respective subclass of these description classes.

The following paragraphs detail the connection between architecture elements of an eventual IRISs framework and the ontology contents. Besides the described aspects, each element is added the IRI of its representative in the ontology in order to provide a link between both and enable the use of the ontological knowledge at runtime.

Value Descriptions   The `ValueDescription` class, which is shown in figure 3.8, has three parameters: the represented data type T, a grounded symbol representing its `semantics`, and a further value description that represents its `base`. The `semantics` parameter connects the value description to the semantic representation of described value, being extracted from the DESCRIBESPROPERTY relation. The data type is read from the HASDATATYPE role, whereas the BASEDON role specifies the `base` parameter.

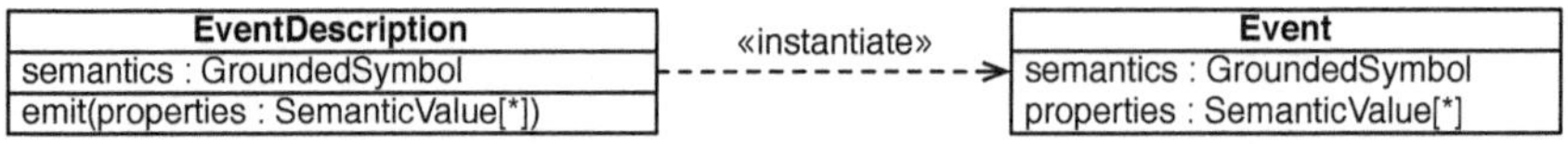

EventDescription
semantics : GroundedSymbol
emit(properties : SemanticValue[*])

«instantiate» - - - - - - - - - - - ->

Event
semantics : GroundedSymbol
properties : SemanticValue[*]

Figure 3.9: `EventDescriptions` act as factories for `Events`, which facilitate inter-module communication.

While the first two relations are mandatory, the BASEDON relation does not necessarily have to be specified. In that case a special base type is used for the base parameter, which is provided by the framework. This way, a type hierarchy that is independent from the one prescribed by the programming language in use is defined.

In addition to the beneficial aspects of semantic links, the utilization of value descriptions fosters decoupling and thus is beneficial for modularity (R1): the instantiated meaningful semantic values can be passed to other modules without loosing information about their semantics. Furthermore, transparency of the KRL is facilitated (R2), since a link to semantics is automatically injected into each instantiated semantic value. This way, a developer does not have to be aware of the underlying ontology (R6).

Relation Descriptions   `RelationDescriptions` can be implemented as a special case of value descriptions (cf. figure 3.8). Their defining parameters are the type of the relation's `subject`, the type of its `object`, as well as the relation's name, which encodes its `semantics`. These are generated from the HASSUBJECT role, the HASOBJECT role, and the HASPREDICATE annotation, respectively. Since only functional and reflexive roles are supported in OWL 2 EL, a fourth parameter that specifies such further `characteristics` may be added.

Due to their relationship to `ValueDescriptions`, `RelationDescriptions` inherit their beneficial aspects regarding the initially state requirements (R1, R2, and R6).

Event Descriptions   The `EventDescription`, visualized in figure 3.9, is identified by its `semantics`. In order to create and send an associated `Event`, the `emit` method is passed a set of `properties`, which consists of entities and semantic values that accompany the event.

`EventDescriptions` are the most important element for uniform inter-module communication. They foster decoupling by hiding the underlying dispatch mechanism. This way, modularity (R1) is facilitated. Since an event carries payload in the form of semantic values, the related beneficial aspects do also apply.

Aspects   Figure 3.10 shows the `Aspect` class. Aspects are used to specify the state values that an entity will contain after it has been instantiated. Each aspect is associated with a certain type of component. The set of components that are involved in the creation and simulation of the entity can be restricted by means of a list, containing the names of included components. In the same way, each aspect can be defined to either provide the initial value for an entity or to be dependent on a different component to specify that value.

The `Aspect` class is defined by six parameters: the `aspectType`, a `componentType` that identifies the components it is associated to, a list of `componentNames`, the sets of `requiredProperties` and `providedProperties`, as well as as list of `parameters`. The latter provide information that is required by a simulation component to instantiate the aspect.

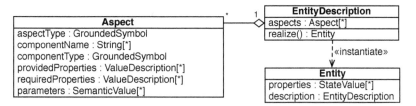

Figure 3.10: `EntityDescriptions` are composed of `Aspects`, which specify the state values that every `Entity` that is instantiated from the description will contain. In this regard, an `EntityDescription` acts as a factory for entities.

The mentioned mapping between concepts from the ontology and program code is indicated in table 3.3, with the following exceptions: in order to allow for different instantiations, the `parameters` have to be passed to the `Aspect` class' constructor. Moreover, the `componentNames` are specified at runtime, wherefore they are not generated from the ontology but also passed as constructor parameters. The `componentType` is not directly taken from the ontology but the components that related to the aspect by a SUPPORTSASPECT role are examined and for each distinct type of component an aspect class is generated. A particular implementation of aspects is discussed in section 5.2.6.

The utilization of aspects is highly beneficial for modularity (R1) regarding simulation components, as it allows to decouple the simulation aspect to which the component is related from others. Furthermore, it inherits the beneficial aspects of the incorporated elements.

Entity Descriptions `EntityDescriptions`, as visualized in figure 3.10, are entirely defined by means of the associated aspects, which are determined by the HASASPECT relation. Hence, the parameters of the used `Aspect` classes have to be provided by the constructor of the `EntityDescription` class. By combining the simulation aspects of the respective simulation modules, entity descriptions inherit the beneficial aspects of these elements.

Action Descriptions As shown in figure 3.11, an `ActionDescription` contains a list of `parameters` as well as two sets that specify its `preconditions` and `effects`. In order to allow for a mapping between parameters and preconditions as well as between parameters and

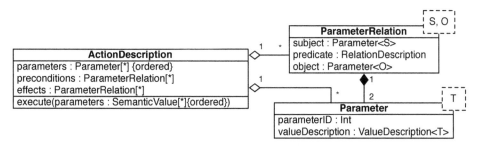

Figure 3.11: An `ActionDescription` contains preconditions and effects (including eventual return values). Both are specified in the form of `ParameterRelations`.

effects, a `ParameterRelation` as well as a `Parameter` class are introduced. Instances of the `Parameter` class combine a `ValueDescription`, which is specified by the HASPARAMETER role, with an identifier. The `ParameterRelation` class is then used to relate these parameters to the sets that are identified by the HASPRECONDITON and HASEFFECT roles in the ontology.

Actions and their descriptions enable uniform access to dynamic aspects that are more specific than the general usage of a simulation module. By providing an appropriate retrieval mechanism this allows to decouple application code from the module that provides a respective action, whereby modularity is fostered (R1).

Components and Application In order to reduce the amount of concepts in use, the application and the simulation components are represented by entities (see section 4.3 for a more detailed explanation). The state variables of the respective entity allow to modify its configuration, e.g., the global gravity could be changed by modifying the physics component's gravity property. Thus, the description of an application or a component is similar to those of aspects and entity descriptions, and the same aspects regarding the initially stated requirements apply.

3.4.3 Cost-Benefit Analysis of the Approach

The concepts and the ontology described in the previous sections facilitate the creation of a deeply integrated KRL, which can be used at compile-time as well as at runtime. The following section will first discuss benefits and costs that relate to compile-time aspects. Afterwards, similar considerations are made with regard to runtime related benefits and issues.

Compile-Time Benefits

The compile-time benefits of the proposed approach are fivefold:

CB1 The communication between different modules is based on the concepts that are specified in the external ontology. Therefore, no interdependencies arise on the programming language level.

CB2 No programming skills are required to specify architecture elements. In this context, graphical user interfaces can reduce the amount of concepts to be learned by a developer.

CB3 The approach is independent from an eventual implementation.

CB4 The validity of the composition of components can (partly) be checked by examining the ontology contents.

CB5 Missing definitions in the ontology can partially be inferred. This reduces the amount of work that is required to specify new concepts.

The next paragraphs will discuss these aspects in greater detail.

CB1: Decoupled Assets   Since all elements that are related to the communication between simulation components are specified externally, the possibility of dependencies at the code level is eliminated. In this context, the ontology provides a means for symbol grounding (cf. section 2.4.2). Thereby, the utilization of the same symbols by each involved component is ensured.

Exchanging a single aspect thus is transparent to the rest of an application. For example, if the physical aspect of an entity is removed or changed, this does only affect the related simulation component, whereas other components can operate without noticing the change. Similarly, adding further aspects as in use case 1.2 or replacing a component in use case 1.1 does not require adjustments except for those involving the respective aspects. This holds true on all levels of an application: completely removing a simulation component does only affect the entities that used the aspects provided by the component.

Decoupling of aspects is especially beneficial in use case 1.3: AI modules that process data in the KRL will automatically be informed about new data. Information that is provided by a new sensor (or AI) module is directly available without requiring changes to either of the modules.

CB2: Independence from the used Programming Language   Since the approach models the architecture elements on a conceptual level and uses human readable symbols, a knowledge engineer or a designer does not have to know about the specifics of the programming language in use. This also implies that the programming language can be chosen by the developers, thus allowing for selecting the language that meets their requirements and skills best.

Furthermore, different simulation modules can be implemented using different programming languages, as long as a means to allow for communication among them is provided. A possible—but presumably not very performant—approach would be to represent the properties of entities in a database that is accessed by the simulation components in use. Chapter 5.5.4 details the variant that was chosen in the context of this work.

CB3: Independence from the Implementation   Since communication between components only occurs by means of either the simulation state or events, different implementations can be combined with one another, if they use the same ontology (or the ontologies are merged). This most certainly requires the conversion of data types, which will be discussed in section 4.1.

In this way, IRIS frameworks that adopt the proposed approach can reuse components from each other by creating a thin communication layer between them. In that case the rendering module from use case 1.1 could easily be exchanged by another one, if the latter has already been integrated into a similar framework before. For instance, the case study from chapter 6 would have required even less efforts, if the external rendering component had already been used in such a framework.

CB4: Validating the Application Configuration   Due to the description-based approach it is possible to check if an application configuration is valid. This begins at the level of entity descriptions: if an entity description only consists of aspects that require a certain property but no aspect does provide it, the entity description can be detected to be invalid. Similarly, if a simulation module is specified to require a certain event but there is no component that emits this kind of event, the application most certainly will not work as expected.

Both is very valuable to a developer, since the use of unknown simulation components might result in configuration errors that can hardly be detected by developers who do not have a holistic knowledge about all used components.

CB5: Inferring unspecified concepts   Inferable assertions can be added to the knowledge base by applying a reasoning module prior to generating program code from the ontology. For example, it is not necessary to assert each individual that represents a value description to be an instance of the value description concept. In this way, the amount of work required to create an application, which is already reduced by transforming ontology content into program code, is lessened even more.

Similarly, the results of the reasoning process can be used to detect incorrect assertions. For example, if a value description is inferred to be an entity description even though it should not, the designer can inspect the particular description and correct possible errors.

Compile-Time Costs

Although efforts were made to reduce the disadvantageous aspects of the approach, the integration of a KRL comes at some cost. Since the utilization of the KRL is optional, these aspects especially involve compile-time issues:

CC1 The ontology introduces an additional concept that has to be grasped by developers. Without appropriate tools for editing its contents this can lead to problems during the development process.

CC2 The combination of simulation modules possibly requires merging the associated ontologies. This problem does also arise in the context of incompatible software interfaces, but with the proposed approach ontology contents need to be modified, too. Since this is an uncommon task for software developers, supporting tools are required.

CC3 The volatile nature of entities prohibits the utilization of static software interfaces, which possibly reduces the understandability of program code.

Runtime Benefits

Although the mentioned compile-time benefits are advantageous to decouple simulation modules as well as tasks of developers, the benefits that are achieved at runtime are equally important. The representation of the application state and available means to apply modifications to it usually have to be carefully planned by the application developer. More specifically, the semantics of entities, their configuration, and possible changes to it have to be specified at compile-time. This forces a developer to decide on the applied methods in advance and prevents dynamic reaction on certain configurations.

By combining the proposed approach with methods from the field of artificial intelligence, e.g., reasoning and planning, the reaction to a certain situation can be chosen at runtime. The benefits that are applicable at compile-time can be summarized as follows:

RB1 The additionally available semantic information allows for dynamic type inference based on semantics.

RB2 The utilization of action descriptions allows to dynamically select modifications to the simulation state at runtime.

RB3 In addition to semantic types, queries that involve the semantics of the application state are facilitated.

RB4 Synchronizing the ontology with runtime information on the application state enables external access to the application.

As before, these aspects are discussed in greater detail below.

RB1: Dynamic semantics-based type inference   The first difference compared to the common approaches is the possibility to check for an entity's meaning at runtime. This is facilitated by the application of a reasoning module. Whereas normally the semantics of an entity's nature has to be specified by asserting variables that encode it, the reasoning module can be used to infer it.

For instance, if a particular composition of multiple entities yields a certain meaning, this could be detected at runtime. In the before-mentioned example of a car, a reasoning component can detect the composition of a chassis and four wheels to be an instance of a car. A rule engine could trigger a certain action (e.g., playing a sound) on each observation of a car being constructed. In this example, which is closely related to use case 1.3, the car entity does not have to be specified anywhere in the application code but only in the ontology. The application developer, who specifies rules for the rule engine, does not even have to know about the components that a car consists of but only has to use the concept of a car.

This way, objects that were constructed by other developers can be reused depending on their specific configuration, instead of their affiliation to a certain class of objects. More importantly, this allows for flexible use of natural language based access to the application at runtime. Instead of checking for a hard coded string that represents an object's identifier, it can be checked against the concept that is identified by an utterance of a user.

RB2: Dynamic invocation of state modifications   In the same way, the representation of actions and functions in the KRL allows to specify the modification of an entity at runtime. This is usually only possible using scripting interfaces, which require the user to be fluent in the respective scripting language. The preconditions and effects of an action allow to check its applicability, or to identify the functions that can be invoked in order to obtain a desired state.

At this point, the possibility to utilize an AI planning module comes into play. If a certain action has preconditions that are not met at the time it shall be executed, a planning component can evaluate the possibility of creating a sequence of actions that creates a situation in which the action can be executed. This is beneficial for natural language interfaces, but it also allows for flexible ways of implementation: instead of invoking the functions that lead to a certain state, a developer can specify that state and let the planning module detect a valid action or sequence of actions to achieve it.

For example, instead of invoking the function `resize(entity, desiredSize)` the desired state `entity has(types.Size(desiredSize))` could be specified. Of course, this comes at the cost of the certainty that the actions are available or that the carried out plan is equal to the functions the developer would have invoked. On the other hand, the developer does not have to know about the particular name and signature of the `resize` method. This is beneficial regarding reuse, since there is no need for searching for the respective method, reducing the temptation to implement it again. Alternatively, the ontology could be queried for available actions by specifying preconditions and effects, allowing the developer to choose between them. Different systems that adopt the latter approach have been developed in the area of software engineering (cf. Devanbu et al., 1991; Rich & Feldman, 1992; Sugumaran & Storey, 2003; Yao & Etzkorn, 2004)).

RB3: Querying the application state In order to be able to query the current state of the simulation by using the concepts introduced in this chapter, a link between the state and the KRL has to be established. As mentioned in section 3.4.2, the basis for this is provided by a link to the associated ontology concepts via their IRI. However, the ontology does only contain the knowledge about concepts and their relations among each other, and possibly the assertions that were made to initialize the application. Consequently, a way to add knowledge as well as to access the (inferred) knowledge at runtime has to be created.

Essentially, there are two options to achieve this: either the internal representation of the application state is extended by a means to allow such queries and updates, or the ontology is loaded by a specific component which updates its contents. While the first approach probably is more efficient regarding computational performance, it would require a customized implementation. Thus, in order to be able to reuse achievements in the field of AI, the second option is adopted in the context of this work. Reasons for this decision include the fact that the approach of implementing a dedicated component, which is responsible for maintaining a semantic view to the application state, can be added and removed without modifying other parts of the application. To avoid proprietary communication with this component, queries can be formulated using SPARQL (see next paragraph). A discussion of a possible implementation is provided in section 5.5.2.

RB4: External access to the application state Due to the adoption of an OWL-based ontology, the *SPARQL Protocol And RDF Query Language* (W3C SPARQL Working Group, 2013) can be used to access and modify its content. SPARQL is a query language developed by the World Wide Web Consortium (W3C), which allows to retrieve and manipulate data in an RDF database.

If the component that is responsible for synchronizing the runtime ontology with the application state is capable of answering SPARQL queries, semantic access to the simulation state can be performed in a uniform way: since changes to the ontology are applied to the simulation state by said component, no further efforts are required to connect the SPARQL interface to the rest of the application.

Although it would be possible to establish SPARQL and the underlying ontology as the central interface between components, the overhead that is introduced by parsing the queries speaks against this. This is mainly because the realtime requirements by IRISs applications do require efficient state value updates. However, applications with less restrictive requirements could adopt this approach.

Even though this was not implemented in the context of this work, the runtime ontology could be stored in a RDF triple store that is accessible via network. In that case, SPARQL queries could be directed to the triple store, thereby allowing for modifications of the application state by another application.

Runtime Costs

The runtime costs of the approach can be summarized as follows:

RC1 Storing a link to the ontology causes overhead regarding the instantiation of semantic values. Although this is limited to the representation of a single IRI, it may be of concern when many values have to be instantiated in a very short time.

RC2 The description-based approaches lead to symbolic access to values (e.g., when retrieved from an entity), which is less efficient than direct access to variables.

RC3 The utilization of semantic information to dynamically evaluate the type of an entity causes considerably more costs than the utilization of the native type hierarchy of the programming language in use. In this context, high expressivity is likely to result in high computational complexity, wherefore only the DL features that are inevitably required should be used.

Conclusion

The integrated KRL provides many benefits regarding decoupling of simulation components and fosters reusability. Furthermore, it provides a basis to decouple the work of different groups of developers. At runtime the approach fosters the utilization of AI methods to draw more benefits regarding decoupling, dynamic access, and semantic queries.

The costs at compile time largely involve a lack of tools that support developers in editing ontology files. In addition, the lack of software interfaces is an issue that requires consideration.

Runtime issues that arise without the utilization of the KRL are relatively small. Its utilization by means of reasoning and planning components, however, can result in lengthy calculations. The introduced ontology structures can be applied to lessen such effects. Nevertheless, sophisticated KRL access has to be avoided in time-critical situations.

In conclusion, the approach provides a solid basis for the integration of an KRL into an IRIS application. However, its integration and use has to performed with care: the type system of the programming language in use should be exploited wherever possible to avoid overly complex calculations.

3.5 Summary

In the beginning of this chapter, the aspects of semantic simulation state representations were discussed. As a result, six requirements for KRLs were detected, which provided the basis for further examinations.

In order to find a model that can serve as a general basis for KRLs and that does comply with the six requirements, the required contents were investigated from an abstract point of view. A set of nine elements that are sufficient to represent the simulation state of an IRISs and changes to it was identified. Building on these findings, the requirements regarding an underlying description logic were analyzed and a knowledge representation model was developed. The model complies with both the OWL 2 RL and OWL 2 EL language profile, wherefore the underlying DL allows for efficient inference processes.

Subsequently, the integration of the developed model into an IRISs framework was discussed. In this context, a modular ontology structure was proposed in order to maximize modularity and thereby reusability of the represented knowledge. In order to reduce the amount of errors that may arise in the process of manual implementation, a concept for the transformation of ontology contents into program code was presented. In doing so, software interfaces for the respective data types were suggested, which constitute a basic model of factories.

Finally, the costs and benefits that can arise from the utilization of the proposed approach were discussed. These split up into aspects that facilitate the development process and those that are advantageous at runtime. Compile-time benefits revolve around decoupling, independence of languages, independence of a specific implementation, validity checks, and inference of knowledge (which will eventually be transformed into program code).

Runtime benefits include the possibility to dynamically perform semantic instance checks, which allow for highly flexible applications. Moreover, the opportunity to let a planning module select a sequence of actions to obtain a certain simulation state instead of having to hard-code it in advance was mentioned.

Costs involve a lack of supportive tools, slight overhead during value access, and possibly length calculations when the KRL is used excessively. These few negative aspects are compensated by the many positive aspects of the approach.

The next chapter will discuss the utilization of the developed model in the context of reusable IRISs. In this context, especially the indicated model of program code elements will be developed further.

Chapter 4

A Semantics-based Component Model for Reusable Intelligent Realtime Interactive Systems

The reason it's about messages and not about objects so much is that the messages are the abstractions. We spend far too much time in our field worrying about what the objects are.

ACM Turing Award Lecture
Alan C. Kay (2003)

4.1 Aspects of Reusability

This chapter illustrates a methodology that allows to turn software modules into reusable components. The latter is commonly addressed by the development of elaborate software interfaces, component models, and similar techniques. In this context, the above-quoted statement by Alan C. Kay suggests to reconsider if the commonly used techniques are the most suited ones for the given task.

This chapter will first contemplate on aspects of reusability in the context of IRIS development to get a clear idea of the approached task. Moreover, possible drawbacks of the commonly used OOP approach are investigated. Afterwards, different methods that facilitate reusability regarding IRISs are presented.

Applying these methods, existing simulation modules can be turned into software components that can be flexibly integrated into the proposed component model. While the task of conducting a systematic reuse program still remains to the entities that eventually implement applications, this work provides the tools that support this intention, for component developers as well as for application developers.

Accordingly, it is concerned with producing reusable resources, more precisely with software development of components for reuse. As opposed to this, the process of software development with reusable components is left to the users of the created framework.

Requirements for Reusability

With regard to the reusability-related concepts that were reviewed in section 2.2.1, the below-stated set of general requirements for IRIS frameworks is established. These requirements as well as the aspects that were mentioned in relation to component-based software engineering (cf. section 2.2.4) have to be kept in mind for the design of an IRIS framework.

R1 In order for simulation modules to be reusable, they should have few dependencies on other modules and reveal low *coupling* and high *cohesion*. A framework hence has to support the developer in creating and using decoupled components.

R2 In order to facilitate *flexibility*, a component has to be implemented in a general way, such that it can be used in different scenarios. Similarly, the framework has to foster *modularity*: it has to be possible to split a component that has multiple purposes into multiple, reusable modules.

R3 In order to facilitate *extendability*, seamless integration of simulation modules with most diverse execution schemes has to be possible. Hence, a framework has to foster concurrency, thereby also taking current multi-core and multi-processor architectures into account. In this context, support for cluster architectures and distributed computing is desirable, too.

R4 The interface between components and the framework should be easy to understand, in order to ensure low complexity and a steep learning curve (*understandability*). Thus, the number of concepts that are required to use the framework should be limited in their number. In this context, the utilization of human-readable identifiers is desirable, too.

R5 Moreover, in order to overcome the opacity of externally produced software, known as the invisibility problem (Brooks, 1987), a mechanism to retrieve information about the program code is desirable.

Aspects of Reusability in IRISs

Achieving a high degree of reuse in IRIS applications is complicated by multiple aspects. Software reuse often has been accomplished with systems that are modular but have a monolithic design in terms of being developed as a single program. More precisely, multiple largely independent modules are used, which are created for a single application. Afterwards, these modules are reused in similar applications.

As opposed to this, RIS development involves the utilization of multiple externally developed components. These components usually do exist in advance and hence have to be adapted to fit the system's requirements. Although each IRIS application utilizes mostly the same simulation modules, they are used in various combinations. Therefore, no subsets of components that have to be compatible with one another can be defined, but each module has to be compatible to every other one.

Since not only reusability but also maintainability, extensibility, and exchangeability are aspects that are desirable for such systems, the mechanisms that are used to adapt external modules have to be reusable themselves. When a module shall be exchanged, the replacement module, more specifically its wrapper, has to match the interface of the old module. Since it cannot be known in advance what module will be used with the system, a *uniform interface* at the system's core is required. Consequently, the majority of presented approaches in this chapter is related to the creation of such an interface.

Data Type Conversion   The most obvious restriction that arises in this context is the use of different data types. Due to the requirement of interactivity, simulation modules that are applied in IRIS applications often utilize highly specialized data structures (impeding R2 and R4). Consequently, the interconnection of these highly specialized structures poses a major challenge for the development of IRIS applications. Moreover, this often results in close coupling of the simulation modules in use (impeding R1). There are two aspects to this issue:

1. The data types that are used to represent a certain concept themselves may differ between the simulation modules in question. For instance, position, rotation, and scale can be represented by using one value for each property or by applying a single matrix.

2. Even if two components use the same data type, the representation in one module may be different from that in another one. For example, a matrix may be stored using arrays of float values, but one module could use a column-major order while the other one applies a row-major order to storage of data.

Access to the Simulation State   Given a mechanism for data type conversion that overcomes the above-mentioned issues, a generic way to access the simulation state is required. This is problematic, since neither the way in which the state is stored by the simulation modules nor the kinds of simulation modules that will require access to it can be known at the time the framework is designed.

A common way to address this issue is to create a centralized registry, which allows for lookup and registration of simulation objects. In this context, the representation of objects that constitute the simulation state is required to comply with a uniform interface. The composition of the objects, in the same way as the composition of simulation modules, highly depends on the application to be developed and, hence, cannot be known in advance. Consequently, the asked for interface usually is individually developed for every application or framework, wherefore it often is too specific to allow its utilization with subsequently added simulation modules (impeding R1 and R2).

Abstraction of Execution Schemes   Besides coupling of data types and state representation, each module that is added to a framework may have its own execution scheme (impeding R1 and R2). In this regard, the calculations performed by one module often depend on the results that are provided by another one (impeding R3). For example, a visual rendering module has to wait for other simulation modules to create a consistent world state before it can display its visual representation. However, the plain serialization of calculations is undesirable, since it neither reflects the multi-core architectures of current processors and concurrent execution schemes nor does it allow different modules to run at different update rates. This is a problem, since especially modules from the area of AI often require lengthy calculations that by far exceed the update rates that are required for a system to be interactive.

Development Environments   IRIS development till recently (mainly due to its novelty) mostly took place in the academic area. Consequently, the developed applications are custom built solutions, which are tailored for the specific use case of the respective research group (impeding R1 and R2). Due to limited resources, the overhead that arises to create reusable components (cf. section 2.2.2) renders the development of such components highly unattractive. Similar to findings in the field of end-user software engineering (cf. Ko et al., 2011) this often results in code that is developed with a "throw away" attitude.

Similar strategies can be observed in the computer games industry: after a successful product has ended its life-cycle, the game engine in use is reimplemented in order to keep up with the customers' growing expectations on subsequent games. This attitude basically impedes R1–R5. In the case of a successful project this is an understandable approach. Instead of investing in reusable software, the profit from a previous game can easily compensate for the expenses that are necessary to create a new game engine. However, this strategy is highly problematic if a project does not pay off and the engine has to be reused to compensate for the previous failure.

Software that is developed in the research area is highly specific and complex by nature. As a result of this, the interfaces that are developed to connect different modules are highly sophisticated and difficult to understand (impeding R4).

Awareness of Existing Functionality   No matter whether software modules are developed by developers in the same team or by an external group, complex modules often contain functionality that a developer either is not aware of or does not understand. Even if sufficient documentation is available, it has to be searched manually for desired functionality. While more prominent functions are detectable with lower effort, specific ones are difficult to recognize (impeding R5). In either case reuse is hardly possible and, as a result, code is reimplemented multiple times.

Comparison to other Sciences

Reusability is closely connected to concepts of decoupling and modularity (see section 2.2.1). Approaches like object-oriented programming, component-based software engineering, and software frameworks have been studied in great depth for years, but—as Alan C. Kay frequently states—the long-desired computer revolution has not happened, yet.

Often comparisons between software engineering and the computer hardware industry or other engineering sciences, like architecture, are drawn. In those fields building upon (i.e. reusing) previous achievements is common: hardware components can easily be plugged together to create bigger systems and knowledge from centuries of construction allows for the creation of stunning architecture.

This raises the question what the difference between software engineering and other engineering sciences would be. The first thing to be observed is the fact that the products that emerge from software development are for the most part virtual and thus invisible (Brooks, 1987). In addition, the foundation of software is largely man-made and thus does not underly the laws of nature. This observation implicates that a software developer cannot be sure that the environment stays the same between two projects. An architect, on the other hand, can rely on the fact that his buildings will almost certainly end up in an environment that complies with immutable laws. In such an environment the ordinary run of things will quickly reveal design flaws and their causes. In contrast, the artificial environment in which a software engineer deploys created products might even be flawed itself.

As indicated by this example, most of the interfaces used in other sciences are based on non-artificial environments, which renders them highly stable. The software engineer, on the other hand, has to build on interfaces that are provided by other engineers, be it from the software or hardware field. Since there is no law of nature forbidding to do so, these interfaces may be changed at will.

The building blocks, which were invented in the field of software engineering to create its own, less mutable environments have been discussed in section 2.2.4. With those tools at hand, the question why reuse in software engineering is put into practice much less often than in other fields remains.

In composition-based scenarios often multiple levels of abstraction exist. A computer is composed of different components, which themselves are composed of integrated circuits. These, in turn, consist of electronic circuits, fulfilling special purposes. The electronic circuits consist (among other things) of logic gates, and so on. All of this is based on findings from the science of physics and electricity (and thus the laws of nature).

Such building blocks can be combined with each other, because their intrinsic functionality allows to do so. Obviously, this aspect is neither affected by asserted names nor by the classification the building blocks fit into. Yet, due to software's invisible nature, programming languages apply these very mechanisms to determine if two assets are compatible.

Two essential observations are of importance here:

1. The interfaces that are used in other sciences are much more stable than those applied in software engineering. This often is owed to the fact that they depend on the laws of nature.

2. The building blocks are characterized rather by their inherent functionality than by their names or classification.

These findings are far from being new and addressed by the OOP approach; classes and object are used to create building blocks and their functionality is covered by adding functions. The difference, however, lies in the way in which characteristics and functionality are represented and accessed.

Drawbacks of OOP-Based Design   In OOP, as in other programming paradigms, an element's characteristic as well as its functions are addressed using references, which in most cases are stored in human readable symbols. Hence, not knowing a reference or its name is equivalent to not knowing the respective element. Since the name is decided on by the developer who implements a program, a uniform naming scheme (and hence a uniform access) is virtually impossible. The only way to realize such schemes would require an agreed on vocabulary that is strictly adhered to.

However, even if a uniform way of naming all variables and functions was present and adopted by every developer, the classification, storing, and retrieval of objects has to be performed manually. Classification is supported by OOP mechanisms like encapsulation and class hierarchies. Yet, these features can be characterized as being *one-way*: while it is possible to derive the set of characteristics and functions of an object by investigating its class affiliation, there usually is no way to derive its class affiliation by identifying its characteristics.

Although this seems to be a negligible feature at first, looking into the implications regarding reusability reveals its importance: similar to the way in which naming issues complicate the access to class members, classification issues complicate the utilization of objects. This is due to the fact that the class of an object is represented by its name rather than by the contained characteristics and functionality.

Another aspect that hinders reusability is the rigid nature of commonly used OOP class hierarchies. These present a means to structure programs, thereby fostering comprehensibility, and facilitate compile-time type checking, which enhances runtime-reliability of the software. Yet, the representation of virtual entities as OOP objects in tree-like type hierarchies often is insufficient to represent the multifaceted and mutable nature of such entities. Unforeseen changes to the type hierarchy often result in redesign and possible partial reimplementation of a RIS, since the implementation is closely coupled to the software interfaces in use.

Recently, the adoption of the ECS pattern (cf. section 2.3.2) eased some of the related problems by favoring a composition-based approach over the inheritance-based one. Nevertheless, the software interfaces in use still result in close coupling of software modules with the contents of the simulation and the requirement of adopting the applied naming schemes hinders reusability. A similar discussion was published earlier (Wiebusch & Latoschik, 2015).

To shed some light on the severity of these issues, consider the following example: In the context of a VR application, all objects that represent vehicles are supposed to be modified (e.g., moved to a certain place). Living up to the concept of software reuse, the application utilizes two software libraries: one that facilitates the representation of trucks and one for the representation of passenger cars. Although the classes representing the respective type of vehicle will most certainly not share the same class hierarchy, they probably share multiple characteristics. In this case, a developer will have a hard time implementing the otherwise rather simple operation, even if the above-mentioned uniform naming scheme is applied.

From the perspective of the two rendering modules to be exchanged in use case 1.1, the implementations of which for now are assumed to follow an ECS-based approach, this is problematic, too. Each rendering module uses its own software interfaces, meaning that the position of the vehicles from above is inaccessible to at least one of the modules. Therefore, even if the developer manages to update these positions, changes are not recognizable by different modules.

Creating a solution to this issue would be a lot easier if the applied programming paradigm would allow to *infer* a common super class and allow for uniform access to its properties.

4.2 A Semantics-based Approach

In this work, the low level concerns that were discussed in the previous section are addressed by the integration of a KRL on a core level. A general model for knowledge representation in IVE applications was presented in chapter 3, which provides the basis for the approach that is introduced in the following sections. A large part of the contents of this section has been presented at the workshop on Software Engineering and Architectures for Realtime Interactive Systems (SEARIS) (Wiebusch & Latoschik, 2015).

The main idea behind the proposed approach is to relax the object-oriented view of representing the simulation state by applying an approach that can be described as semantic duck typing with compile-time aspects. As mentioned before, object-oriented design has multiple benefits on the object level and complies with the human notion of things. To keep these beneficial aspects, a semantic layer is added on top of the object-oriented implementation, as described below.

4.2.1 Ontological Grounding

The most basic addition on top of the object-oriented approach is the integration of a central repository of symbols. Obviously, the stored symbols cannot be expected to be used throughout all program code: the constant requirement to identify available symbols would restrict programmers and reduce their efficiency immensely. The use of such symbols is hence meant to be limited to those parts of program code that are part of an interface to other components, i.e. for semantic values and events.

The compilation of such a dictionary is a complex and laborious task. Especially the agreement on the symbol used for a specific concept is difficult, since different programmers tend to use different terminology for the same object. At best, an ontology for all concepts and their relations can be found, which is used by every programmer working with the developed framework. Since they originate from the ontology, the symbols identifying those concepts will be called *grounded symbols* (cf. section 3.4.2).

While some concepts share a terminology among different groups of developers, others do not. A practicable way to approach this issue is to partition the ontology into common and domain specific parts. The first will then be used by every user of an eventual framework, whereas the latter can be selected to one's needs. Previously discussed features of OWL (cf. section 3.2.6) are highly beneficial for the creation of an ontology as well as for the intent of partitioning it.

Although OWL files are well suited, their content cannot be directly used during programming tasks, wherefore the code transformation process indicated in section 3.4.2 is desirable. Multiple aspects are addressed by this: for one, the approach becomes independent of the utilized programming language. In addition, features of code editors, like autocomplete or suggestions, can be used by accumulating the generated symbols inside a dedicated namespace. Moreover, the number of errors due to misspelling of symbols is reduced, because the compiler will take over the task of a spell checker.

4.2.2 Semantic Values

By describing basic features and combining these descriptions with type definitions from the used programming language, previously meaningless values are assigned a meaning. In compliance with the terms introduced in the previous chapter, the *semantic values* that represent the application state will be called *state values*, whereas the semantically enriched descriptions of those values will be referenced as *value descriptions*. By combining a value with an appropriate value description a semantic value is created. In addition to these concepts, *semantic types* are introduced. A semantic type is the semantic representation of a value description and thus can also be used to instantiate semantic values. Figure 4.1 provides an overview of the introduced concepts and their relations, each of which will be discussed in the following paragraphs.

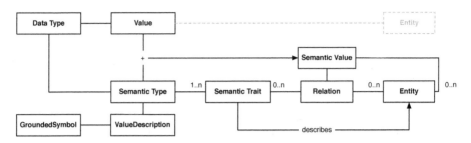

Figure 4.1: Conceptual overview of the semantics-based approach. The top row shows the common way of data representation in an object-oriented design. The bottom row shows the elements added by the presented approach. Each of the shown elements is discussed in section 4.2.

To some extent, a value description represents an OWL data or object property: it specifies an attribute that is associated with an object. However, OWL properties are quite restricted when it comes to additional information, e.g., they are not integrated into a class hierarchy.

The following example is helpful to get an idea of the application of these concepts: a floating point value that represents the radius of a round object (e.g., a sphere) can now be assigned the value description RADIUS. This certainly does not add valuable information for the computer or compiler (see the discussion of semantics in section 3.1), but a programmer is able to distinguish between the meanings of RADIUS and DIAMETER.

Of course, this can also be achieved by choosing appropriate variable identifiers, but these usually have a limited scope: it cannot be ensured that the same identifier will still be used after the value was passed to a method. Using semantic values, the identifiers of used variables loose importance, since the value itself does carry its meaning.

A compiler, to some extent, can perform semantic checks by integrating this concept into the programming language's type system: a method parameter, for example, can have the type `SemanticType[Radius]`, allowing only semantic values with this exact value description to be passed. In this example, the value description `Radius` is used as a type parameter of the `SemanticType`.

Listing 4.1 shows the benefits of such definitions: an variable `someVariableName`, the name of which does not reflect its content, does contain a float value which was intended to reflect the diameter of an object. Passing this value to the function `setRadius`, which is meant to update the radius of an entity, can now be detected to be erroneous by the compiler. In this context, the transformation process of ontology content into program code relieves the developer of manually specifying `SemanticTypes`.

4.2.3 Semantic Traits

While semantic values can help to integrate semantics into a programming language, the concept itself is quite limited. Besides associating grounded symbols to values, no further benefits can be drawn from it. A desirable feature would be to allow the creation of more complex descriptions from existing ones; an idea that is similar to composition and inheritance in object-oriented programming languages.

```
def setRadius(e : SemanticEntity, value : SemanticType[Radius] ){
  e set value
}

val someVariableName = Diameter(1f)
// assume more code here
setRadius(someEntity, someVariableName) // --> compiler error
```

Listing 4.1: Detection of a mistakenly passed diameter value to a setRadius function (Scala syntax).

A central concept that is exploited in combining the OOP approach with the semantic one is the idea of traits (Ducasse et al., 2006). Developed as a means to increase reusability by facilitating multiple inheritance, traits allow for a more finely granulated modularization of a class's functionality.

Semantic traits allow to combine multiple value descriptions to create a new one. However, the values described by semantic traits are different from those described by value descriptions. While a value description is meant to entirely describe an associated value, a semantic trait does rather specify a set of requirements to the described value. Compared to OWL ontologies, semantic traits are equivalent to class descriptions (and intersections thereof).

An essential feature of semantic traits is the fact that they do not inherit value descriptions but aggregate them, thus choosing composition over inheritance. Thus, strict type hierarchies are escaped and a modular structure that better reflects the multifacetedness of IRIS applications can be achieved. It is worth mentioning that at this conceptual level all values are assumed to be represented uniformly throughout a whole application. A later implementation, however, will require a way to convert between different representations (cf. section 4.5.1).

The idea of semantic traits aims at decomposing objects into their (semantic) properties. For example, a virtual object could be decomposed into a color trait and a shape trait. It is important to mention that this does not include part-of (or other) relations directly; a wheel entity is not a semantic trait of a car entity.

4.2.4 Relations

In order to represent such and other associations, the concept of a *relation*, which was introduced in section 3.2.4, is applied. Relations are used to link a semantic trait or semantic value to another semantic value. In the car-wheel example from above the two semantic values wheel and car would be connected by a partOf relation. Semantic traits that involve relations can be interpreted as partial descriptions of entities, wherefore they can be used to retrieve matching entities.

As shown in figure 4.2, a relation is a semantic value itself. This is a reasonable representation, since all interface elements are meant to be represented by semantic values, and a relation might belong to the described entity's interface to the application. Accordingly, the grounded symbol that is associated with a respective RelationDescription is the relation's name from the ontology.

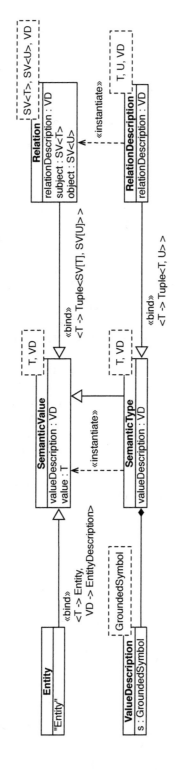

Figure 4.2: Overview of the predefined semantic values. Relations are semantic values, as are entities. In addition, each value description has an associated semantic type. Both relations and semantic type instances are created by means of associated descriptions. The used abbreviations for type parameters are: VD = ValueDescription, ST = SemanticType, SV = SemanticValue. T and U represent arbitrary data types.

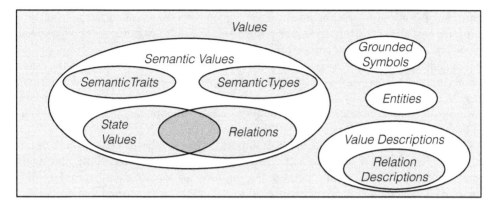

Figure 4.3: A schematic overview of an application's state representation: the ellipses represent the intersecting sets of different types of values.

In addition to relations, figure 4.2 shows two further predefined classes: `Entity` and `ValueDescription`. The `Entity` class, being a semantic value itself, is the programmatic representation of the entity concept introduced in section 3.2.4. As opposed to the object-oriented approach, entities of different types do not necessarily create a class hierarchy in program code. Their interconnections and the assertions of attributes are achieved by the use of relations. Since the data type of an entity is arbitrary, a preexisting entity data type can be wrapped and reused.

A `ValueDescription` is basically defined in the same way it was in section 3.4.2, except that it does not necessarily have to contain the associated data type. The latter is instead reflected by the `SemanticType`, which is a semantic value that encapsulates a `ValueDescription`. It might at first seem a little counterintuitive to let the `SemanticType` class derive from the `SemanticValue` class, because the former is conceptually used to describe the latter. However, creating a hierarchy like this does enable very flexible definitions, like expressing the fact that an entity has a certain property without asserting its value.

Although it would not be very efficient, this approach also allows to build data structures by using semantic values and relations only: an IN relation could connect any semantic value with a `set` entity. Retrieving values from that set then would require to detect all entities with that exact relation.

Figure 4.3 visualizes the intersections of the discussed concepts. The outside box represents all values that currently exist in the context of the application, whereas the presented, more specific concepts are visualized in the form of ellipses.

4.2.5 Methods

So far, the semantics-based approach only allows for the description of entities, their attributes, and relations between them. However, a program also consists of methods that (especially in the object-oriented case) are often tailored for specific objects.

With regard to entities, relations and semantic traits can be used to specify both preconditions and effects of a method. Since a semantic trait captures a (possibly partial) view on an entity but also allows to describe single values, all parameters of a method can be specified in the form of such traits. This way of describing parameters also captures the need to specify preconditions that have to be met before executing a certain method.

Similarly, effects of a function can be described using semantic traits. While the description of preconditions is for the most part achieved by means of the method's parameters, effects have to be stored externally. In the end, two sets are created for each method, one containing the semantic traits representing its preconditions and the other representing its effects on the entities in the parameter list.

The implementation of a particular method, which in OOP-based design would be part of a class, is linked to a semantic trait. The semantic trait then represents the view on the entity that supports the specific method. For instance, the semantic trait `movable` will be accompanied by a method `moveTo(destination)`. It has to be ensured that every entity that matches that trait is compatible to the method. Then the `movable` trait allows to reuse the `moveTo` method with every compatible entity.

Similar to the retrieval of entities, semantic traits that describe preconditions and effects of a method can be used to retrieve it. On a small scale, this could even enable the automatic combination of methods into a more specific one, given an elaborated description of entities and methods.

4.2.6 Example of Application

Entities are not required to be structured in a class hierarchy. The reason for this is the fact that not the entity itself carries its description but the semantic values it comprises do. Hence, the class affiliation of an entity can be detected by checking it against a semantic trait.

This implies that an object that was not designed to be an instance of a specific class in the first place can become such an instance by being added the missing semantic values and relations. On the other hand, a subsequently implemented semantic trait can describe existing entities, when the contained semantic values and relations are matched.

Returning to the example from previous section, the trucks and passenger cars that do not share a common class hierarchy can now be represented as follows: the truck and passenger car instances are represented by entities. They possibly still do not share the same class hierarchy, but they could either share the same base ontology (e.g., for vehicle parts) or a developer could specify a new ontology that merges the existing ones. This can be achieved by importing the ontologies used by the two libraries and detecting as well as marking equivalent classes. By means of such a shared ontology, a semantic trait that describes both trucks and passenger cars can be defined.

Figure 4.4 provides an overview of this example: in the passenger cars library and the associated ontology the car is specified as a movable thing that has a position as well as wheels. Of course an actual implementation would be more detailed, but for the given example this representation is sufficient. The second library uses the term vehicle to describe a truck entity, which is specified to have coordinates and wheels. Each library provides a method to modify the position (or coordinates) of the respective entity.

For the sake of the example coordinates and position are assumed to have exactly the same representation. The transformation of data types and forms of representation will be discussed in section 4.1. For the same reason the utilization of a common base ontology, which provides

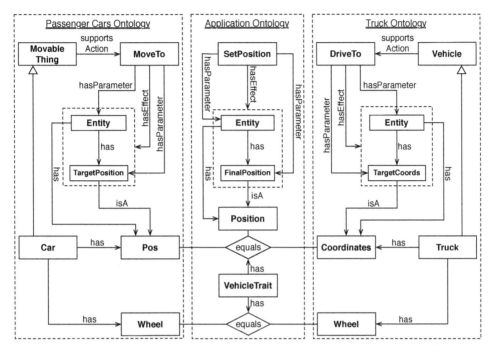

Figure 4.4: Exemplary use of the semantics-based approach. Two libraries with unrelated class hierarchies are connected by means of an application ontology. Despite different naming schemes uniform access to the entities' position value is enabled.

the used relations, is assumed. If different relation identifiers were used, the application ontology would have to define equalities for these, too.

In order to use both libraries, a developer has to create an application ontology, which is shown in the center of figure 4.4. Therein at least the equality of the wheel concepts of both libraries as well as of the position and coordinate concept have to be specified. In the figure an additional SetPosition function is defined by the application developer.

With this information at hand, multiple opportunities of combining the libraries arise. First, both passenger cars and trucks match the (extremely underspecified) VehicleTrait, which is shown in the lower center of figure 4.4. It is defined to describe entities that have wheels and a position. The latter can be modified manually, wherefore the desired functionality (moving trucks and passenger cars) can be implemented.

Furthermore, the SetPosition method that was implemented by the application developer can be applied to cars and trucks. Due to the specified equalities it can be detected to implement the above-mentioned functionality. All three, the MoveTo, the SetPosition, and the DriveTo method, can be inferred to be equivalent according to their parameters (i.e. preconditions) and effects. Moreover, all three of them can be applied to both trucks and cars.

In the presence of multiple methods that could be applied to obtain a desired effect a heuristic is required to select the most appropriate one. Besides the obvious possibility to select the first detected one, a distance measure can be applied: the closer the specification of a method is to the entity it shall be applied to, the more appropriate it is. Distance (or proximity) in this context is expressed by

1. being directly related (e.g., by a `supportsAction` relation),

2. the number of effects that are part of the target state,

3. the extent to which the parameter types of the methods preconditions are matched (i.e. the total sum of classes that separate the parameter types and the actual parameters in the class hierarchy), and

4. being defined in the same ontology.

Regarding the specification of semantic traits, it is desirable to describe the minimal set of requirements that have to be met to allow for the respective functionality. In the given example this could, e.g., be the fact that the respective entity has wheels, a position, and can be steered. Subsequently, a function that allows to move the described entity to the desired position would be implemented (or retrieved), which works for all entities matching the semantic trait. Later, e.g., a motorcycle could be moved using the exact same method, since it will (probably) match the same trait.

Each semantic trait can be interpreted as a partial entity description. Using this description all instances of matching entities can be wrapped and then used uniformly. Compared to an OOP-based design, such entity descriptions relate to classes. Yet, in contrast to OOP classes, the proposed concept allows for dynamically changing objects and their properties, and thus their position in the class hierarchy.

4.2.7 Annotations

The above-mentioned building blocks are sufficient to overcome some of the issues that were found with OOP-based designs. However, a programmer will feel restricted when it comes to expressiveness and flexibility of the proposed approach. Especially the possibility to hide information is a valuable feature, which will be missed by programmers who are used to OOP languages. The restriction to use a limited set of symbols, which should not be extended as rashly as new variables are defined and additionally requires the extension of the underlying ontology, will also be perceived as rather hindering.

To allow more specific descriptions of objects without creating specific symbols for every possible case, the concept of *annotations* is introduced. It enables to specify more precise semantic descriptions and, in combination with relations, to specify scope.

An annotation basically is a semantic value that is assigned to another semantic value. For example, a value can be added a timestamp by annotating it with a respective semantic value. The link between a value and its annotations is established by means of a `hasAnnotation` relation.

Regarding the specification of scope, a special semantic value SCOPE can be defined. A semantic value can be annotated with an arbitrary number of such scope values. This can be done either manually by the programmer or implicitly by the framework in use. If this feature is supported by the framework, the retrieval mechanism of said framework can filter results by means of the defined scope in which the retrieval took place.

4.2.8 Benefits and Drawbacks

The presented approach opens up new possibilities. Due to its flexibility a developer can easily access different aspects of the simulation. Such access, of course, has to be handled with care to avoid unexpected side effects. The next sections will discuss such benefits and possible drawbacks in more detail.

Benefits

Applying the techniques presented above a programmer can break out of the restrictions enforced by strict class hierarchies: an object can be declared as an instance of multiple classes, which are represented by semantic traits. It also can exist without being an instance of a specific class and become the instance of a class, retrospectively. This is highly beneficial if previously defined objects shall be reused in different contexts (R2).

The use of a coherent vocabulary will foster reusability of developed programs. Not only will the understandability of program code increase (R4), but also will the support for retrieving classes and functions. In addition, it allows for the integration of symbol-based AI methods, e.g., from the fields of reasoning and planning.

Furthermore, if the used framework provides adequate storage and retrieval mechanisms, a programmer can focus on implementing application logic instead of planning how to store the used objects. The use of semantic traits for method retrieval purposes allows to specify *what* shall happen instead of *how* it should happen, which is beneficial for requirement R5. This approach requires additional efforts to define method descriptions, but an elaborated retrieval mechanism for methods, which may be applied for an object that is only defined by the description of its attributes, will allow for more easy reuse of previously defined functionality.

Drawbacks

The loosened restrictions also do pose a drawback: enabling the programmer to leverage scope restrictions, like those known from object-oriented approaches, allows to modify values without understanding eventual side effects.

With respect to performance, the proposed technique is in an inferior position compared to other paradigms. While most elements can be wrapped by appropriate classes (or other first-order objects of the applied programming language), at least the retrieval mechanism will need to compare semantic traits, which is more costly, e.g., than the comparison of keys in map-like data structures.

Integration of the Proposed Approach   The above mentioned drawbacks may lead to the desire to create a new programming language that provides features that mitigate if not even compensate the raised issues. However, this is contrary to the aim of this work, which is to foster reuse.

Multiple reasons against creating a new programming language can be named: first, creating another programming language would require to re-implement many features that exist in libraries, or at least create a mechanism to use features implemented in other languages (e.g., using shared libraries, etc.). Moreover, the creation of (another) programming language will require eventual developers to learn this language, wherefore it rather does require additional efforts than lighten their workload.

Especially in the field of complex software components, like physics simulation and 3D rendering engines, it is much more convenient to create an approach which can be

- applied to a wide range of programming languages to enable easy use of existing components, and

- used to wrap existing software components and reuse previously implemented functionality.

In order to provide guidance to how the approach can be integrated in the field of virtual environments and therein fulfill the two above mentioned requirements, the following section introduces a uniform access model. This model especially addresses the needs of interactive systems and focuses on its application for the creation of virtual environments.

4.3 A Uniform Access Model

The semantics-based approach presented in the previous section provides the basis for a methodology that can foster the reusability of software programs. However, its sole existence does not guarantee the creation of reusable software, wherefore a way to direct an eventual developer to its efficient use is required.

For this purpose a uniform access model is presented, which aims at reducing the number of concepts to be learned by a developer. The underlying idea is that reusing and maintaining software is fostered by its understandability. Accordingly, overly complex software interfaces that prohibit comprehensibility are counted as an inhibitor of reusability. This is supported by the findings presented in section 2.2.2. In consequence, the goal of the uniform access model is to provide a single, uniform, easy to understand interface that can be used throughout a whole application.

The intention to create such an interface introduces further requirements, since multiple actors will be utilizing the interface: apparently software developers, more specifically application developers, will be its most frequent users. However, the aspect that the interface essentially connects software modules that are being (re-)used in an application also has to be taken into account. Since this work focuses on IRISs, other actors, such as virtual agents, also belong to it users.

Implications of these observations include the requirement that the interface must allow to access the complete simulation state. Optimally, the simulation state itself constitutes this interface. Further requirements include human-readability to allow for its utilization by developers and high flexibility to enable its usage for most diverse applications. In addition, the integration of a KRL is highly desirable to cope with the integration of AI methods and virtual agents. Therefore, the model presented in chapter 3 provides its basis.

Since the research environment this work was conducted in dealt with the development of VEs, the examples used in the subsequent sections will mostly originate from that area. However, it has to be pointed out that the access model as well as the semantics-based approach presented in the previous section could also be utilized for other kinds of applications. Parts of this section have been presented in Wiebusch and Latoschik (2014).

4.3.1 State Representation & State Transitions

The conceptual elements that are used to represent a VE have been discussed in section 3.2.4. As indicated, each application run can be viewed as the composition of events, which transfer a start state into subsequent states. Each of these states is exhaustively represented by a set of state values. State transitions, on the other hand, are represented by events, which specify a set of modifications to the current state.

Events To relieve a developer of handling events, their processing can be hidden. Using a uniform software interface, callback methods can be registered for the handling of events of any kind. Since value updates are represented by events, this interface has to be implemented by both state variable and event representations. This way, event handling code can be attached directly to a respective event source's representation (e.g., an updated state variable).

It may not always be completely clear if a certain aspect should be represented as an event or a state value. For example, a collision could be thought of as a state (being in collision) or an event (detection of the collision). The reason for this duality is the fact that two different things are being represented: the event that initiates a certain state as well as the state itself. Hence, both has to be represented, the state value which represents the collision state as well as the events adding and removing it. Allowing for the observation of both, state values and events, an eventual developer can choose the representation of interest.

Entities In order to create a more comprehensible representation of the simulation state, entities were introduced as a structuring element. Each entity consists of the state values that belong to the concept it represents. Besides plain properties, the contained state values can also represent relations, thereby allowing for interconnection of entities and other state variables.

In this context, the uniform access model makes use of relations introduced in section 4.2.4. As opposed to the earlier definition, which allows to specify higher-order relations (i.e. relations that reference other relations), this is not permitted in the context of the proposed uniform access model. In consequence, relations can only be used to link entities with state values (which, in turn, may represent entities). The model does not explicitly state how these relations are to be represented. Depending on the type of relation, aspects like symmetry and transitivity have to be taken into account. One possible way of implementing relations is presented in section 5.2.7.

Due to the fact that the complete simulation state is meant to be accessible by means of entities, not only virtual and real objects but also simulation modules are represented by entities. In this regard, a module itself is related to an entity that contains its configuration parameters. Consequently, changing the state values of the entity will result in a modified behavior of the simulation module.

4.3.2 Uniform Access to the Simulation State

Given the concepts introduced in previous sections, the interface that is used to access and modify the current simulation state can be reduced to have very low complexity. Since all architecture elements as well as the objects that reside in the simulated environment are

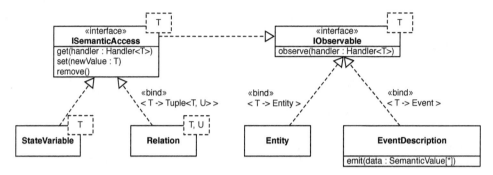

Figure 4.5: The software interfaces that are proposed in the context of the uniform access model. The shown functions are sufficient to access and modify all parts of an application.

represented by entities, the `Entity` class is the main element of concern. The operations that have to be supported are threefold:

1. `set` properties (i.e. state values): This includes adding new properties and updating values of existing properties. The information required to perform this task consists of the entity to be updated, a reference to the property, and the new value to be set.

2. `get` values/`observe` value changes of properties: accessing the value of a certain property of a single entity can be interpreted as the polling implementation of observing value changes. The latter does, in addition to the entity of interest and a reference to the property, require a callback function that is executed each time a value update is observed.

3. `remove` properties: Although the removal of a single property from an entity is performed rather rarely, it is necessary in some cases. For example, if the inferred type of an entity depends on the existence or non-existence of a certain property, changing its type affiliation may require to remove the property. Similar to the `get`/`observe` operations, the required information contains the affected entity as well as a reference to the property to be removed.

The `set` as well as the `observe` method can also be used to handle events: setting (or rather emitting) an event requires to send the event and the values that represent its payload. Observing an event is very similar to observing a value update. Hence, it requires a description of the event to be observed and a callback function that is invoked each time the event occurs.

In comparison to entities, two differences exist for events. First, the `set` method should conveniently be named `emit`. Second, as an event does not share the persistent nature of an entity, a surrogate has to be defined. For this purpose, events are associated with *event descriptions*. The above-mentioned interface is then implemented by such descriptions, allowing to emit and observe matching events. Using such descriptions, the actual event is just a carrier for the payload, all other interactions are performed by means of the associated description. After all, referring to the event description as an 'event' obviates this way of looking at things. The resulting software interfaces of the uniform access model are shown in figure 4.5.

4.3.3 Simulation Modules

The simulated environment comes to life by means of the utilized simulation modules. In the case of an IRIS, this could, for example, be a graphical rendering module, a physics engine, a sound rendering module, an AI module, or input-/output-modules.

As mentioned before, these modules are meant to be as independent from each other as possible. However, many such modules require to work on a consistent simulation state. For example, in use case 1.1 all position updates that a physics engine computes have to be integrated into the (internal) representation of the graphical renderer before a consistent image can be created.

Hence, an execution scheme for all modules has to be specified. Common approaches include serialization of the module's simulation loops, utilization of data-flow graphs, or more complex definitions in configuration files (see section 2.3.2).

The entities that are associated with simulation modules provide access to the modules' internal configuration, e.g., rendering rate of a 3D-renderer or simulation sub-steps of the physics engine. In order to allow for the specification of an execution scheme for modules, the addition of *successor* state values to this entity is suggested. By means of this value a module can signal the therein specified successors to start calculations as soon as it has finished its own. In addition, this allows for flexible adaption of the execution scheme at runtime. Although this feature is rarely required, it allows for dynamic adaption to the available hardware resources.

Central Registry

The proposed model relies on the existence of a central registry for architecture elements. One of its tasks is to instantiate the utilized modules. Besides this, it serves as the sole counterpart that modules can contact at runtime. This is beneficial, e.g., for handshaking-processes, like the announcement of events and registering for their observation.

Furthermore, it is a valuable element for registering entities that are infrequently required. For example, access to entities like a keyboard or other input devices can be decoupled from the module providing them (which in most cases will be the rendering module). A detailed description of the central registry implemented in the context of this work is provided in section 5.2.8.

4.3.4 Benefits and Drawbacks

With the presented techniques, the interface to the application is reduced to five methods, namely `get`, `set`, `emit`, `observe`, and `remove`, thus answering requirement R4. Exemplary usage of these methods is shown in listing 4.2. While this is a rather simple example, more detailed usage is shown in the examples of the next chapter.

In combination with the semantics-based approach from section 4.2 the uniform access model is highly valuable for all presented use cases: each component now can be loosely coupled (R1) by utilizing only the presented five methods, wherefore modifications to the simulation state become interceptable.

Regarding use case 1.1 this enables the seamless replacement of the rendering module. This is because the symbols that are used to access certain properties of an entity are specified in

```
1   CollisionEvent.observe{
2       coll => println("observed collision event " + coll)
3   }
4
5   entity1.observe(types.Mass){
6       newVal => println("observed value change: " + newVal)
7   }
8
9   CollisionEvent.emit(Set(types.Entity(entity1), types.Entity(entity2)))
10
11  entity1.get(types.Mass){
12      oldMass =>
13          entity1.set(Mass(oldMass + 1f))
14          entity1.remove(types.Mass)
15  }
```

Listing 4.2: Example usage of the uniform access model. Registering for events and state variable updates is performed using the `observe` method (line 1–7). Updating state variables and emitting events is achieved by means of the `set` and `emit` methods (line 9 and 13), access to state variables requires invoking the `get` method, which redirects the value handler to the accessed state variable (line 11). Removal of state values is achieved by means of the `remove` function (line 14)

an external ontology and thus can be adapted if necessary. Moreover, the uniform interface allows to perform necessary data type conversions automatically.

Similarly, newly added modules (use case 1.2) can easily access and provide new information about the simulation state by means of the developed interface. In the example of a heart rate sensor the user entity can be retrieved and a value for the hear rate be added and updated. Other modules can then observe this state value and benefit from the newly added data. In this context, it is advantageous to allow to observe non-existent state variables (resulting in the registered callback not being invoked). This way, sensors can be added at runtime, resulting in the subsequent invocation of callbacks. For the same reason an entity is observable for changes to its composition.

Finally, the AI modules that cooperate in use case 1.3 can adopt a behavior similar to the blackboard model (Nii, 1986): when one of the modules adds new knowledge to the state, others are informed about that fact and can incorporate this information into their calculations. For instance, if heart-rate sensor data arrives and the rule engine detects the user to be in an anxious state, a reasoning module can (possibly) infer reasons for this situation. This way, general purpose AI modules can be utilized in different applications (R2).

Compared to, e.g., SPARQL, the expressiveness of the uniform access model is rather restricted. The model is intended to provide access to single properties and relations, whereas query languages allow to formulate arbitrarily complex requests.

However, an extension that allows to utilize semantic traits to perform more complex queries is conceivable: a semantic trait could possibly be transformed into a SPARQL query, which is answered by a reasoning module in the form of an appropriate data type (e.g., a special kind of entity).

Besides all these beneficial aspects, some drawbacks exist: the symbol-based access to state variables and the invocation of the `observe` callbacks, which commonly update the internal representation of a module, introduce an overhead. However, since most of the time only small parts of the simulation state are subject to change, this overhead is kept in reasonable limits. Using hash table-like data structures the time complexity for required lookups remains constant and manageable.

Moreover, the callback nature of the proposed model is not exactly conforming to the OOP style that most programmers are used to. This may lead to developers being reluctant to adopt the new mechanism, wherefore it is desirable to wrap it into further, more adequate interfaces, making the transition process as smooth as possible.

This issue is picked up on in the next sections in which the adoption of the actor model is proposed. Since this model restricts interaction between so called actors to message-based communication, similar issues arise.

4.4 Concurrency: Adoption of the Actor Model

Both approaches presented in the previous sections do not rely on a certain programming language, paradigm, concurrency mechanisms, or similar. Although the OOP approach facilitates the concept of entities, it can be implemented using other paradigms as well.

The same holds true for any concurrency mechanisms to be implemented. Commonly, a closely coupled approach that relies on shared memory is applied to avoid overhead concerning both memory consumption and access times. In this scenario multiple threads of computation access the shared simulation state, wherefore the application of synchronization mechanisms, such as mutual exclusion locks or semaphores, becomes necessary. While this approach is beneficial regarding mentioned overheads, it comes at the cost of maintainability and comprehensibility (cf. Lee, 2006).

Due to the fact that this work is addressing the reusability—and, hence, maintainability and comprehensibility—of software, this approach is inadequate. A possible way to address this is to serialize the execution of simulation components. However, recent developments on the hardware sector, which more and more encourage the exploitation of multi-core and multi-processor systems, prohibit this approach.

An alternative way, which is inevitably applied in the context of distributed systems, is the application of message passing mechanisms. This is performed on a large scale in clustering (i.e. networked) scenarios. For example, different message oriented middleware and frameworks that allow to execute procedures and services on remote servers, e.g., CORBA (Vinoski, 1997), and in the Semantic Web (cf. section 2.4.3) have been developed. However, message passing also is a common approach in non-distributed applications, as indicated by the overview of VR frameworks in section 2.3.2.

In the field of VR, besides applications running on a computer cluster, especially event systems are implemented using message passing approaches. Moreover, the graphs of graph-based architectures, like FlowVR (Allard et al., 2004) and Avango (Tramberend, 1999), can be interpreted as message-based systems by viewing the outputs of a graph node as messages that are sent to the connected nodes.

In this context, the *actor model*, which introduced by Hewitt et al. (1973), is applicable. It is, e.g., used by the SCIVE framework (cf. section 2.3.4). The model does not only adopt the message passing paradigm but also addresses decoupled elements of computation, which are called *actors*. Such an actor can be thought of as a single thread of computation, which can exclusively communicate with other actors by sending messages. Besides creating new actors, an actor can react to received messages and send messages to other actors that it is aware of.

It has to be mentioned that, although it is safe to think of each actor as an independent thread of execution, it does not necessarily have to run in its own thread or process. Similarly, the idea of message-passing does not necessarily involve an elaborate message serialization mechanism and the involved overhead but may be implemented by a queue-like data structure that is added a reference to a sent/received message.

Having a close look on the concept of actors it becomes evident that this model is highly desirable for decoupling simulation modules. By representing a module (e.g., the sensor module from use case 1.2) as an actor it can be informed about the current world state via messages, thus being maximally decoupled from the simulated environment. Data flow in the opposite direction can be realized by sending update messages to other modules. This approach is a perfect match for the event-based state updates discussed in section 3.2.4. The remaining task is to manage message addressing, as actors do not know each other in advance (except if one actor instantiated the other). Due to the low coupling adding, removing, or replacing (cf. use cases 1.1 and 1.2) a simulation module would not even be noticed by other elements of the application (except for the absence or occurrence of events the module emits).

Besides facilitated removal and/or replacement of simulation modules, the application of the actor model also eases the implementation of such decoupled modules. With the application of synchronization mechanisms it often is necessary to acquire mutex locks on different elements of the simulation state. Thus, developers need to have an understanding of the internals of other modules to implement the locking mechanisms. Furthermore, the understandability of program code decreases, since the synchronization code complicates the initially intended application logic.

The actor model obviates such mechanisms. The only elements that have to be synchronized are the actors' mailboxes, which is usually hidden in the utilized actor library. Using immutable data types in all messages that are sent from one actor to another no possible points of concurrent access remain. Thereby, the model facilitates decoupling: component developers do not have to be aware of the processes executed by other actors (i.e. simulation modules).

In consequence, the adoption of the actor model is beneficial with regard to requirements R1 (low coupling) and R3 (extendability and concurrent execution of simulation modules).

4.4.1 Issues to be faced

Although these benefits sound very tempting, different issues have to be faced when the actor model is applied. These will be discussed in the following paragraphs.

Unfamiliarity The probably most problematic aspect that arises with the adoption of the actor model is the fact that programmers are not used to its usage and peculiarities. Consequently, existing program code is understood less easily compared to more common approaches, wherefore programmers tend to be reluctant to adopt the model.

For example, in most OOP-based languages the program flow can be inferred by reading line by line and possibly following method calls. As opposed to this, the message-based paradigm that comes with the actor model requires to handle messages at unknown points in time. The fact that a message sometimes is not processed instantly, but enqueued first and processed later, complicates to backtrace the origin of the message. The callback-based way of handling messages rather matches the functional than the imperative programming paradigm; return values are ignored and the use of global variables (and, hence, shared state) is prohibited. Callbacks are, of course, also common in OOP, but the actor model requires to use them much more excessively. Therefore, it requires a certain time of familiarization before developers adapt to the new paradigm.

Since this issue inherently arises with the model's application, there is no uniform solution to it. Nevertheless, some implementation specific ideas will be provided in chapter 5.

Message Ordering   The order in which messages will be processed is not transparent to the programmer. The actor model itself does not make guarantees regarding the ordering of messages, which makes grasping the ongoing processes even harder.

The possible unreliability of message ordering is evident in the context of multiple senders, since each actor (theoretically) runs its own thread of execution. Regarding two messages originating from the same actor, on the other hand, the possible absence of order is not as obvious. A networked scenario is a reasonable example for a situation in which the order of messages may be disturbed: a network packet containing a message may take a different route than a subsequent one, wherefore the two packages might arrive in reverse order.

In the context of a VE framework one minor assumption concerning the ordering of messages has to be made: two messages that were sent from one specific actor to a single other actor have to be processed in the order they were sent (i.e. the mailbox of each actor is implemented as a first-in-first-out data structure with respect to the order of outgoing messages of a single sender). This issue will be addressed in the subsequent sections.

Supported Messages   An actor does not inherently implement a certain software interface that can be inspected to look up supported methods or, in this case, supported messages. The use of such an interface, in terms of direct method calls, is not desirable after all, since it would cancel out many of the benefits regarding decoupling. In the absence of a software interface a programmer has to know about the internals of the receiving actor, which is highly undesirable, too. One possible solution to this issue is the externalization of the message-handling procedures, which will be detailed below.

Immutability of Messages   Since the payload of a message leaves the scope of one actor and enters the scope of another one, it must not be changed by the receiver as long as the sender holds a reference to it and vice versa. Consequently, the complete message payload as well as the message itself has to be immutable in order to avoid the necessity of synchronization mechanisms.

This can be achieved by simple mechanisms provided by the applied programming language, e.g., immutable data types, copy-on-write, or similar techniques. However, this requirement has to be kept in mind when implementing the actor model. During the development of the

Simulator X framework (see chapter 5) it was found that especially developers who are new to a framework adopting this model have to explicitly be introduced to this fact, since it has been a major source of errors.

In cases in which the transferred data is small in terms of memory consumption the requirement of using immutable data types usually does not create an issue. If, however, large amounts of data that are modified by the sender as well as the receiver have to be transfered, performance optimizations have to be considered.

Debugging   Related to the problem of deferred message processing, which was mentioned in combination with the problem of unfamiliarity, problems concerning debugging the created software arise. This is mainly due to the fact that stack traces are not inherently supported, since message processing is decoupled by means of the mailbox of an actor. One possible solution to this is to store the origin (in terms of the related stack trace) with each message. However, this would cerate a high amount of processing overhead and, hence, is undesirable.

Although this problem is related to the usability of the proposed approach, it does not directly affect the reusability of implemented software. Therefore, it will not be discussed any further in this work.

4.4.2 Integration with Previously Mentioned Approaches

The semantics based representation as well as the uniform access model do not assume a specific way of implementation. However, the discussed benefits of the actor model led to its adoption for the implementation of the Simulator X framework (see chapter 5).

Message Ordering and Consistency

Among the enumerated issues that arise with the utilization of the actor model, the ordering of messages is an important one. Although it addresses a lower layer of the implementation, it does affect the work of developers of later layers (i.e. simulation modules and applications).

In order to enable the possibility of a consistent application state, the assumption that two messages that are sent by one actor to one other actor are processed in the same order they were sent has to be made. If this is not the case, value updates of a state variable might occur in reverse order. As a result, faulty message ordering would result in an incorrect view of the simulation state.

Consequently, the mailbox of an actor has to be implemented as a first-in-first-out data structure (e.g., a queue). This is the case for most actor software libraries, since a last-in-first-out structure would result in counter-intuitive behavior: messages would be processed in reverse order and if too many messages are received old messages might never be processed. Furthermore, in networked scenarios the order of packets has to be maintained. This could either be ensured on the network protocol level (e.g., using TCP instead of UDP) or within the actor library (e.g., by numbering messages consecutively).

Simulation module and application programmers can then—keeping the asynchronous nature of the actor model in mind—treat a dispatched message like an asynchronous function call. As a result, by using the state variable layer application development becomes similar to non-actor based programming.

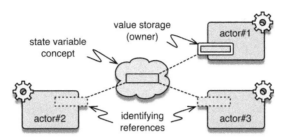

Figure 4.6: The *State Variable* concept based on Latoschik and Tramberend (2011), ©2011 IEEE. The state variable's owner (`actor#1`) stores its value and guards access to it. Using messages and an identifying reference other actors can request value updates, the current value, and update notifications.

The internals of the state variable implementation, however, have to be built carefully: even if the order of messages is ensured for two communicating actors, unexpected effects may occur as soon as a third actor comes into play. For example, if one message is forwarded by a third actor and a subsequent message is directly sent to the same final receiver, the order may be disturbed, even though there was only one sender and one (final) receiver. Therefore, it is desirable to send messages directly instead of forwarding them. One implication of this is the fact that event handling requires a handshaking process, which is mediated by a central component.

Virtual Shared State

Given such sender-related message ordering, the concept of state values, as introduced in section 3.2.4, can be extended to create a virtual shared state. Since an actor must not access the internals of another actor, it has to maintain its own representation. To keep this representation synchronized with the global state each change to that state has to be signaled by means of a message.

In this context, the responsibility for such notifications has to be asserted to one actor. A valid approach is to create one designated actor that informs every actor in the system about state changes. Alternatively, each state variable could be assigned a dedicated actor that takes over that task for the specific variable.

In scenarios in which many state variable updates are preformed the first approach might create a bottleneck, since all actors have to wait for the notifying actor to dispatch updates. The second approach, on the other hand, requires a lot of context switches, if many state variables are maintained. Since both scenarios cannot be ruled out, a compromise has to be found.

A reasonable way to handle this issue is to assign an *owner* to each state variable, which is responsible for dispatching updates to its *observers* (see figure 4.6). This owner initially is the actor in whose context the variable was created, thus no additional actors have to be instantiated for the creation of new variables. Since the owner holds the state variable's value, message traffic is highly reduced, if each variable is created by the actor that is concerned with most of the variable's value updates (however, the owner could—for whatever reason—be changed at runtime).

An identifying reference to the state variable is then used by each actor to register with its owner for updates or to request a value update. If the owner of the state variable is stored within the reference, most of the required handshaking processes can be hidden behind the software interfaces that are implemented by the state variable class. Since the whole (shared) simulation state is represented by means of state variables, a virtual shared state is created, which can be accessed by every actor in the system.

A major benefit of this implementation is the fact that registered callbacks may not block the execution of other modules of the program. Callbacks allow for inversion of control, which is a beneficial feature in non RIS applications. However, when a thread of execution's continuation is required to retain interactivity, e.g., to render the next frame, the execution of an arbitrary callback in that thread can break this requirement.

With the proposed model, the callback is executed in the context of the actor that registered it and not in that of the actor that triggers the callback. This way, inversion of control can be achieved with minimal effect on realtime-related processes, whereby requirement R3 is taken into account.

Event System Support

The integration of an event system into an actor-based framework is straightforward, since the message-based architecture inherently supports the notification about events. However, the event-emitting actors have to be informed about the actors that are interested in their particular type of event.

At this point, two afore-mentioned aspects prove advantageous. First, the central module registry (cf. section 4.3.3) can be used to support handshaking mechanisms. Second, the approach of using event descriptions (see section 4.3.2) allows to announce certain kinds of events without actually instantiating them.

The functionality of sending an announcement message to the central registry, which is the only actor that has to be a priori known to every other actor in the system, can be hidden behind the software interface of the event description. Similarly, every actor that is interested in a certain event can send a request to the central registry using the same description. The central registry can store all such announcements and requests, and inform the matching emitter/receiver pairs about their existence. Further messages may subsequently be directly sent between those two actors.

In a way, the central registry for events takes on the role that state variable references have for state updates. Both using the central registry as well as state variables yields the situation that no actor has to know any other actor in advance, thus maximizing decoupling of functional components.

Missing Interfaces

The fact that the communication of actors is restricted to sending messages creates another issue: a missing software interface creates the problem of invisibility, i.e. the functionality of an actor is not obvious to a programmer who wants to invoke functions of that actor.

As stated before, the solution to introduce a common software interface is not feasible. This is owed to the fact that such an interface would require the implementing module to be known in advance (i.e. at compile time). However, this is not always possible as exemplified by the following situation: during the course of an application a physical impulse shall be applied to a virtual object. If the common approach to call a method from a module's interface is applied, the programmer needs to know which module is responsible for the application of impulses, access that module, and invoke the correct method.

Regarding reusability this is problematic in two different ways. First, during development the programmer of the application in question might not be aware of the components that will finally be used. Even if the components are known, it is not necessarily clear which module is responsible for a certain functionality.

Second, if a module should be exchanged afterwards, both modules have to implement the exact same interface, even if some functionality might not be needed. This especially is an issue if a module shall be replaced by two components that split the same functionality (cf. requirement R2). For example, a physics engine could be replaced by a dedicated collision detection module and a module that computes the other aspects of the physical simulation.

Regarding the simulation state the previously introduced virtual shared state is sufficient to obviate such an interface. The responsible module can update the respective parts of the simulation state without other components even being aware of its existence.

Method Registry

In terms of dynamic aspects, such as function calls and behavior simulation, a solution to the problem of the missing interface is required, too. As indicated above, it is desirable to render knowledge about other components' responsibilities unnecessary. This way, the developers' understanding of parts of the application that were developed by others is obviated and simulation components can be decoupled.

One possible solution is to decouple function calls using a similar approach as introduced with the registration of event providers and event handlers. The new system can be used to register functions instead of events (or rather their descriptions). Using semantic traits (cf. section 4.2.3) to specify preconditions and effects of a registered function a developer can request a certain functionality by specifying the desired effects. When a matching method has been selected from the registry, a message is sent to the associated actor which then invokes the function.

Similarly, each method can be associated with a trait that has to be mixed in by the function registry. Thus, a programmer can bypass the lookup functionality and directly invoke the desired function, eventually resulting in a dispatch of the same message that would have been sent using the lookup method. Obviously this approach does not depend on the actor model: direct function calls instead of message based invocation would work in the same way.

For traceability reasons it is desirable to make sure that only one function is registered for a certain functionality. Although multiple registered functions would not break the system, a possibly random choice has to be made among the matching functions, which could result in unexpected performance issues or other negative effects. Unique functionality among registered methods can be verified using the semantic traits that are used for its registration. If a second function has the same preconditions and effects, the registry can either be implemented to replace the existing function or to ignore the new one.

Given a sufficiently large repository of functions and associated components, issues related to retrieval of appropriate functionality can be mitigated. A noteworthy aspect of this approach is the fact that AI components, like an automated planner, can access the registered functions in the same way a programmer does. This opens up new possibilities for implementing, e.g., virtual agents, which can modify the virtual world by invoking the registered functions. This way, complex and redundant implementation of agent behavior can be simplified.

As indicated before, the feasibility of the presented approaches has been tested in the course of the implementation of the Simulator X framework. Details concerning its implementation and characteristic features are presented in chapter 5.

4.5 A Component Model for IRIS Frameworks

So far, the elements presented in this and the previous chapter each address a rather isolated aspect of an IRIS application:

- The knowledge representation model, which was presented in section 3.3, provides the basis for semantics-based representation of the application state.

- The semantics-based approach, which has been introduced in section 4.2, utilizes a fixed set of symbols to enable semantic type checks.

- The uniform access model from section 4.3 provides a means to access and modify the application state in a uniform way.

- The adoption of the actor model, which was discussed in section 4.4, allows for the creation of highly decoupled, concurrent simulation modules.

Clearly, a possibility to interconnect these single aspects is required. Different possibilities exist for this purpose: the least desirable approach is to manually design every element from scratch; the link to the KRL, semantic traits that are supported, as well as uniform access to both. This would require huge efforts and cause redundant work, since a developer would have to implement every aspect over and over again.

Alternatively, software interfaces can be applied to create a basis on which components and entities are built. In that way, features like encapsulation facilitate reuse and allow to easily exchange components that are implemented using the same interface. However, such interfaces are meant to be immutable after their implementation and complicate exchanging components if these do not exactly match the interface. To some extent, these interfaces constitute the atoms an eventual application is build of: indivisible elements which can be aggregated to create more complex parts.

The ECS pattern addresses this issue by assuming a different perspective. All aspects of an entity, which are addressed by a certain simulation module, are determined by the set of components the entity consists of. This way, the simulation modules (called 'systems' in the ECS pattern) are decoupled from the particular instance of an entity and bound to components only. While this turned out to be a step into the right direction, it shifts the problem from the implementation of the entity class to that of the component classes. Still, the implementation depends on used data types and requires simulation modules to be compatible with interfaces they do not provide themselves. Obviously, this can not be fully avoided, since a common ground has to be created to allow inter-module communication.

As motivated before, this communication should be performed using the entity data structure. In the context of the ECS pattern this means that a shared area in memory is created by means of utilized components, which the (ECS) systems can operate on. In order to gain most flexibility, these elements should be as versatile as possible. Consequently, they also should be as atomic as possible.

The techniques proposed in this work provide a means to overcome these issues: a common ground for inter-module communication is created by the KRL from chapter 3. It provides a well-conceived foundation that reflects the nature of RIS applications. Therefore, it allows for specification and semantic augmentation of atomic architecture elements.

The generation of program code from ontology contents ensures consistent interfaces, which act as factory methods (cf. Gamma et al., 1994) for further architecture elements. This way, mistyped identifiers can be avoided, required programming skills can be reduced, and incompatibilities can be detected early. Instead of applying rigid, inheritance-based OOP interfaces, semantic traits and a uniform access model were introduced to overcome the inflexibility of common approaches.

The next sections discuss the generated factories and their characteristics, whereas their usage and the created elements are discussed in section 5.2.6.

4.5.1 Semantic Values, Events, and Automatic Type Conversion

The most basic elements that are provided by the proposed approach are semantic values and events. In order to benefit from the symbols that are grounded in the application's ontology, each is associated with such a symbol. This way, the utilization of a common set of identifiers can be assured.

Semantic Values   Besides the grounded symbol, value descriptions do contain a description of the data type which the instantiated semantic value will have. They furthermore contain a reference to another value description which they are based on. This is essential for the provisioning of a data type conversion mechanism: every simulation module that introduces new data types has to provide a set of type converters. Such a converter has to be able to convert the data type that is contained in the newly introduced value description to the uppermost data type in the hierarchy, which is created via the base parameters of the value descriptions.

For example, assume that a physics engine introduces an additional value description `Transformation`, which has the data type `physics.Matrix` and is based on another `Transformation` value description with data type `core.Matrix`. Then a converter has to be specified that can transform those two data types into one another. Due to the utilization of value descriptions it is possible to automatically select a matching converter, assuming that it was registered at the application startup.

This way, each simulation module can use its own data types without having to know about the data types that are used throughout the rest of the application. The basic idea of this technique was already mentioned by M. Shaw (1995). By the introduction of value descriptions its automatic application is facilitated.

```scala
class ConvertedVariable[L, G](vd : ValueDescription[L, G],
                             wrapped : StateVariable[G]){
  // detect converter once
  private val converter = Converters.findConverter( vd, vd.base )

  def set(newVal : SemanticValue[L]){
    // convert to global type using already detected converter
    val globalTyped : G = converter.convert( newVal.value )
    // set global type to state variable
    wrapped.set( globalTyped )
  }
  def observe(vd : ValueDescription[L, _], handleValue : L => Unit){
    // redirect observe call to variable with global type
    wrapped.observe {
      globalTyped : G =>
        // convert global type to local type each time it is updated
        val localTyped : L = converter.revert( globalTyped )
        // call handler with local type
        handleValue ( localTyped )
    }
  }
}
```

Listing 4.3: An example of the automatic type conversion process in Scala syntax: a converter is retrieved according to a given value description and used to perform conversions in order to encapsulate a state variable.

The application of the uniform access model from section 4.3 enables to completely hide the conversion process from the developer. Since each semantic value is instantiated by means of the associated description, it can be provided with the proposed access methods. Using the above-mentioned automatic lookup procedure for converters, the get and observe methods can convert data into the local format on access. An example for this approach is given in listing 4.3.

If, for instance, the Transformation value of an entity in the above example is accessed, the related program code could look like this: entity.get(Transformation). The information stored in the Transformation value description allows to select the appropriate converter and to perform the conversion. Similarly, the set method allows to convert the data type in the opposite direction.

As shown in listing 4.3, in case of the set and observe methods the search for an appropriate converter has to be performed only once, since it can be stored and directly used afterwards. Similarly, the use of the same data types for a certain semantic value throughout the application will reduce the overhead to a minimum, since in that case no conversion is necessary at all. In the same way that converters can be used for state variables they are applicable for semantic values: by implementing the dedicated function as[T, B](vd : ValueDescription[T, B]) : SemanticValue[T] each value can be automatically converted to the desired type.

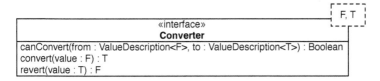

Figure 4.7: Converter Interface: the `canConvert` method is used during converter lookup, afterwards only the `convert` and `revert` methods are invoked.

Relations   As mentioned before, relations are specific versions of semantic values and vice versa. However, a relation does not necessitate a conversion mechanism, since it is uniquely identified by the associated grounded symbol.

Events   Descriptions for events are much simpler than those of semantic values, since each event type can be identified by the associated symbol. Events can carry payload in the form of semantic values, e.g., the entities affected by the event. If desired, the event description can include a set of value descriptions, which describe the semantic values the event is ensured to be accompanied by.

Events do also benefit from the type conversion process that was described above. Assume that a simulation module that uses different data types emits an event that is received by the physics engine from the previous examples. If the event contains a transformation (think of a collision event which might contain the location of the collision), retrieving the transformation from the event will invoke the same procedures as mentioned above.

The description based approach also is beneficial for the registration in a publisher/subscriber system: a simulation module can register for a certain kind of events by utilizing the associated description. In the same way, the description can be used to inform the system about the fact that a simulation module does publish a certain kind of event. Thereby, an eventual handshaking process is enabled.

Converter Interface   The interface for converter classes, which is shown in figure 4.7, is concise: a `canConvert` method enables to check if the converter is capable of performing the conversion between two value descriptions, which are specified by the `from` and `to` parameter. The converter allows conversion from the source type to the target type as well as the opposite direction by invoking the `convert` and `revert` method, respectively.

The conversion is not applied to semantic values but operates on their data types to allow for higher performance in possible subsequent calculations. However, the caller of the method can use a value description to create a semantic value after the conversion process.

4.5.2 Entity and Component Descriptions

Since entities essentially are a collection of relations and state values, an entity description consists of a set of value descriptions and relation descriptions. The plain combination of such descriptions, however, would be incomprehensible and their construction would require a great deal of work. In order to ease the specification of entity descriptions, the intermediate layer of aspects is used.

Aspects

Adhering to the concept of reusability, a simulation module has to be as independent from other modules as possible (R1). Therefore, a uniform specification mechanism that is independent of the respective module and its implementation is required.

This is complex for different reasons: While the instantiation of entities and state values should be decoupled, it is entirely possible that one module requires values that are provided by another one in order to be able to instantiate the entity. For example, the position of a virtual object might be stored in a file that is loaded by the rendering module. At the same time, the physics engine does require an initial value for the position of the object to create its internal representation, as well. While this example is easily solvable, more complex dependencies that necessitate alternating provision of values between modules can arise.

Furthermore, a simulation module might not be involved in the simulation of an entity from the start, but integrated at runtime. Similarly, certain aspects of the simulation may have to be turned off and be re-enabled later on. Thus, the mechanism to integrate an entity into the simulation loop of a module has to be independent from the actual state of the application.

Apart from that, the initial values for an entity, more precisely for the state variables it contains, have to be specified. In some cases this does require more information than plain values, e.g., configuration or model files that have to be parsed. Since these are usually specified by the application developer, a description-based mechanism is a reasonable approach.

In accordance with the event-based approach, the instantiation of an entity is triggered by a designated event that contains the mentioned initial values. Depending on this information, the responsible authority has to be detected. For the creation of new modules this is a central element of the respective RIS framework, e.g., the proposed central component registry. For any other entity the involved simulation modules have to be requested to instantiate their local representation of the entity.

The essential observation is that the only information that is required to instantiate a new entity—be it a simulation module, an input device, or any other object—is the set of initial values as well as information on the involved modules. Therefore, all entities can be created using the same mechanism.

The application developer has to specify which modules will be concerned with the creation and simulation of the entity as well as initial values that are used by these modules. For this purpose, the `Aspect` class, which has been introduced in section 3.4.2, is used.

Each such aspect is related to a single component type and does specify the state values and relations of the entity that are used by the component. In addition to the associated set of value and relation descriptions an aspect contains a grounded symbol, which identifies its semantics. For example, a `PhysicalSphere` aspect could be defined to tell the physics component that the associated entity should be simulated as a sphere-like rigid body by using a SPHERE symbol.

Since the state values and relations that are described by an aspect can overlap, the simulation module that is responsible for providing the initial values for a particular state value has to be specified. For this purpose an aspect contains two sets of descriptions: the ones for which the associated module will provide initial values and the ones that are required by the module but for which the module cannot provide initial values itself. Figure 4.8 exemplifies this concept by visualizing an entity description that consists of four aspects.

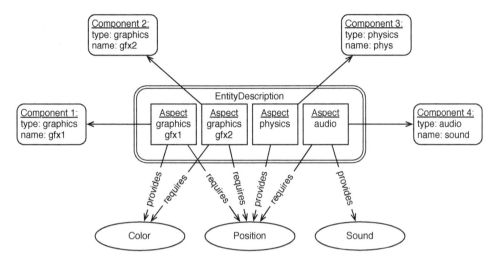

Figure 4.8: An entity description that consists of four aspects, each of which is associated with one of the four components. The association is created via their names. For each aspect a set of required and provided initial values is specified.

Moreover, four components are depicted: two graphics modules, a physics engine, and an audio renderer. The four aspects are each associated with one component by matching the given component types and, if provided, names. Furthermore, each aspect is specified to provide or require certain initial values.

When the described entity is instantiated, the associated components of each aspect will be requested to specify dependencies on initial values. Based on this information a build order is calculated, resulting in further dispatch of events to resolve all initial values and eventually in the instantiation of the entity. This way, simulation modules can instantiate the entity without being aware of one another. A more detailed discussion of the entity creation process is given in section 4.5.3 and a possible implementation is addressed in section 5.2.6.

Analogies with Aspect Oriented Programming   The created approach can be compared to the ideas introduced by the *Aspect Oriented Programming* (AOP) paradigm (Kiczales et al., 2003). With aspect oriented programming, the concepts of aspects, join points, advices and pointcuts are introduced. In order to separate orthogonal parts of the software, new code that is specified by an aspect can be woven into the program. By means of pointcuts it is decided at which location (join point) in the program the code (advice) of an aspect shall be applied. This is, for example, beneficial if a logging mechanism shall be introduced, since aspect oriented programming allows to insert code before and after calls to a method. In this way, an aspect can define points in the program code where logging should happen without changing the main program code.

In general, this concept is beneficial for developing reusable RISs. *System-level concerns*, such as physical simulation or graphics rendering, can be implemented generically by component developers, whereas an eventual application developer can define the objects that shall be affected by the respective module.

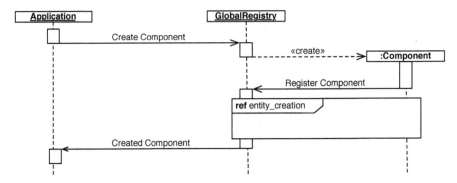

Figure 4.9: Creation process for components: except for the initial instantiation of the component, which is performed by the global registry, the process is identical to the entity creation process depicted in figure 4.12 on page 136.

This can be achieved in a similar way by utilizing the aspects defined in this work. Furthermore, the `observe` method provides an opportunity to weave in code into the simulation without changing other program parts. Although this approach is not as powerful as the aspect oriented programming one, it allows for easy integration of simulation aspects without referencing the corresponding component itself or even changing its program code. Consequently, one might say that the developed approach introduces AOP on a higher level, restricting its application to the simulation loop.

As with AOP, the more often such methods are applied, the harder it gets to understand the program code. Thus, the features should be used with care and, even though it is possible to use them throughout the whole program, an eventual developer is advised to do so in a localized way to maintain understandability. In other words, the application logic concerning one specific entity should not be distributed over the whole program code but ideally be contained in a single source file.

Component Description

Besides the software interface between a simulation component and the framework, the former is represented as an entity at runtime, whereby an interface to its configuration is provided. This implies that a component is described by means of an associated entity description and the respective component aspect.

The following example is helpful to shed some light on this concept. An application is said to feature a physics engine and a rendering component. The screen configuration is provided to the rendering module in the form of a specialized configuration class, whereas the physics engine does only require an initial value for the `Gravity` property. In order to realize this setup, an application developer does utilize the component aspects that are provided with each component, respectively. The above-mentioned parameters are passed to these aspects and the usual entity creation mechanism is performed to instantiate both components.

Figure 4.9 provides an overview of the component creation process: inside the application an entity description that at least contains the respective component aspect is utilized. Since the global registry component possibly is the only existing module at that time, it creates the new component. Afterwards, it starts the entity creation process as described in following sections. On the completion of the process, the application is informed about the newly created component by being passed the associated entity.

The above-mentioned mechanism provides a single interface for the instantiation of every desired entity, including simulation components. As with the creation of entities, the specifics of a possible implementation are discussed in section 5.2.6.

4.5.3 Components

One goal of this work is to create a mechanism to decouple simulation modules. Up to this point, mechanisms to allow for uniform access to the simulation state, to provide a set of grounded symbols, as well as to enable semantics based access have been discussed. Building on the observation that all modifications to the application state can be represented as events, the actor model was suggested as a possible means to allow to decouple communication by adoption of a message-based approach.

The following section will complete this proposition by providing the final component model, which is facilitated by the previously introduced techniques. At first, a more abstract way of communication between components is introduced, in order to allow for more a comprehensive description of the proposed interfaces.

Inter-Component Communication

There are multiple possibilities to look at the proposed communication architecture:

- *Message-Passing*: every event is a message and the receivers are known to the sender. This is in line with the perspective that is assumed by the actor model and used in the Simulator X framework. The possibility to directly address the receiver of an event potentially allows for efficient implementations. However, due to communication in a peer-to-peer manner, this view tends to be confusing when an overview of an application is required.

- *Blackboard*: simulation modules can publish information (including requests), which is added to the simulation state. Other modules subsequently process the information and update the simulation state accordingly. While this is a highly understandable model regarding state representation, representing events that are not directly related to state changes is not inherently supported.

- *Event Bus*: all communication is managed via one bus to which all modules subscribe. This does not fully reflect the approach's potential for concurrent programming, but the fact that the bus represents a single interface that is concerned with the dispatch of event notifications allows for a comprehensible representation.

In the following sections the communication by means of an event bus is assumed in order to allow for more concise representation of data flow. More precisely, every event description, state variable, or other source of events is assumed to publish the event to a logical event bus that can be subscribed by any element of the application. Every time an event is published

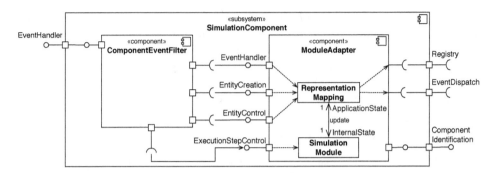

Figure 4.10: UML component diagram for simulation components. It is the component developer's task to implement the `ModuleAdapter`, which synchronizes the internal state of the simulation module with the representation of the framework.

all subscribers to the bus are informed and may decide to react and possibly emit further events themselves. As discussed before, this bus can be assumed to be managed at a clock that subsumes all real clocks in order to simulate concurrency (cf. section 3.2.4). Aiming for approximation of the more efficient message-passing design, the act of ignoring a message is assumed to cause no computational effort at all. An actual implementation, however, is suggested to adopt the actor model and its inherent message-passing architecture, as discussed in section 4.4.

Component Interface

By the adoption of the event bus perspective all communication is viewed as the occurrence of events. Since it is common practice to provide software developers with interfaces that prescribe the methods they have to implement, a mechanism that turns the observation of a specific event into a method call of such an interface is created.

Figure 4.10 visualizes the internals of a simulation component: a framework has to provide a `ComponentEventFilter`, which translates specific events to method invocations of the different interfaces that are implemented by the component (see figure 4.11). Similar event filters are provided for state variable updates and event descriptions, resulting in the invocation of the callbacks that were registered using the `observe` method. By concatenating these filters all occurrences of framework dependent events are turned into respective method invocations.

Events that are not handled by any filter are passed through to the `ModuleAdapter`. The latter has to be implemented by component developers. Its task is to create a layer that connects the simulation module's internal representation with the application state that is maintained by the framework. For this purpose, the `observe` methods of state variables and event descriptions are highly useful: callbacks that update the module's internal state can be registered, regardless of which element of the application caused the variable's change or emitted the event. Similarly, updates that originate from the simulation module can be redirected to other modules using the `set` and `emit` methods. In order to gain knowledge about existing entities a component can either rely on entities in the creation process of which it was involved or query the global registry.

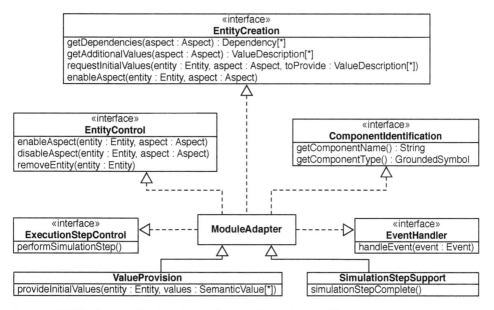

Figure 4.11: UML diagram showing the interfaces to be implemented by a `ModuleAdapter`. The creation of responses to asynchronous events is facilitated by inheritance from the `ValueProvision` and the `SimulationStepSupport` class.

Figure 4.11 shows the interfaces that have to be implemented by a `ModuleAdapter`: First, a simulation component needs to specify its component type as well as its component name. The former is required to facilitate assigning a component to respective aspects, whereas the latter is used to distinguish components of the same type.

Moreover, a component is involved in the entity creation process. Figure 4.12 shows this process, using the example of an entity creation process that involves a graphics module and a physics engine. Subsequent to the call to the `createEntity` method, which optionally can provide a callback function that is invoked after the process was completed, communication can be performed in a message- or event-based manner.

Events that are related to the creation of entities are treated by the `EntityCreation` interface. In the initial step the `getDependencies` method is invoked, which has to return combinations of value descriptions that specify which values the component requires before it can provide further values. For example, if a component would require an entity's size before it can provide an initial value for its mass, the dependency would specify that mass is dependent on size. Furthermore, the `getAdditionalValues` method will be called, allowing the component to announce additional initial values that it will provide even though they where not specified by the aspect.

The second step in the creation process is concerned with providing initial values for the state variables of the created entity. Since the process of obtaining these values, e.g., by loading a file, may be performed asynchronously, the `requestInitialValues` function does not return values directly. Instead the `provideInitialValues` method has to be called to specify the respective set of values. Depending on the build order that was calculated based

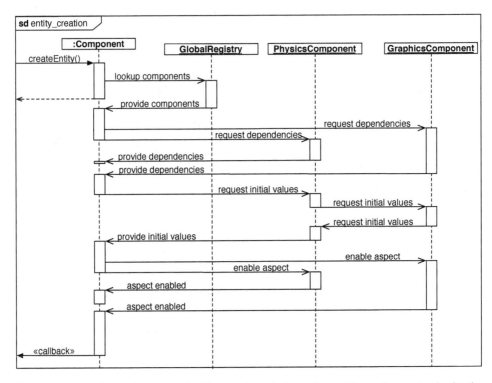

Figure 4.12: The entity creation process. In this example, a physics and a graphics module are involved in the creation of an entity. Prior to the actual creation process, these components are retrieved from a central registry.

on the announced dependencies, the invocation of the requestInitialValues function may occur multiple times. For that reason, a set of values that has to be provided during a certain invocation is passed to the function.

After an entity has been created, all components that are involved in the creation process are notified and their enableAspect methods are invoked. At this time each component has to include the entity into its simulation loop.

During its lifetime an entity can be modified in multiple ways. Obviously, it can be destroyed, which is signaled by the invocation of the removeEntity method. Furthermore, a single component can be notified to enable or disable the simulation of a certain aspect of a single entity. For this purpose, the respective method from the EntityControl interface will be invoked.

Observably, the enableAspect method is shared by the EntityCreation and the Entity-Control interface. This is due to the fact that—from a simulation component's point of view—no difference exists between the initial creation of an entity and enabling an aspect. Consequently, adding an aspect to an existing entity is possible, too. For this purpose, all required initial values either have to be contained in state variables or be provided by the aspect that is passed to the enableAspect method.

```
abstract class ModuleAdapter
{
    // Identification
    def getComponentType() : GroundedSymbol
    def getComponentName() : String

    // Entity Creation
    def getDependencies(aspect : Aspect) : Set[Dependency]
    def getAdditionalValues(aspect : Aspect) : Set[ValueDescription[_, _]]
    def requestInitialValues(toProvide : Set[ValueDescription[_, _]],
        entity : Entity, aspect : Aspect)

    // Entity Control
    def enableAspect(entity : Entity, aspect : Aspect)
    def disableAspect(entity : Entity, aspect : Aspect)
    def removeEntity(entity : Entity)

    // Event Handling
    def handleEvent(event : Event)

    // Simulation
    def performSimulationStep()
}
```

Listing 4.4: The component interface from figure 4.11 shown in Scala syntax.

Virtually all events are redirected to invocations of event handlers that are part of architecture elements, for example, callbacks registered via the observe methods of state variables and event descriptions or methods of the component interface. Nevertheless, in some situations it might be required to forward incoming events to a dedicated event handling interface or to observe all incoming events (e.g., for logging). For this purpose, all observed events for which no particular event handler is registered are processed by the handleEvent method of a ModuleAdapter.

The final method that has to be implemented is called performSimulationStep. As its name indicates, each invocation of this method has to result in a single simulation step of the wrapped simulation module, including respective updates of the simulation state. For example, a visual rendering module has to render a single frame or a physics engine has to compute a single time step (nevertheless it may calculate substeps internally). Similar to the provideInitialValues method no return value is provided but an invocation of the simulationStepComplete method is necessary to signal the finalization of the simulations. This is because calculations may be performed asynchronously but the simulation component has to remain reactive to handle further incoming events. Listing 4.4 provides an overview of the proposed interface using Scala syntax.

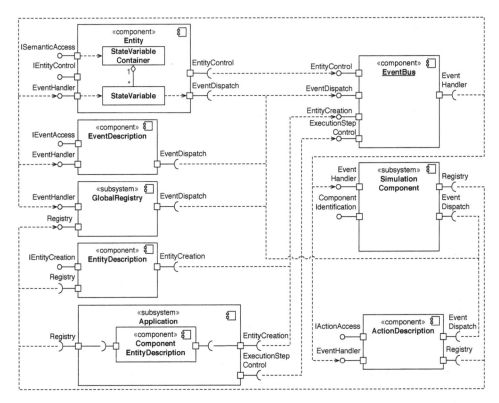

Figure 4.13: A UML component diagram depicting the integration of a simulation component into an application: the application uses `ComponentEntityDescriptions` to instantiate `SimulationComponents`. Conceptually, all communication is mediated by the `EventBus`.

4.5.4 Application Composition

Having defined the way in which elements can be described and instantiated, the instantiation of the application itself remains to be discussed. Adhering to 'everything-is-an-entity' concept, the application is represented by an entity, too. In the previous section it was not clearly specified to which entity description the component aspects were added to. With the application entity a container is present to which all simulation components are connected by means of a `hasPart` relation.

This rather odd way of representing the simulation modules as entities inside the application opens up interesting ways of reflection: for example, the entity that is associated to the physics engine could be added a visual aspect that allows to render its current state inside the application. Furthermore, its properties could be modified inside the virtual environment: for example, a virtual on/off switch could enable or disable the physical simulation. All of this is possible without any further efforts, because it is sufficient to add the required aspects to the respective entity description.

The overall interaction of elements in an application is visualized in figure 4.13: in the top left-hand corner, the entity class is shown. It provides the `ISemanticAccess` interface, enabling access to state variables (cf. section 4.3.2). Moreover, the IEntityControl interface enables the functionality of the EntityControl interface for one particular entity (cf. figure 4.11). State update events are dispatched from and to the contained state variables via the event bus.

The task of the EventBus is to translate method invocations into events and publish them. Observers of these events subsequently use appropriate event filters to turn the observation back into (callback) method invocations. In the figure such filters are not visualized for the sake of brevity. An example was given in the form of the ComponentEventFilter in figure 4.10 on page 134.

Event descriptions provide the EventHandler interface to define callbacks that are registered for the described events. The created events are published to the event bus, wherefore the EventDispatch interface is required. In order to enable a developer to observe and emit events, the IEventAccess interface is implemented (which prescribes the observe and emit methods that were introduced in section 4.3.2).

The global registry component implements the Registry interface and thus provides facilities for registration and lookup for architecture elements. Similar to all other elements, it requires a connection to the event bus in order to announce registrations. Depending on the eventual implementation, the event bus (i.e. the lookup mechanisms for message dispatch) and the global registry can be realized as a single component.

Entity descriptions as well as component entity descriptions, the latter of which are used inside the application component, are visualized in the bottom left-hand corner of figure 4.13. Both require the EntityCreation and Registry interfaces to trigger the entity creation process and register created entities. The application component provides the ExecutionStep-Control interface, allowing to trigger the execution of simulation components externally.

An ActionDescription requires access to the global registry to obtain information about the simulation state. Since it needs to emit events to announce results of the performed action as well as to receive events to be triggered externally, the EventDispatch interface is required and the EventHandler interface provided. Finally, the IActionAccess interface allows to invoke the action manually. The EventDispatch interface, the Registry interface, as well as the IActionAccess interface are provided in appendix B.

Due to the communication via the event bus new simulation components can easily be integrated. As shown on the right-hand side of figure 4.13 this does only necessitate the connection to the event bus and the global registry, which is facilitated by the provided interfaces. Entities, entity descriptions, action descriptions, and event descriptions provide the means to access the respective concept and encapsulate the underlying event mechanisms. In this way, a component developer can utilize these elements to create a wrapper around a preexisting simulation module to create reusable simulation components.

4.6 Summary

In this chapter, the knowledge representation model that was introduced in the previous chapter was extended into a component model for reusable IRIS applications. In the course of its development, the analysis of VE development aspects led to the proposition of a *semantics-based approach*. As a part of this approach the concept of semantic types and semantic traits was introduced. Both address restrictions that are commonly observed in the context of

IRIS development. They especially extend the type system of the underlying language by the integration of semantic type checks. Furthermore, the possibility to detect the type of an entity at runtime by checking it against a description from an underlying ontology is added.

In this way, the semantic reflection paradigm (cf. section 2.3.4) is extended: the proposed approach provides a set of grounded symbols, the consistency of which is fostered by means of an ontology. Using these symbols, semantic access to central programming primitives as known from the semantic reflection paradigm can be achieved. Moreover, a description of software interfaces is provided, which ease the implementation of such an approach.

The second contribution of this chapter is the *uniform access model*. It addresses the observation that overly complex software interfaces hinder reuse (cf. section 2.2.2). Expanding on the state value- and event-based representation that was developed in the previous chapter, a comprehensible interface to access and modify the simulation state is provided. The introduction of event descriptions creates a mechanism to observe events, which is nearly identical to the access to the simulation state.

The inherent requirement for exploiting all available hardware resources that are provided by up-to-date multi-core architectures as well as the development of potentially networked applications was then addressed by the proposition to adopt the actor model. After a short review of the issues that have to be faced in this context, the integration of the approaches that were mentioned in the preceding sections were discussed and hints for an implementation were given.

Finally, a component model that allows for the integration of all presented approaches was introduced. The model guides the developer in creating a reusable simulation component from a preexisting simulation module. In this context, the automatic conversion of data types as well as the instantiation of entities in a decoupled IRIS application were discussed.

The five requirements for frameworks for reusable IRISs, which were established in the beginning of this chapter, are answered by the proposed component model as described below:

R1 *Support for creating decoupled simulation modules:* The combination of the uniform access model (cf. section 4.3) and the actor model (cf. section 4.4) enables the creation of a module wrapper, which allows to turn preexisting simulation modules into decoupled components. In this regard, the uniform access model provides a means to apply the automated type conversion process, which was introduced in section 4.5.1. While this addresses the static aspect of decoupling, the message-based interface that is introduced by the actor model provides an approach to treat the dynamic aspects. The proposed component model (cf. section 4.5) provides the software interfaces that guide a component developer in the process of creating the decoupled component.

R2 *Support for the creation of generalized components:* Combining the concepts of semantic types and semantic traits (cf. section 4.2) with the uniform access model allows to decouple simulation modules from the specifics of the application content. This way, a simulation module can be flexibly used in most different situations. Applying the description-based approach, which was discussed in the context of the component model (cf. section 4.5.2), allows to decouple the creation of entities from the involved components. In this regard, simulation components can be split into multiple reusable modules, which address separate concerns by creating associated aspects.

R3 *Support for concurrent execution of simulation modules:* The adoption of the actor model and its inherent support for message-based architectures is highly beneficial for decoupling the execution schemes of simulation modules. A component that is represented as an actor can run in a completely independent thread of execution. In this way, addition and removal of components is facilitated with minimal effects on other parts of an IRIS.

R4 *Support for human-readable identifiers and high understandability:* Both the uniform access model and the semantics-based approach foster understandability of an IRIS application. The former introduces semantic type checks, which is beneficial for viewing a certain facet of an entity, whereas the latter provides a concise interface to access the simulation state. This interface can be used by developers as well as AI modules and virtual agents, since it provides uniform access to the complete simulation state. The component model fosters an 'everything-is-an-entity' view, whereby the uniform interface is extended to every element of an application. Thus, simulation modules as well as virtual (and real) entities can be accessed using a concise interface.

R5 *Support for retrieval of information about program code:* Although the proposed approaches do not directly permit to retrieve information about the program code, the description of actions that was introduced in the previous chapter provides a similar feature. It provides the opportunity to lookup functionality by specifying desired effects, thus reducing the efforts that are necessary to search for implemented functionality. By implementing respective tools this information becomes accessible at compile-time as well as at runtime. Similarly, the underlying ontology can allow to search for available semantic traits and entity descriptions.

Each of the techniques that were introduced in this chapter can be considered separately from the others. Nevertheless, the biggest advantages can be taken by their combination in the form of the component model. The following chapter will overview the Simulator X framework, which represents an exemplary implementation of this model.

Chapter 5

Simulator X

I remember seeing an elaborate and complicated automated washing machine for automobiles that did a beautiful job of washing them. But it could do only that, and everything else that got into its clutches was treated as if it were an automobile to be washed. I suppose it is tempting, if the only tool you have is a hammer, to treat everything as if it were a nail.

The Psychology of Science: A Reconnaissance
Abraham H. Maslow (2004)

5.1 Simulator X - A VR Research Platform

Simulator X (Latoschik & Tramberend, 2011) is a VR research platform that has been developed in the context of the project entitled *Semantic Reflection for Intelligent Realtime Interactive Systems* (SIRIS). The framework's main purpose is to facilitate research in the areas of multimodal interaction, intelligent graphics, and RIS development. In addition, it is being used to develop methods for the analysis of distributed systems (cf. Rehfeld, Tramberend, & Latoschik, 2013).

In the beginning of its development the project members felt that the frameworks at hand were not suited for their respective research needs. Software that had been developed in previous projects had become unmaintainable over the years and eventually disappeared completely. Although the knowledge that was gained in these projects was preserved in the form of publications and films, the huge efforts that had been made to implement applications were in vain. These experiences urged the project members to reflect on the development tools in use.

It was observed that existing approaches did not allow for access and modification of low level architecture elements. Reasons for this bear resemblance with the above-quoted commentary by Abraham H. Maslow: game engines and virtual reality frameworks are highly optimized for specific kinds of simulation, e.g., visual rendering, physics simulation, and animation, rendering them inappropriate for other cases of application. As a result, they force developers to wrap extending concepts around the internal data structures, often leading to closely coupled solutions that provide access to only parts of the simulation state. These findings as well as other hindering aspects that were mentioned in previous chapters led to the idea to create the Simulator X framework.

The SIRIS Project

The SIRIS project was conducted by the *Beuth Hochschule für Technik Berlin* and the *Intelligent Graphics Group* at the *University of Bayreuth*, which later moved to the *University of Würzburg* and became the *Human-Computer Interaction* group.

   The project's defined goal was to develop alternative and novel approaches to software techniques and architectures for Intelligent Realtime Interactive Systems (IRISs). A central idea of the approach was to build on the concept of *Semantic Reflection* (see section 2.3.4), which accounts for the first letter of the project's acronym. Accordingly, it provided a perfect environment for implementing the ideas developed in this thesis. The main contribution to the project is the design and conceptual development as well as the implementation of the core features of the Simulator X framework, especially focusing on the computational utilization of knowledge about the application state.

   The next sections will provide an overview of the design decisions taken as well as the resulting architecture of the Simulator X framework.

5.2 Architecture

Simulator X was designed as a test bed for alternative IRIS architectures. Consequently, the core ideas, concepts, and techniques developed in this thesis have been implemented in its current version. They now provide the central features of ongoing (I)RIS architecture research as well as a solid basis for many applications built on top of it.

   Adopting the introduced component model, active elements are restricted to message-based communication, thereby decoupling both data representations and control flow. Since the actor model (Hewitt et al., 1973) basically follows the same intention, it has been chosen as the basis for the current version of the Simulator X framework.

5.2.1 Actors

The model defines an actor as an entity of autonomous computation, which can communicate with other actors by means of messages only (cf. section 2.3.4). In fact, it promotes the idea that *everything is an actor*. This implies that no communication between two independent units of computation can happen other than by exchanging messages. Since message-based communication constitutes the lowest level of coupling, it inherently fosters the design principles of low coupling and high cohesion.

   Consequently, each Simulator X application is constituted of a set of actors. In fact, the application's main class is an actor that can receive messages and react to them. This way, a distributed structure is facilitated, allowing to use the nodes of a computer cluster to perform single computations or distribute simulation modules among them (some details regarding the feature of distributed applications are given in section 5.3.1).

   The application actor instantiates further actors, which represent the simulation modules utilized by the application. These comprise common elements, like a 3D rendering module, a physics engine, or application logic. Each of the simulation modules, in turn, can create further actors that concurrently fulfill specific tasks. For example, a stereoscopic 3D rendering module can spawn one actor for each of the computed views. Since an actor is only aware of

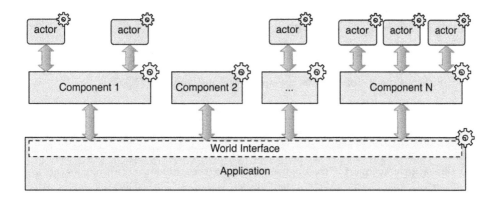

Figure 5.1: The Simulator X architecture: actors (indicated by gear wheels) are aware of other actors on neighboring layers and can exchange messages. Further reaching communication requires requesting the respective actor's address from adjacent actors.

its creator and its children, the knowledge about other actors has to be acquired by querying these actors. A typically created hierarchical application model is shown in figure 5.1.

5.2.2 Scala

Initially, four programming language candidates were considered for the implementation: C++, Java, Haskell, and Scala. Before the final decision was made, exploratory implementations in C++, Haskell, and Scala were carried out. Java, due to its resemblance to C++, was excluded from these implementations.

The advantage of C++ over the other languages was its assumed higher performance and wide distribution. Moreover, all project members had been in programming in C++ before. However, aspects like low level memory management, pointer arithmetics, and similar concepts were considered to have negative impact on the development process and quality of the final software.

Java was considered a good candidate, since all of the project members were experienced Java programmers and its platform independence was considered a desirable feature. On the downside, doubts were raised as to performance limitations of Java.

The idea of choosing Haskell was brought up due to its support for the functional programming paradigm. It eventually got rejected because of the long learning curve and complexity of program code that was anticipated by some project members.

In the end Scala (Odersky et al., 2006) was chosen, especially because its syntax promised concise programs. This was a reasonable aspect: since the development was to take place in an academic context, fast prototype development was one of the main tasks to be carried out. Moreover, the fewer amount of required program code promised to result in higher quality of the developed software, since the chance to create erroneous code usually decreases with the lines of written code. Aside from that, Scala's integrated implementation of the actor model, support for the functional as well as the object-oriented paradigm, and compatibility with the Java Virtual Machine constituted further positive aspects.

Especially the following of the features of the Scala programming language turned out to be highly advantageous (Wiebusch, Fischbach, Latoschik, & Tramberend, 2012):

- support for both the OOP as well as the functional programming paradigm

- inherent support for creation of Domain Specific Languages (DSLs)

- concise program structure

These aspects are dicussed in more detail in the following paragraphs.

Multi-Paradigm Support   Today, most programmers are used to write programs that adopt the object-oriented paradigm. Consequently, a programming language that forces them to comply to a different paradigm is likely to evoke reluctance to utilize it. Nevertheless, a single paradigm is usually designed for a specific purpose and impedes the realization of other aspects. For example, the creation of callback functions often is accomplished by complex constructs in pure OOP languages.

However, the very feature of callbacks is highly relevant in the context of VR frameworks. Arrival of new sensor data, reaction to certain events, handling user input, etc. are often accomplished by registering callback functions for the respective event. It becomes even more important in the context of message-based architectures, such as the actor model, in which nearly every action is a reaction to the receipt of a message. Especially the opportunity to define anonymous functions in place fosters locality. The code examples that are presented throughout this chapter provide examples for this feature.

Since the Scala language supports both the object-oriented as well as the functional programming paradigm, programmers that are familiar with one of them can slowly accustom themselves with the other.

Support for DSLs   An important factor for reusability of software is its understandability. Domain specific languages support this requirement by allowing for the creation of easily readable program code. This is achieved by hiding complex syntactical properties as well as by using more understandable expressions for otherwise incomprehensible operators and identifiers.

Whereas other languages often require external tools to utilize DSL features, Scala facilitates their creation and utilization inside program code. This is mainly achieved by Scala's opportunity to omit the dot operator as well as leaving out parentheses for functions that take at most one parameter.

Listing 5.1 provides a simple example of a DSL that allows to perform basic calculations using easily understandable program code (cf. lines 17–19). The DSL definitions in lines 2–14 use multiple features of the Scala language, including the in-place definitions of functions mentioned in the previous paragraph. Since similar concepts will be used in subsequent examples, a detailed explanation is given below. A very basic understanding of the Scala syntax by the reader is assumed, though.

The And class (line 2) serves as a provider for the and keyword, with the help of which the result of an addition or subtraction can be computed. The public constructor parameter and serves as a reference to the function that eventually performs the calculation.

```
     // begin DSL definitions
     class And(val and : Int => Int)

     object Sum {
        def of(i : Int) = new And(j => i + j)
     }

     object Difference {
        val between = (i : Int) => new And(j => math.abs(i - j) )
     }

     object Compute{
        def the[T](calculation : T) = calculation
     }
     // end DSL definitions

     val three = Sum of 1 and 2
     val two   = Sum of 1 and 1
     val one = Compute the Difference between two and three
```

Listing 5.1: A DSL example in Scala. The definitions in lines 2–14 allow for the easily understandable specifications in lines 17–19.

The two objects Sum and Difference (lines 4–10) provide the static methods of and between. Each of these returns an anonymous function, which takes an integer value as a parameter and returns an instance of the And class. The constructor parameter of the And class is the function that finally computes the result of the given expression. In the given example this constructor parameter will be an addition or subtraction function, respectively.

The instance of the And class that is returned by the of method in line 5 is passed an anonymous function. This function takes the of function's parameter i and adds its own parameter j to it. As mentioned above, this anonymous function could be passed to methods that register callbacks in the same way that it is passed to the constructor of the And class.

The definition of the between value of the Difference object essentially works the same. It represents a function that takes a parameter i and creates an instance of the And class by passing another method that calculates the difference between i and its own parameter j. As opposed to the of method, between is a constant that holds a reference to a function. Effectively, of and between are used in the same way. The Compute object (cf. line 12-14) simply provides a function named the, which returns the parameter it was passed. Its type parameter T is required to preserve the type of the passed parameter.

With these specifications the easily understandable expressions 'Sum of 1 and 2' and 'Compute the Difference between two and three' are supported. Admittedly, the expression 'val three = 1 + 2' is shorter and equally understandable, but an expression like 'val one = math.abs(2 - 3)' is already a little harder to grasp. As indicated by the example, complex concepts can be made easier to understand by means of DSLs.

```
import java.util.function.Function;

public class And{
   final public Function<Integer, Integer> and;

   public And(Function<Integer, Integer> and){
      this.and = and;
   }
}
```

Listing 5.2: Java version of the And class from listing 5.1.

Conciseness The definitions in listing 5.1 also exemplify the way in which Scala program code is concise. For example, the Java version of the And class will look similar to the implementation shown in listing 5.2. In C++, the implementation could possibly involve an additional header file. Similar to the concise definition of classes, other language constructs also tend to require less program code compared to other programming languages. Especially the utilization of aspects introduced by the functional programming paradigm are conductive to conciseness.

The benefits of such concise program code include

- less implementation effort and hence more time to focus on the initial problem,

- higher locality of code, due to compactness, and

- higher understandability, since less code has to be read.[6]

5.2.3 Semantic Values

The intention to introduce semantics on a core level is addressed by the concept of *semantic values*. A semantic value, as introduced in section 3.2.4, essentially is a plain value that is associated with a value description.

In Simulator X a value description is abbreviated SValDescription. It serves as a factory for semantic values, provides a link to the ontology, and connects the represented value with the data type hierarchy that is specified therein. This way, the feature of automatic type conversion is rendered possible, since the value descriptions can be utilized to look up respective converters.

Listing 5.3 shows the definition of a SValDescription (line 1) for semantic values that represent (affine) transformations. It is based on the Matrix description (line 3) and inherits the associated data type ConstMat4. Moreover, it is associated with the grounded symbol transformation. The set of available grounded symbols is established by transforming the concepts that are defined in the application ontology into plain Scala objects. Similarly, the value descriptions are automatically generated from ontology contents (cf. section 3.4.2).

---

[6] However, this can change to the contrary when code gets too dense.

```
object Transformation extends SValDescription(Matrix as
    Symbols.transformation definedAt Example.link("Transformation"))

object Matrix extends SValDescription(NullType as Symbols.matrix withType
    classOf[ConstMat4] definedAt Example.link("Matrix"))

object Example{
    def link(in : String) = "http://www.hci.uni-wuerzburg.de/ontologies/" +
        "simx/concepts/BasicTypes.owl#" + in

    val semanticValue = Transformation(Mat4.Identity)
}
```

Listing 5.3: Example for a transformation type description in Simulator X. A new semantic value instance is created using the description's apply function. The result is automatically linked with the description.

Altogether, the data type (here: `ConstMat4`) is decoupled from the semantics (represented by the `transformation` symbol). As shown in line 8, the value description does serve as a factory for semantic value instances, which are automatically linked with it.

5.2.4 Events

Besides the representation of a value that belongs to the application state, Simulator X supports the concept of *events*. An event denotes one certain incident that has no lifespan but rather happens at a certain point in time. Examples for this are collisions, the start or end of a process, and other application logic related occurrences.

Every Simulator X event is associated a symbol, which identifies its semantics. Furthermore, a (possibly empty) set of affected entities is part of the Event class. As shown in listing 5.4, events are created by means of event descriptions (line 1) using their `emit` method (line 7–9). Moreover, every `EventDescription` can also be used to register callbacks that are called on each occurrence of the event (cf. line 3-5).

```
object Collision extends EventDescription(Symbols.collision)

Collision.observe{
    cEvent => println("observed collision between " + cEvent.affectedEntities)
}

def publishCollision(e1 : Entity, e2 : Entity) : Unit =
    Collision.emit(Set(e1, e2), Force(10f))
```

Listing 5.4: Usage of events and event descriptions in Simulator X. Similar to semantic values (cf. listing 5.3), events are instantiated via the associated description class. Line 8 exemplifies this concept by emitting a collision event, which references the two entities in collision and specifies the collision force.

Events can be emitted by every `EventProvider`, the latter being a Scala trait that can be mixed into any actor class. As shown in the example, the required handshaking processes are completely hidden from the developer. As a result, events can be used at any point in an application.

Since handling every value update in the form of an event would result in an uncommon and incomprehensible program structure, a mechanism to represent *state* is introduced. The next section introduces a mutable variant of semantic values that encapsulates update events and thus provides a more convenient way to access the simulation state.

5.2.5 State Variables

Building on the actor model and the concept of semantic values, *state variables* (abbreviated *SVars*) are introduced in Simulator X. State variables (besides events) provide the basis for the implementation of the uniform access model that was introduced in section 4.3. Hence, they implement the three methods `observe`, `get`, and `set`. In addition, each state variable is assigned a Universally Unique Identifier (UUID) for identification purposes as well as an `ignore` method to unsubscribe from further update notifications regarding that state variable.

Moreover, each state variable is assigned a dedicated actor, its *owner*, which is responsible for controlling value updates, sends out notifications about such updates, and handles value read requests. In Simulator X each actor has an associated map data structure, linking the owned state variables' data with their UUIDs.

Except for the local owner's representation, only immutable references to a state variable are used. Each such reference contains the state variable's UUID as well as its initial owner. In this way, requests to update or access its value can be communicated to the owner. If the owner has changed (which, in theory, is possible to allow for load balancing), the previous owner will inform the requesting actor about this circumstance. The requesting actor stores this information internally and directs subsequent requests to the new owner.

The immutable reference also acts as a proxy, by providing a software interface that encapsulates the underlying message-based communication. Additionally, it allows to access the values in a callback-like manner. Listing 5.5 exemplifies the access to state variables in Simulator X, which is in line with the uniform access model from section 4.3.

At this point, the benefit of anonymous functions in Scala becomes evident. The possibility to specify the operations that are performed with a retrieved value at the same line of code in which the access occurs (cf. lines 4 and 14–16) allows for much more understandable programs than the use of externally specified functions would.

To some extent this work adopts the idea of a blackboard model (Nii, 1986) to represent global state and access to it. Such a model facilitates decoupling of knowledge sources by means of a centralized data base (the blackboard). All knowledge sources exclusively communicate via this blackboard and opportunistically react to changes. The simulation modules in an IRIS application can be interpreted as such knowledge sources, which communicate by reading and updating the simulation state. However, as opposed to a blackboard model, simulation modules do not necessarily have to act opportunistically. Furthermore, Simulator X's event system provides an alternative way of communication, enabling components to bypass the communication via the blackboard.

```
def incrementValue(sVar : SVar[Integer]) = {
    // using callbacks
    sVar.get {
        value => sVar.set(value + 1)
    }
    // using continuations
    val value = sVar.read
    sVar.set(value + 1)

    // observing values
    val sVarValues = mutable.Map[SVar, Integer]()
    sVar.observe{
        updatedValue =>
            println("change: " + (updatedValue - sVarValues.getOrElse(sVar, 0)))
            sVarValues.update(sVar, updatedValue)
    }
}
```

Listing 5.5: Exemplary access to state variables in Simulator X.

The Scala language supports continuations by means of a compiler plugin. Using continuations essentially permits to stop the execution of a method, capture its context, and store it for later execution. The read method that is applied in line 7 of listing 5.5 makes use of this feature. Although it allows for an even more conventional way of programming, the underlying mechanisms remain the same. Moreover, since Scala provides delimited continuations, the scope of a continuation needs to be specified. For this reason, continuations can be used in each top-level message handler that is attached to a Simulator X actor, since it automatically delimits the scope of the continuation.

Some aspects should be kept in mind when state variables are used:

- The underlying message-based access leads to the introduction of a delay between the request of a value or its update and the eventual execution of the specified callback. In the context of the incrementValue method in listing 5.5 this implies that a different actor can modify the state variable after its value is sent to the actor that invoked the get method. The increment operation is hence executed using an outdated value, which most certainly will lead to an unexpected result.

- Creating a local representation of the required state variables by means of the observe method should always be preferred to the use of the get method. Lines 11–16 in listing 5.5 exemplify this procedure. The beneficial aspects are the instant access to the most recent value as well as the more common way of value access.

The set of all state variables allows to observe all changes to the application state. As motivated before, the utilization of plain state variables would, however, result in an incomprehensible application design. Hence, a state variable is always associated to an *entity*. The next section will provide the details of the entity model that is applied by Simulator X.

```
def handleTransformationOf(entity : Entity){
   // accessing values
   entity.observe(Transformation) foreach {
      newTransformation =>
         println(
            "Entity " + entity + " got new transformation " +
               newTransformation
         )
   }

   // adding / updating values
   entity set Transformation(Mat4.Identity)
}
```

Listing 5.6: An entity does allow to create comprehensible access to its properties by pass-through of the access methods of the state variables.

5.2.6 Entity Model

Entities are the central building block of Simulator X applications: while the actor model, which is utilized to handle functional elements in Simulator X, promotes the view that 'everything is an actor', static elements are represented assuming the perspective that 'everything is an entity'.

Entities

Regarding stored data, an *entity* is nothing more then a set of state variables that represent its properties. To identify state variables inside the entity the associated value description is used. The approach of assigning a value description to each state variable inside an entity accounts for the fact that a state variable is meaningless as long as it is not associated with an entity.

In order to allow for multiple state variables with the same value description, the concept of *annotations* is added. Each annotation is basically an arbitrary semantic value (e.g., a timestamp) that is used to particularize the semantics of a value description.

Listing 5.6 exemplifies the way in which the properties (i.e. the state variables) of an entity are accessed: read access is accomplished by means of the entity's observe method (the get method is handled analogously). Since multiple state variables can match the value description Transformation, a set of state variables is returned. The foreach method invokes the observe method on all of these state variables, applying the anonymous function that was passed to the foreach method.

Updating a state variable is performed by means of a state value, as shown in line 11: the entity is passed a state value which automatically is inserted into the matching state variable. If no such variable exists, a new one will be created and the currently active actor will become its owner. In order to add a second state variable, the respective value description has to be added an annotation, since otherwise the already present state variable would be overwritten.

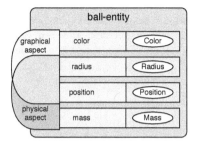

Figure 5.2: Exemplary entity description of a ball entity, which is specified to consist of a physical aspect as well as a graphical aspect (adapted from Wiebusch & Latoschik, 2012).

Aspects

Persisting with the description-based approach, entities are instantiated by means of associated descriptions. For this purpose, the concept of *aspects* that was introduced in section 2.2.3 is applied. A Simulator X aspect identifies the properties that an entity has to have to enable a particular simulation aspect. For example, entities that are created by means of a description which contains the PhysicalSphere aspect (cf. listing 5.8) will be treated as sphere-shaped rigid bodies by the utilized physics engine. In order to enable this kind of simulation, at least a radius and a mass property are required and will thus be inserted into the respective entity.

Figure 5.2 exemplifies the concept of aspects in the context of an entity description: the ball entity description consists of a graphical as well as a physical aspect. While the color and mass property are only used by either the graphical or physical aspect, the radius and position properties are shared by both. Note that each of the state variables is assigned an identifying concept that carries its semantics.

Besides the question which of both components (graphics or physics) will become the owner of the shared variables, the initial values for all properties have to be specified. Since the simulation modules are meant to be easily exchangeable, they must not directly depend on one another. As indicated in section 4.5.2, such interdependencies cannot be avoided in every case, e.g., if a simulation module loads information that another module depends on from an external file. In that case, a build order has to be established to ensure that every module is provided the information it needs to instantiate the entity.

To support this process, aspects specify the values a component will provide as well as the values it does require. For this purpose, two sets have to be specified by each aspect, as shown in line 6–10 of listing 5.7:

- the set of *provided values*, which consists of state value descriptions for which initial values will be provided by the respective component. In the given example, this set contains the mass and the position of the entity.

- the set of *features*, which contains value descriptions that are required by the respective component to enable treating the entity in the desired way. In listing 5.7 this includes the values provided by the component as well as the entity's radius.

The set of required values can be calculated as the set of features that are not provided by the component.

```
case class PhysicalSphere(position : ConstVec3f, forComponents :
    List[Symbol]) extends EntityAspect(Symbols.physics, Symbols.sphere,
    forComponents)
{
  def getCreateParams =
    Set(Position(position))

  def getProvidedValues =
    Set(Mass, Position)

  def getFeatures =
    getProvidings + Radius
}
```

Listing 5.7: The (simplified) version of an aspect for physical rigid body spheres used in Simulator X.

Furthermore, a set of parameters, which are required for instantiating the entity, is specified in lines 3 and 4. This set does not necessarily match the set of provided values. For example, if the physics engine estimates the mass of an object by its size, or if the value is obtained from a model file, no value needs to be provided initially.

In addition, aspects contain two symbols in order to identify the related component type and the semantics of the aspect, respectively. In listing 5.7 these are Symbols.physics and Symbols.sphere, which are linked to the grounded symbols PHYSICS and SPHERE in the ontology. By means of these symbols the aspect is decoupled from the component that will finally receive. Ideally, all physics components support a common set of aspects, whereby they would become easily exchangeable.

Finally, a list of symbols can be specified, which contains the names of the components that should receive the aspect when the entity is created. If this list is empty, all components of the given type will be involved in the entity creation process. Otherwise, only the components that have the correct type and name will receive the aspect.

Since only the developer of a simulation component has sufficient knowledge to specify the aspects it supports, these aspects are to be supplied with the component. The final composition of the provided aspects is subsequently accomplished by the application developer.

Entity Descriptions

Listing 5.8 shows the description of a ball entity in Simulator X. It consists of the Physical-Sphere aspect, which was introduced in listing 5.7, as well as a ShapeFromFile aspect. The latter is expected to cause the rendering engine to load a 3D model from a COLLADA file and render it at the same position where the physics engine assumes the entity to be. Due to the physics engine's dependency on the radius property, which was expressed in the aspect, the size of the simulated sphere is the same for both modules.

At this point some important observations have to be made: first, the entity description does not implicitly mention any of the simulation modules that are involved in its simulation. Hence, simulation components with the same component type that do support the used

```
case class Ball(name : String, position : ConstVec3)
   extends EntityDescription ( name,
      ShapeFromFile( // visual aspect
         file      = "assets/vis/ball.dae"
      ),
      PhysicalSphere( // physical aspect
         position = position
      )
   )

// instantiation of the described entity at position (0, 1, 0)
Ball(position = Vec3(0, 1, 0), name = "ball#1").realize{
   ballEntity =>
      println("instantiated " + ballEntity)
}
```

Listing 5.8: An exemplary description of a virtual ball, which uses the `PhysicalSphere` aspect introduced in listing 5.7. The utilization of named parameters is a feature supported by the Scala language.

aspects, e.g., two physics engines, can be exchanged without adapting the entity descriptions. In this context, supporting an aspect means to support the required and provided values as well as to recognize the aspect type. This way, the definition of an application's content is decoupled from the simulation modules accessing it.

Secondly, the constructor parameters of used aspects are either filled with default values or passed from the entity description's constructor. This structure facilitates the generation of complete entity descriptions from external formats.

Finally, the utilization of named parameters (a feature of the Scala programming language) effectively increases the readability and usability of program code. For example, note that the order of parameters in line 12 of listing 5.8 does not match that of the Ball class in line 1. However, due to the specification of parameter names, the correct assignment is possible. Thus, the exact order of parameters does not have to be known in the first place, and later programmers can easily distinguish between parameters without inspecting the invoked function. Using parameter names that match the grounded symbols from the ontology improves understandability even more.

Entity Creation

In Simulator X the instantiation of an entity from its description requires multiple steps. The entire process is visualized in figure 5.3. At first, messages that contain the respective aspect are sent to all simulation modules that are related to the entity. Each module answers this query with the list of dependencies that will arise when the module loads or computes the initial values for the entity. Furthermore, it can declare to provide further properties (which is not the case in the given example). In figure 5.3 the physics engine announces that it requires a value for the radius parameter before it is able to provide a value for the mass property.

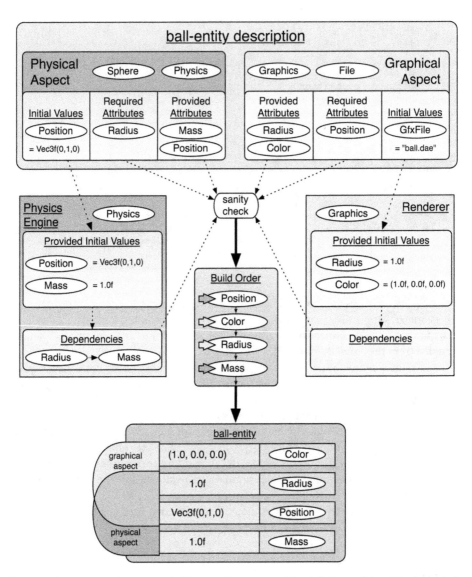

Figure 5.3: The entity creation process in Simulator X. By means of the definitions of the utilized aspects (see 5.2.6) a build order is created. In the shown example, a physics engine and a renderer are queried for the initial values they can provide. The renderer loads information from a file that is specified by the aspect, whereas the physics engine uses the position from its aspect and notifies about a dependency of the mass property on the radius property (i.e. it guesses the balls mass from its radius). The resulting build order is shown in the center, which eventually results in the instantiation of the ball entity visualized at the bottom. Figure adapted from Wiebusch and Latoschik (2012).

After a response was received from each component, a sanity check is performed. To pass this check, the set of values that are provided by all components has to match the set of required values. It furthermore is ensured that only one initial value will be provided for each property.

If the sanity check is passed, a build order is created from the lists of required values, provided values, and additional dependencies. In the example from figure 5.3 this leads to the order shown in the center: the physics engine first provides the position, then the renderer provides color and radius, and finally the physics engine provides the mass property. This eventually results in instantiation of the ball entity shown at the bottom.

In the given example there is more than one sorting that yields a valid build order. For example, the renderer could also first provide the radius and the color property. However, it would not be able to create its internal representation, because it depends on the position property and, thus, would have to be notified about that value, as a last point.

The heuristics of the algorithm that calculates the build order is to minimize the amount of messages to be sent. In the example four messages are required: one to the physics engine (1), which will notify the renderer (2) about the position value. The renderer in turn loads the COLLADA file, creates its internal representation of the entity, and provides the radius and color properties to the physics engine (3). The latter now creates its internal representation of the entity, since it is informed about all values that it needs for this purpose, and eventually notifies the actor that initiated the creation process (4) about its completion.

As a final step, all related modules are concurrently notified about the completion of the entity. At this point it is integrated into each component's simulation loop.

5.2.7 Relations

As discussed in section 3.2.4 and 4.2.4, relations are implemented as a special variant of semantic values, which are stored in state variables. A relation consists of a symbol, which identifies the relation's type, and the two values it connects. Due to their resemblance to semantic values, relations are accessed in the same way, using the get, set, and observe methods.

In order to specify a relation, the DSL-like convenience functions that are shown in listing 5.9 are used. Although it would be possible to instantiate relations without associating them with an entity, this is not intended in Simulator X. Hence, a relation either connects an entity with another entity or creates a special relation between an entity and a state value.

In line 2 and 9 of listing 5.9 the '?' object is used to represent the participant of a relation that shall be identified. The first example indicates how to register for notifications about new occurrences of the HasArm relation. The ? object does implement the interface that is prescribed by the unified access model and serves as a proxy object to formulate requests for the left-hand side of a relation.

Instantiating a relation is performed using the set method, similar to creating common state variables. The only difference is the utilization of the -> operator instead of the parenthesis operator, which is a convenience function supported by the relation description class.

Finally, in line 9 the ? class is used to specify a query for the right-hand side of the HasArm relation. From this example the resemblance of relations to state values becomes evident.

```
def relationExample(user : Entity, arm : Entity){
   ?.observe(HasArm -> arm) foreach {
      retrievedUser =>
         println( retrievedUser + "has arm")
   }

   user.set(HasArm -> arm)

   user.get(HasArm -> ?) foreach {
      retrievedArm =>
         println("user has arm " + retrievedArm)
   }
}
```

Listing 5.9: Simulator X relations example: relations are used in the same way as state variables are. The introduction of a DSL allows to handle them more easily.

5.2.8 Components

The previous sections have introduced the architecture elements of Simulator X that are used to represent the application state as well as changes to it. In order to allow for dynamic changes, components (cf. section 4.5) are implemented. Simulator X components are objects that are often called engines (e.g., physics engine) in the game context, or (sub-) systems in the context of the Entity-Component-System pattern.

In order to facilitate encapsulation every component is implemented as an actor. This implies that the component can perform all of its computations asynchronously and is not coupled with the control flow of other components, per se. Moreover, the component is free to start an arbitrary amount of actors that perform calculations to support the component's task.

Essentially, every module of computation that accesses and/or modifies one or multiple aspects of the simulation state is realized as a component. This includes common simulation modules, like a 3D renderer or a physics engine, but also includes arbitrary other aspects, for example, game logic, input/output handling, or character movement.

It is possible to create two simulation components that wrap a single simulation module. For instance, a complete game engine that provides both rendering and physical simulation capabilities could be represented by a physics and a rendering component. The functionality can be separated by creating two module adapters, each of which synchronizes the associated simulation aspect. This way, is is possible to decide on using either one or both features, thus facilitating reusability.

Regarding the question of adding aspects to an existing component, as opposed to creating a new component, a component should be extended by an aspect if it already provides similar aspects, otherwise a new component should be created. For example, if an existing physics component does support force-based simulation of sphere-shaped rigid bodies and the same feature should be added for box-shaped rigid bodies, it is reasonable to extend the physics component by a respective aspect. If a behavior simulation for certain entities should be added,

```
abstract class Component(
    val componentName : Symbol,
    val componentType : GroundedSymbol)
{
    // component configuration related
    def configure(params: SValSet): Unit
    def requestInitialConfigValues( toProvide: Set[ConvertibleTrait[_]],
            aspect: EntityAspect, e: Entity): SValSet
    def finalizeConfiguration(e: Entity): Unit

    // entity related methods
    def requestInitialValues( toProvide: Set[ConvertibleTrait[_]],
            aspect: EntityAspect, e: Entity, given: SValSet): Unit
    def entityConfigComplete(e: Entity, aspect: EntityAspect): Unit
    def removeFromLocalRep(e: Entity): Unit

    // externally triggered simulation loop
    def performSimulationStep(): Unit
}
```

Listing 5.10: The interface to be implemented by every Simulator X component. The super classes as well as the protected keywords are omitted for brevity.

a new component should be created, which can modify the acceleration state variable of the entities in order to affect their position. In some situations this decision is not as obvious. For example, if the above-mentioned physics component—which can only apply forces to sphere-shaped rigid bodies—is used and a collision detection mechanism is required, this would, according to the given heuristics, require to implement a new component.

Of course, physics engines do usually include collision detection as well as force simulations and are capable of handling a variety of different object shapes. Nevertheless, the mentioned separation into multiple simulation components allows for using single aspects.

The Component Interface

Each Simulator X component has to implement the software interface that is shown in listing 5.10. It is mainly guided by the methods that were proposed in the component model in section 4.5.3. Some of these are pre-implemented with empty method bodies in order to ease the process of implementing a new component. Besides the performSimulationStep and configure methods, the remaining method definitions are concerned with the entity creation process.

The configure method is passed a set of semantic values (SValSet), which are used to set a new or update an old configuration of the component. It is invoked each time the properties of the component entity change.

As discussed in section 4.5.2, a component is created in the same way that entities are. Thus, the methods requestInitialConfigValues and finalizeConfiguration as well as

requestInitialValues and entityConfigComplete essentially have the same semantics. The former are concerned with the creation of the component entity and the latter with
the creation of any other entity.[7]

The methods that are concerned with performing the entity creation process are implemented as suggested in section 4.5.3, with the exception that the enableAspect method in
the EntityCreation interface is called entityConfigComplete (for historical reasons).
In the requestInitialValues method each component has to create its representation
of the entity, as soon as sufficient information is available to do so. This is important, since
the invocation of the entityConfigComplete method is performed at the same time by all
components and no delays must occur at that point. Otherwise, the entity would be included
in the simulation loop of some components earlier than in that of others.

The performSimulationStep method is triggered externally every time the component
is meant to provide an updated state of its simulations. This does not necessarily mean that all
computations have to be performed when the method is called. Instead, precomputed values
could be published by means of either events or state variables. However, it is important that
these values are valid at the time they are published: e.g., a physics engine must not publish a
state that was up to date 100 milliseconds ago.

Since an actor can process only one message at a time, callbacks that have been registered by
means of an observe method are invoked outside the performSimulationStep method.
This implies, that computationally expensive calculations should not be performed in such
callbacks, because it could delay the beginning of the simulation step.

Component Creation

Pursuing the 'everything is an entity' metaphor, components are instantiable and accessible
like entities. More precisely, every component is described by a component-entity description
and its properties are accessed by means of the state variables of that entity. For example, the
gravity setting of a physics engine is changed in the same way that the gravity value of any
other entity is.

Since usually all components are instantiated during an application's startup, a convenience
function is added that takes a set of component aspects as a parameter and collectively starts
the associated components. Listing 5.11 shows a component aspect as well as its usage in a
Simulator X application.

As shown in the example, a component aspect is structured much in the same way as other
entity aspects are. In addition to common entity descriptions, it has a type parameter that
specifies the component's main class (i.e. the one that implements the Component interface
from listing 5.10). Another difference is the circumstance that a component description cannot
specify provided and required values but only the set of value descriptions, which specify the
properties that will be contained in the associated entity. Finally, if the component requires
any values passed to its constructor, these can be passed to the ComponentAspect class in
the form of a sequence (cf. end of line 3 of listing 5.11).

---

[7] This distinction was made due to a request of the framework's users, who preferred a clear separation between
entity and component creation.

```
// provided by component
case class JBulletComponentAspect(name : Symbol, gravity: ConstVec3)
    extends ComponentAspect[JBulletComponent](Symbols.physics, name, Seq())
{
  def getComponentFeatures = Set( Gravity, SimulationSpeed )
  def getCreateParams = Set( Gravity(gravity) )
}

// inside application main class
val displayCfg = BasicDisplayConfiguration(1280, 800, fullscreen = false)

def applicationConfiguration = ApplicationConfig withComponent
    JVRComponentAspect(Symbol("renderer"), displayCfg) and
    JBulletComponentAspect(Symbol("physics"), ConstVec3(0, -9.81f, 0))
```

Listing 5.11: Component creation in Simulator X. The shown JBulletComponentAspect is a simplified version of that used in Simulator X in the way that less parameters are specified.

The component aspect for the JBullet[8] physics component (lines 2–7) is used in line 14 to specify the configuration of an application that utilizes two components. In this context, the ApplicationConfig object conveniently allows to combine multiple component aspects using the and keyword. That configuration is specified to be the return value of the applicationConfiguration method (lines 12–14), which is part of every Simulator X application. This way, both components are automatically created on the application's startup, using the provided parameters.

World Interface

One essential observation that was made during the development of the Simulator X framework is that there needs to be a central authority that

1. manages the instantiation of components,

2. allows for registration of architecture elements, such as components, actors, event publishers, event subscribers, and entities, and

3. manages hand-shaking procedures (e.g., in the context of the event system).

The main reason for this requirement is the fact that no architecture element should need to be aware of others, to achieve minimal coupling. In Simulator X this component is the so-called *World Interface* (Wiebusch, Latoschik, & Tramberend, 2010). It does exist only once per process and is automatically started with the application.

---

[8] JBullet is available via http://jbullet.advel.cz.

All instantiated components are automatically registered with the world interface. This way, it can be queried for components that match a certain aspect, each time an entity is instantiated. In this context, component aspects are processed by the world interface, which is responsible for the instantiation of components.

The registry functionality is also required for hand-shaking processes in the context of the event system: every actor that emits an event is automatically registered in the world interface as an `EventProvider` for the particular event type. In the same way, actors that call the `observe` method of an entity description are registered as `EventHandlers` for the described type of events. Each time the set of registered `EventHandlers` or `EventProviders` changes, the world interface initiates a handshake between new matching pairs. Afterwards, events are directly sent between these pairs in a peer-to-peer manner.

A further situation in which the world interface is applied is the access to existing and newly instantiated entities. This is especially relevant in the context of handling entities that represent real world objects. For example, the component that is performing the visualization of the virtual environment often is also providing mouse and keyboard input. Since these entities[9] do exist only once, there is no sense in instantiating them multiple times. Using the world interface, the graphics component can instantiate entities on its own and register them using symbols from the ontology. These entities can subsequently be accessed at any point in an application, without knowing about their origin. In the same way, any other entity can be registered and accessed, thus allowing for queries to the world state from any point in the application.

5.2.9 Ontology

As motivated in section 3.2.1, the integration of semantics into a VR framework has multiple benefits. In Simulator X this integration is achieved by means of value descriptions that are linked to an ontology. This way, the knowledge that is encoded in the ontology is linked with the simulation state without the need for data duplication.

A second beneficial aspect of the integrated ontology is the possibility to utilize grounded symbols. These ensure that a consistent set of identifiers is used throughout an entire application. Since every simulation module is wrapped into a component, a layer that translates between the module's internal representation and the globally used one is created.

Structure and Composition

As shown in figure 5.4, the structure of the ontology used in Simulator X is guided by the model presented in section 3.4.1. The *core ontology* contains all concepts that describe architecture elements. It is imported by the *basic types* ontology, which contains common concepts that are shared among components but do neither belong to the core framework nor are specifically designed for a certain component. In a way, this file establishes common sense knowledge about concepts in the context of VR frameworks. Ideally, it is continually extended by the community, thus creating an ontology of common sense VR knowledge.

Building on these files an additional ontology file is created for each component type. In figure 5.4 this are the *graphical concepts* as well as the *physical concepts* ontologies. These

---

[9] Since everything is an entity, so are the mouse and the keyboard.

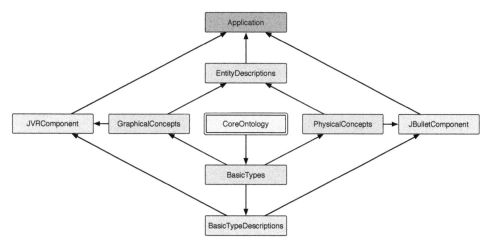

Figure 5.4: Structure of OWL files: The inner files (green) contain general concepts. The outer files contain knowledge that is related to a certain implementation of the core framework (bottom) and the components (sides). Each arrow indicates an import relation between the connected ontology files.

files include component-specific knowledge and assertions. For example, the *physics concepts* ontology contains the specification of physical aspects on an abstract level. In the example of a sphere-shaped rigid body (cf. section 5.2.6), the set of features that is provided by a PhysicalSphere aspect is described in this file.

Using these files, which contain abstract concepts, the entity description in listing 5.8 can be specified. For this purpose, the concept of a ball has to be contained in an *entity descriptions* ontology. Multiple of these ontologies can be created to, e.g., create different sets of entity descriptions. Each of them would import the required concepts, which in this case are the graphical and physical concepts ontologies. Using the imported assertions about aspects, the intersection of the PHYSICALSPHERE concept and the SHAPEFROMFILE concept—both being subconcepts of the aspect concept—could be declared as a subclass of the ball concept, as shown in listing 5.12.

```
SubClassOf (
   ObjectIntersectionOf (
     physicalConcepts:PhysicalSphere
     graphicalConcepts:ShapeFromFile
   )
   entityDescriptions:Ball
)
```

Listing 5.12: OWL contents for the ball entity description from listing 5.8, asserted in the entity descriptions file (cf. figure 5.4).

```
Declaration ( NamedIndividual ( application:BallEntityDescription ) )

ClassAssertion (
  ObjectSomeValuesFrom (
    basicDescriptions:describesProperty
    entityDescriptions:Ball
  )
  application:BallEntityDescription
)

ObjectPropertyAssertion (
  Annotation (core:overridesProvide basicTypes:Position)
  simxCoreOntology:hasAspect
    application:BallEntityDescription
    jvrComponent:SimXJVR_ShapeFromFileAspect
)
```

Listing 5.13: OWL contents for the ball entity description from listing 5.8, asserted in the application file (cf. figure 5.4).

In order to create more concrete information that can be used to generate program code, the *basic type descriptions* ontology is specified. This ontology imports the basic types ontology and asserts axioms concerning the value descriptions in use. For example, the fact that a value description should be created for the transformation type, involving a particular matrix data type, is specified in this file.

Each component provides at least one additional component specific OWL file, which includes information about the aspects that are implemented by the component. The information in these files is based on the concepts that are defined for the respective component type (cf. figure 5.4). For example, the exact implementation of the PhysicalSphere aspect, which is used in previous examples, is specified in this file. The properties that are required by the aspect are specified in shared concept files (cf. listing 5.7 on page 154). These are extended by the component specific files, which contain additional information about the provided and required initial values.

Finally, each application provides another OWL file, which imports the files provided by the components in use as well as the entity descriptions ontology. In the example in section 5.2.8 the JVRComponent and the JBulletComponent are used, wherefore their associated ontologies are imported. Based on the accumulated concepts, the application developer can specify a set of entity descriptions in the application OWL file.

Listing 5.13 exemplifies the required assertions to specify the description of the ball entity. First, an individual that represents the entity description has to be specified. This individual is subsequently asserted to belong to the class of individuals that describes a ball entity. Finally, the entity description is specified to involve the SIMXJVR_SHAPEFROMFILEASPECT.

In situations where only one single individual is specified for a certain aspect type, e.g., if the SIMXJVR_SHAPEFROMFILEASPECT is the only SHAPEFROMFILE aspect, the general assertion from listing 5.12 is sufficient due to unambiguity. Consequently, the last assertion from listing 5.13 is only required in two situations:

1. if multiple SHAPEFROMFILE aspects are specified, or

2. if conflicting provide/require schemes arise by the combination of aspects.

In the first case, it is sufficient to assert the HASASPECT object property. In the second case, however, a way to resolve the arising conflicts has to be specified. This can either be done by modification of the SIMXJVR_SHAPEFROMFILEASPECT or in the way it is shown in listing 5.13. In that case, the OVERRIDESPROVIDE annotation is used to annotate the HASASPECT property assertion, indicating that the specified aspect should be the one that is used to specify the entity's initial position. The alternative approach is to annotate the aspect in question, in which case it would be always the one by which an entity's initial position is specified. Depending on the combination of components and aspects in use, the one or the other approach might be more adequate.

Code Generation

The intention to decouple components is facilitated by the generation of most of the description classes mentioned in the previous sections. Starting with grounded symbols, value descriptions, aspects, entity descriptions, and even functions can be generated from the contents of the ontology. In this context, the description based approach that was proposed in section 4.5 is highly beneficial, since it provides a clearly defined interface between the ontology and program code.

The modular structure of ontologies, which was introduced in section 3.6 and detailed in the previous paragraphs, simplifies the process of exchanging a component by a similar one: when the ontology file of the previous component is exchanged by the new one, the value descriptions and aspects therein are automatically generated into program code. Furthermore, the entity descriptions automatically use the specific aspects of the component, as long as there were no explicit overrides regarding provided values. The tasks that have to be performed to replace a component in Simulator X are detailed in section 6.2.2.

Consequently, the generation of program code is part of the compilation process of a Simulator X application. Since the core ontology as well as ontologies of implemented components do rarely change, they are loaded from a web server. In order to allow for offline compilation, the code generation application caches the used ontology files and uses the stored version if no connection to the Internet is available.

5.3 Features

Since Simulator X is meant to facilitate the decoupling and usage of simulation components, most of the specific features are implemented in the form of components that can be attached to an application. Some of these components will be discussed in section 5.5.

Nevertheless, there are three noteworthy features that are integrated into every Simulator X application, which will be discussed in the following sections.

```
1   // local machine
2   val displayCfg = BasicDisplayConfiguration(1280, 800, fullscreen = false)
3
4   override protected def applicationConfiguration = ApplicationConfig
        withComponent
5       JVRComponentAspect(gfxName, displayCfg) and
6       JBulletComponentAspect(name = physicsName,
7                            gravity = ConstVec3(0, -9.81f, 0)) on "physicsNode"
8
9   // remote machine
10  class SimxRemoteApplication(args : Array[String])
11      extends SimXApplication with RemoteCreation
12  {
13    protected def configureComponents(){
14      registerComponentCreationSupport[JBulletComponent]("physicsNode")
15      registerComponentCreationSupport[JVRConnector]("renderNode")
16  }
```

Listing 5.14: Remote component example: only the specification on "physicsNode" is added to the local application configuration, resulting in it being executed by the remote application shown in lines 10–16.

5.3.1 Distributed Computing

Due to the underlying actor model all state synchronization in a Simulator X application is achieved by means of messages. Thus, each application is inherently capable of being deployed in a networked setup. While this is indeed a desirable feature in the context of VR frameworks, it also is beneficial regarding reusability. If, for example, a particular component relies on certain outdated hardware, this component can be run on an external node while other parts of the application are executed on an up-to-date system.

Listing 5.14 shows the specification that is required to run components on a remote machine. The upper half of the definition specifies the application configuration on the machine that runs the application initialization. In comparison to listing 5.11, the only difference is the addition on "physicsNode" which is attached to the physics component aspect.

On the remote machine(s) only the code that is shown in the bottom of listing 5.14 has to be executed. In line 14 and 15 the remote machine announces to be capable of creating a JBulletComponent as well as a JVRConnector and that these services are accessible using the identifiers "physicsNode" and "renderNode" respectively.

In the example only the JBulletComponent service is used. If the rendering should also take place on the remote machine, an on "renderNode" specification has to be added to the JVRComponentAspect. Since Simulator X actors communicate with each other directly, no messages besides initialization specific ones would be sent via network in that case.

Although this might suggest that complex mechanisms are underlying this feature, this is not the case. In fact, no modification to a simulation component is necessary to enable its usage on remote machines. Yet, it has to be kept in mind that the data that is dispatched

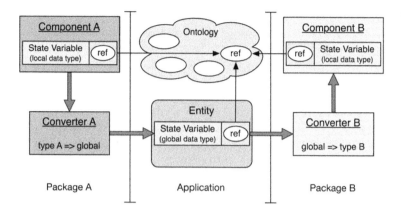

Figure 5.5: Overview of the automatic type conversion process. Figure taken from Wiebusch and Latoschik (2012), ©2012 IEEE.

between actors during network-based communication obviously has to be serializable. Due to the message-based architecture of Simulator X, only two modifications are required:

1. The utilization of the JmDNS library (van Hoff, 2015), which allows for service registration and discovery in local area networks. In this way, the services can be registered using simple strings, instead of supplying detailed information (e.g., a computer's IP address).

2. An adaption of the world interface (see section 5.2.8) to register as an mDNS service and synchronize with other world interfaces. The latter basically requires forwarding all messages regarding the registration of architecture elements to the remote world interface instances.

The dispatching of messages to (remote) actors is conveniently handled by the akka actor library (Typesafe Inc., 2015). This is feasible, since Simulator X does only use serializable references to actors. Currently the Simulator X framework relies on the serialization mechanisms that are provided by Scala and the Java Virtual Machine. However, the akka library does allow to replace this implementation with a more efficient one without modifications to the rest of the Simulator X framework.

5.3.2 Automatic Type Conversion

The second feature of Simulator X to be discussed in detail is its capability to automatically convert types between different representations. In this context automatically means that the conversion is performed without a developer having to explicitly invoke the respective functions. The basics for this feature have been introduced in section 4.5.1. The actual conversion functions have to be implemented by a component developer or application developer. Although the action descriptions, which are provided by means of the ontology, could be used to automatize the process even further, this feature is not implemented in the current version of the Simulator X framework.

As shown in the center of figure 5.5 on page 167, a Simulator X application specifies a format that is used as a common ground for data types and variable identifiers. These identifiers and data types are specified in the *basic types* and *basic type descriptions* ontologies that were introduced in section 5.2.9. As mentioned before, each component provides its own implementation specific ontology, which is based on the basic type descriptions and contains further component specific type definitions.

In the example of figure 5.5, each of the two components *A* and *B* is assumed to provide its own internal data types. Since the value descriptions, which are used in the context of state variables, constitute an internal type hierarchy (cf. section 4.5.1), related types can be identified. If component *A* updates a state variable of an entity by using its set method, the component's converter is automatically applied to transform the value into the global data format. When the second component *B* accesses the state variable (using the get or observe method), its converter does convert the global data type into the one that is used by the component.

Listing 5.15 shows an example implementation of a converter which converts data between the internal format and the global format. By using the value descriptions LocalTrafo and Transformation the converter can automatically be retrieved when semantic values are applied. The convert function shown in lines 7–8 transforms a locally represented value into the global format, whereas the revert function, which is shown in lines 10–11, reverses the transformation.

Each converter is registered at the time it is instantiated and subsequent lookup processes are performed automatically. Note that, in the case of the observe method, this lookup does only have to be executed once, since the revert function is automatically wrapped around the provided callback function and executed on each value update. Due to the fact that most state variable access is performed in this way, the introduced overhead is minimized. Furthermore, if no conversion process is necessary, there is no overhead at all, since the value is passed as is.

Lines 16–17 and 20–21 of listing 5.15 show the access to the same variable, using the global value description and the local value description, respectively. In the first case, no conversion is applied, whereas in the second case the revert method, which is defined in lines 10–11, is applied.

It is important to note that the conversion process is not limited to data type conversion: if, for example, a component applies a left-handed representation, whereas the global representation is assumed to be right handed, the converter can be applied even if the type of data is the same for both representations.

The automatic type conversion process does facilitate exchanging components in the way that it provides a means to decouple the globally applied data types from the ones that are used internally. For that reason, exchanging a component by another one is independent with regard to applied data types.

5.3.3 State History

A feature that is highly desirable in the context of applications that involve multimodal interaction, and more specifically multimodal fusion, is the possibility to access an earlier version of the simulation state. If, for example, a pointing gesture as well as the utterance of the word 'that' is detected in the context of a user who wants to select a moving entity, the detection of both speech and gesture will probably be completed after the entity moved

```
 1  // local type definition
 2  object LocalTrafo
 3      extends SValDescription(Transformation withType classOf[ConstVec3f])
 4
 5  // converter definition
 6  val localConverter = new Converter(LocalTrafo)(Transformation){
 7      def convert(i: LocalTrafo.dataType) : Transformation.dataType =
 8        ConstMat4f(Mat4x3f.translate(i))
 9
10      def revert(i: Transformation.dataType) : LocalTrafo.dataType =
11        ConstVec3f(i.m30, i.m31, i.m32)
12  }
13
14  // examplary access
15  def accessValue(entity : Entity){
16      entity.get(Transformation).foreach{ // no conversion
17        globalType => println(globalType)
18      }
19
20      entity.get(LocalTrafo).foreach{ // localConverter is used
21        localType  => println(localType)
22      }
23  }
```

Listing 5.15: Converter example: the specified converter is automatically invoked if necessary (line 20). Alternatively, the value can be passed through without alterations (line 16).

further. In that case, the direction detected from the pointing gesture at the time at which the utterance occurred has to be computed. The result has to be applied to the simulation state that was valid at the time of the utterance. Obviously, this feature is also beneficial for other aspects, such as AI methods and IVAs.

Implementing a state history is a highly complex task with almost any existing VR framework. On the one hand, it is virtually impossible to store the last states that occurred in a given timespan. This is due to the fact that every aspect of the simulation state would have to be accessible to the respective simulation module. In other words: every variable that is part of the simulation state has to be known and accessible. Depending on the required information, this can be limited to the position of an object but could also include environmental lighting, coloring, and any other features.

On the other hand, the span of time that needs to be stored may vary not only per application but also per property type (and possibly even per property). One solution to this is to store every information as long as the maximum desired timespan requires. This would, however, result in huge amounts of data to be stored and thus can easily cause performance issues. Alternatively, a highly elaborated mechanism to select, store, and retrieve the state history could be applied. As a result of these issues, existing approaches are often tailored a the specific use case.

The architecture of Simulator X, and especially the concept of state variables, allows to achieve the desired behavior much more easily. Building on the unified access model, which ensures that access to the simulation state is performed by means of a fixed interface, a simple implementation is rendered possible.

Two aspects were adjusted to enable the described functionality:

1. The data structure that is used by the owner of a state variable (cf. section 5.2.5) was changed to store a collection of timestamp-value tuples instead of a single value. The maximum size of the collection is set at the time of the state variable's creation and can be dynamically adjusted at runtime. If no size is specified, the collection is set to contain exactly one element, resulting in the same behavior that is observed with the state variables introduced in the previous sections.

2. The methods that are provided in the context of the unified access model were extended by two parameters. The first is used to specify the time at which the retrieved value should have been valid, whereas the second allows to specify a mechanism how values should be interpolated, if necessary. Both parameters are optional; the default behavior remains to access the latest known value.

Using this modified variant of state variables a developer can decide on a per variable basis which property should be stored for which amount of time. This enables flexible use of the Simulator X framework for applications in scenarios that involve multimodal interaction.

5.4 Project Structure

As mentioned in section 2.2.2, multiple organizational aspects were found to inhibit software reuse. Among these, a lack of regulations regarding the storage and classification of reusable assets as well as changes (or their absence) are especially relevant for modular VR frameworks. In Simulator X these issues are addressed in the form of used software repositories and the project structure.

5.4.1 Version Control and Project Structure

Each Simulator X project consists of multiple git repositories.[10] The main repository contains the application specific files as well as configurations that combine the utilized components, whereas each component is located in a sub-repository (see figure 5.6).

This structure has shown to be beneficial for multiple reasons. Since each sub-repository is a stand-alone repository, each component can be integrated into any Simulator X application independently. Furthermore, the application repository always links to a specific version of the component repositories. Thus, even if the application is incompatible with an updated version of a component, it still can be deployed on different machines. This allows the application developer to postpone adaption to updated components. In this context, the structure does also benefit modularity, since a component must only depend on the Simulator X core component, which is guaranteed to be available in every application.

---

[10] git is available at https://git-scm.com.

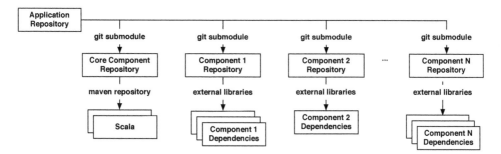

Figure 5.6: Simulator X project structure: each component is located in its own git repository, which is added as a git submodule to the main application repository. External dependencies are managed by each component repository, ideally using dependency management tools like Apache Maven.

Besides from being stored in a stand-alone repository, a component also has to provide its own settings for compilation (e.g., makefiles, dependency management, etc.). Since Simulator X is implemented using the Scala programming language, every application is compiled using sbt.[11] Therefore, each project repository contains a build configuration that includes the build settings in every component. Nevertheless, the addition of other build systems is possible, too: the main project repository simply has to be added the necessary configuration files.

5.4.2 Dependency Management

Developers often voice their misgivings regarding the dependence on external software libraries. On the one hand, this is understandable, since external assets may change and become incompatible, be no longer supported, or even become completely unavailable. On the other hand, software reuse obviously cannot work without reusing software, wherefore dependencies are inherently inevitable.

Besides software libraries that are included in the repositories, Simulator X applications make heavy use of the Apache Maven dependency management, especially relying on *The Central Repository* by Sonatype, Inc.[12] Maven's built-in dependency management allows to link external software libraries to a component without requiring developers to deal with their retrieval. Since old versions are kept in Maven repositories, the risk of them becoming unavailable is reduced. Obviously, new versions of a library can be incompatible, but since the retrieval mechanism allows to specify a specific version of the library, the release of a new version does not affect the component as long as the dependency is not updated. This way, the management and retrieval of dependencies is left to the developer of a component, thereby facilitating the separation of developers' tasks.

---

[11] sbt is available at http://www.scala-sbt.org.
[12] http://search.maven.org

5.5 Implemented Components

The approaches that have been introduced in the previous chapters and have been implemented in the Simulator X framework were used to create diverse applications, some of which will be presented in chapter 6. In order to build these applications, multiple simulation components were implemented. These include a VRPN (Virtual-Reality Peripheral Network, Taylor et al., 2001) component, an OpenAL (Hiebert, 2005) sound component, a rendering component (Roßbach, 2010), and many more.

Except for the components that deal with specific application logic, each of these components was created by wrapping a pre-existing library. In some cases, Java bindings had to be created, in others such binding already existed or the library was written in Java or Scala in the first place.

The next sections will first discuss the task of adding a sensor to an existing application and then present three implemented components that are of special interest; either due to the added value or due to their exemplariness. With these considerations the three use cases that were mentioned in the introduction of this thesis are covered.

5.5.1 Adding new Sensors

Adding a new sensor that provides new data is the least spectacular, but one of the most useful aspects. The setting is specified by use case 1.2: an existing application is said to be added an arbitrary sensor, to enhance the applications capabilities of reacting to the current situation. The most common sensors for VR applications are position tracking systems, which inform the system about an object's or the user's position.

The acquired data often has to be transformed into the correct coordinate system, in order to match the representation that is employed throughout the application. In the Simulator X framework this is an easy task: the component that provides the sensor data will specify a converter and subsequently use its local representation, while the framework takes over the conversion processes. Hence, adding this type of sensors (e.g., a Microsoft Kinect sensor, a Razer Hydra, or more expensive motion capturing systems) to the system simply requires to implement a respective component and to add the associated aspect to an entity. Since most components are in some way using spatial information about objects, the added information can instantly be used.

A much more interesting case is the integration of less common sensor data, like the heart rate sensor from use case 1.3. The initial step (creating the associated component) is identical to the above-mentioned situation. However, the data from such a sensor most probably is not of any use for other modules, if it is not preprocessed. There are two options to do this: either the sensor component processes the data itself or it emits events on the arrival of new data. In the latter case, a second component can observe this type of event and eventually process the incoming data, possibly utilizing information from other sensor modules.

The important observation here is that the coupling is realized via the type of the emitted event. Therefore, the second component could have been in the system before and now would simply be processing further data. Thus, in the optimal case data is processed automatically without further changes to the system.

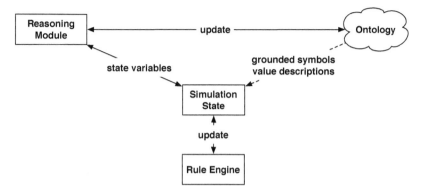

Figure 5.7: Overview of the connection between the application, a rule engine, a reasoning module, and the ontology.

5.5.2 Reasoning

Due to the deeply integrated ontology, the most obvious addition to the Simulator X framework is a reasoning component. As motivated in chapter 3, usually the most problematic issue with regard to the addition and use of a KRL is the fact that it is added retrospectively, wherefore the synchronization with the application state is complicated.

The architecture of the Simulator X framework facilitates this synchronization in the way that it allows for observing updates of semantically annotated values. This is not limited to a fixed subset of the application state but can be performed for each of the properties that constitute that state. The most important difference to other approaches, however, is the fact that the access to the application state is two-way. Thus, newly inferred knowledge about the state can easily be integrated and used by any component that is part of the application. In this regard, added reasoning components can also be considered as sensors that add new information to the simulation state (cf. use case 1.2).

Rule Engine

The *rule engine* is a very simple, but also very effective component, which makes use of the semantic information that is attached to properties. It observes all value changes that occur at runtime and applies the rules it was provided. In this context, a rule is very much like an action, since it has preconditions and effects. For example, a rule that identifies two entities that are close to each other can be checked each time the transformation of an entity is changed. If the preconditions of the rule are matched, its effects are applied. In this case, the fact that they are close to each other is asserted by means of an adequate relation.

In addition, a more elaborate rule engine was implemented in the context of a master thesis (Eckstein, 2014). That component especially focuses on the domain of physics, allowing for common sense reasoning in the context of physical simulations. Both rule engines are capable of introducing important changes to the application state. However, their ability to infer more complex facts is quite limited. For this purpose, a reasoning component was added, which makes use of the application ontology to infer new knowledge about the application state.

Reasoning Component

The implemented reasoning component utilizes the OWL API (Horridge & Bechhofer, 2009) to access the contents of the application ontology. This software library allows to attach different reasoning modules to an application. Out of the available modules, Pellet (Sirin, Parsia, Grau, Kalyanpur, & Katz, 2007) and HermiT (Shearer, Motik, & Horrocks, 2008) have been used in Simulator X.

Similar to the rule engine, the reasoning components observe the properties of every entity that is instantiated. Since these properties are linked to the ontology concepts via their value descriptions, synchronizing the ontology is straightforward: for each entity and every state variable an individual is added, which is identified by the UUID that is associated to it in Simulator X. These connections are visualized in figure 5.7: the ontology provides grounded symbols and value description for the application, which utilizes them to represent the simulation state. AI modules, such as a reasoning module, then can easily synchronize this state with the concepts in the ontology.

The amount of information that is added to the reasoner's knowledge base can be specified by the configuration of the component. In this context, there are three choices:

1. Only relations between entities are added.

2. Relations between entities as well as properties with OWL compatible data types are added.

3. All properties and relations are added.

In the latter two cases properties have to be serialized in order to be added. In this context, data types that are not supported by OWL are converted to strings.

```
object AttachAction{
    import Symbols.{attach, actionObject}

    def definedFor(target : simx.core.entity.Entity) =
      new ActionDescription(
        identifier = attach,
        preconditions = List(
            Entity asParameter actionObject is compatibleWith the target,
            Entity asParameter actionObject is CloseTo the target
        ),
        positiveEffects = List(
            Entity asParameter actionObject is PartOf the target
        ),
        negativeEffects = List()
      )
}
```

Listing 5.16: An `AttachAction` specified using the action DSL.

The most reasonable choice depends on the respective application. Representing relations between entities is probably sufficient when a rule engine is used, since value related inference can be performed by that engine. In a different scenario, the ontology itself could contain further rules, requiring to store the required properties. If SPARQL queries that include specific values of properties shall be answered by the reasoning component, all properties have to be serialized and added to the knowledge base.

In either case the reasoning component periodically infers new knowledge and updates the simulation state. Similarly, the reasoning process is initiated each time a SPARQL query arrives. At this point, the uniform access model is highly beneficial, because all updates can be achieved by means of the set method. Since entities and state variables are identified by UUIDs in the knowledge base as well as in the application, the matching process is straightforward.

5.5.3 Planning

In order to allow to use the action definitions from the ontology more effectively, the planning4J library (Cerny, 2012) was used to implement a planning component. Planning4J provides an abstraction layer between Java and PDDL enabled planners, by creating PDDL files and passing them to the planner in use. In this way, the latter can easily be exchanged, thereby providing the developer with an opportunity to use the most efficient planner at hand.

Planning DSL

In addition to the planning4J library, a domain specific language was implemented to allow for higher understandability of action definitions as well as preconditions and effects. It is based on the value descriptions used in the Simulator X framework, wherefore no additional mechanisms to establish links between the ontology contents and program code are necessary.

Every action description in the DSL contains an identifier, a list of preconditions, a list of positive effects, and a list of negative effects. Each list consists of `Predicates`, which are the representatives of relations in the DSL. A predicate is defined by means of the language keywords `asParameter`, `is`, `has`, and `the` as well as semantic values and value descriptions.

Listing 5.16 exemplifies the application of this DSL using the example of an attach action. The action is assumed to have the effect that a second object is part of the target entity. In line 8, 9 and 12 the second entity is specified by means of the `asParameter` keyword. The parameter name `actionObject` is subsequently used to identify the same entity. The precondition that requires the action object to be compatible with and being close to the target entity is specified using the `is` keyword. Internally, these specifications are mapped to the respective planning4J concepts.

In the same way, the effect of the described action is specified in lines 11–14: the action only does have positive effects (i.e. no `NOT` operator is used). Since effects are represented by predicates, too, the same DSL from above is applied: in line 12, the `PartOf` value description is used to specify the results of the action.

Action descriptions are registered with the planning component: its interface allows to register tuples of action descriptions and functions, linking the description to the function to be invoked. Listing 5.17 shows the usage of the planning component.

```
def testAttachAction( clock : Entity, battery : Entity ){
    def attach(target : Entity)(params : Map[Parameter[_], SVal[_]]) = {
        val part = params(Entity asParameter actionObject))
        part.set(partOf -> target)
        Continue calling NextAction
    }

    registerAction( AttachAction definedFor clock, attach(clock) )

    Planning4jComponent.createPlan( battery is PartOf the clock ){
        case Some(plan) => plan.execute()
    }
}
```

Listing 5.17: Exemplary usage of action descriptions: in line 8 the attach function from lines 2–6 is registered using the action description from listing 5.16. The planning component then is utilized to create a plan that results in the battery entity being part of the clock entity (lines 10–12).

Combining AI components

Figure 5.8 sketches a scenario in which multiple AI components collaborate to create an IVE, whereby use case 1.3 is covered. The overall goal is to activate a clock by attaching a battery to it. For this purpose, the ontology is assumed to contain the concepts CLOCK and BATTERY. Moreover, a POWEREDCLOCK is a member of the class of OPERATIVEOBJECTS, which in turn is a subclass of the class of objects that are OPERATIVE. Finally, a POWEREDCLOCK is defined as a CLOCK that contains a BATTERY. With these concepts at hand, the reasoning component observes the simulation state and updates it when new facts are inferred.

The planning component is given the goal that was shown in listing 5.17: the battery shall become a part of the clock. Assuming that it is not asserted to be close to the clock, the planning component generates the plan to move it there before it is attached. By triggering the MoveAction, which has to be defined similar to the AttachAction shown in listing 5.16, the animation component is requested to move the battery to the position of the clock.

In the meantime, the rule engine constantly observes the application state, checking for objects that have moved and applying the IsCloseTo rule. It checks if the distance between an entity that has moved and any other entity has dropped below a given threshold. If this is the case, a CloseTo relation is asserted. Depending on the application, rules can be restricted to observe only particular entities, in order to maintain reactivity.

If the position of the clock was changed while the animation component moved the battery, the closeTo relation will not be asserted. In that case, the planning component will re-plan the action sequence, resulting in the execution of the same plan (with an updated target position). Otherwise, the AttachAction is triggered. In this context, the animation component might play an animation and will eventually set the desired PartOf relation.

At this point the reasoning component comes into play: it will infer that the clock now has a part that is a battery, since the HASPART role is the inverse of the PARTOF role. Accordingly, the

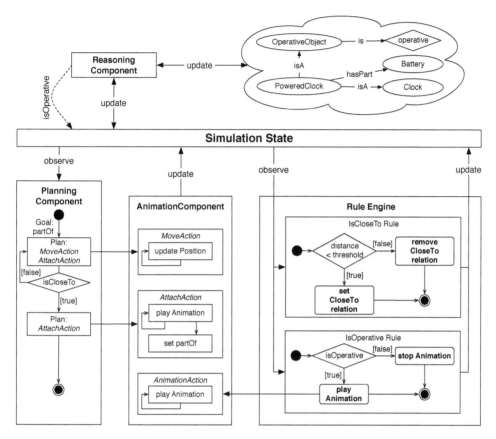

Figure 5.8: Collaboration of the AI components: the planning component creates a plan that results in invoking actions provided by the animation component. The rule engine and the reasoning component observe the world state and add inferred knowledge.

clock is inferred to be a POWEREDCLOCK and thus OPERATIVE. These facts are subsequently added to the entities in the simulation state.

Finally, the new state is recognized by the rule engine, applying the IsOperative rule. This will eventually trigger the playAnimation action in the animation component, which could animate the hands of the clock.

In order to fully cover use case 1.3 and integrate actions of the user, consider the following alteration of the example: instead of moving the battery automatically by the animation component, the user is asked to but the battery in place. This means, instead of triggering the MoveAction, the planning component informs the user about the task and then switches into a waiting state. It then regularly checks if the preconditions of the next action in the calculated plan are met, before it continues its execution. The rest of the application remains exactly the same. Assuming that the users motions are tracked, an appropriate input metaphor can be applied to allow for moving the battery. As soon as it is close to the clock, the application will react as described before.

As shown by this example, different AI components can be connected without even knowing about one another. Since the execution of actions is triggered using events, every component is easily replaceable. Moreover, manually attaching the battery to the clock has the same effect as triggering it via actions. Consequently, the virtual environment reacts to user interactions in the same way it does to execution of plans (e.g., by a virtual agent).

Reusability through Planning

The example that is described above exemplifies the possibility to achieve software reuse through the utilization of action descriptions. Instead of specifying the actions to be invoked, the desired state can be defined and a planning module evaluates if this state can be obtained with the registered methods. This opportunity has benefits and drawbacks, as discussed below.

Benefits of a Planning-based Approach   Besides a reduced amount of work regarding reimplementation and integration, further benefits of the chosen approach exist:

- The amount of work related to retrieval of reusable code is reduced, since a developer is allowed to describe what should be achieved instead of specifying how to achieve it.

- For the same reason, the amount of work related to understanding existing program code, which is necessary to reuse it, is reduced.

- Intelligent entities in the virtual environment can apply functions based on the current world state and thus become reactive.

In a general sense, method descriptions and automatic invocation of methods constitute a more abstract way of programming and thus accounts for the finding by Kim and Stohr who state that "while most reuse has been concerned with concrete resources, many researchers contend that larger savings can be obtained by the reuse of more abstract resources" (Kim & Stohr, 1998, p. 6).

Drawbacks of a Planning-based Approach   Although automatic method invocation is a tempting approach, there are at least two aspects which prohibit its frequent application:

- One of the benefits of the approach at the same time is a drawback: since the developer surrenders control over the way in which code is composed to accomplish a certain task, this also reduces his influence on this composition. Especially in complex systems with a large amount of registered actions the risk of unexpected program behavior increases.

- Automatic planning requires high computational efforts and thus is only applicable for non time-critical situations.

Consequently, automatic method invocation has to be used with care and further work is necessary to evaluate to what extent it can be used to facilitate reusability of Simulator X applications.

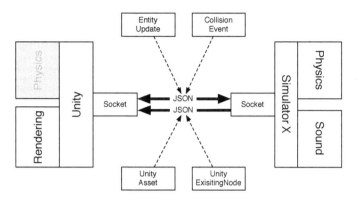

Figure 5.9: Overview of the used components in the Unity setup. Either physics engine can be utilized; in the shown setup the Unity physics engine remains unused.

5.5.4 Example Component: Unity

Multiple components were implemented for the Simulator X framework, many of which have a specialized feature set, such as providing sensor data, rigid-body physics simulation, or stereoscopic 3D rendering. In order to demonstrate the applicability of the approach one of these will be discussed in further detail: the Unity engine (cf. section 2.3.3) was prototypically linked to Simulator X. Besides the opportunity of using the physical simulation and 3D rendering features of Unity, this also allows to use the Unity content editor for the creation of VEs. The following section describes the steps taken to implement the connection, thereby exemplifying the methods that have to be applied to create a reusable Simulator X component. This example will be continued in the next chapter, and eventually it will fully cover use case 1.1.

Connection to Unity   Initially, a means to connect to the Unity engine has to be chosen. Besides the implementation of a Unity plugin, the possibility of a connection via network exists. While the first promises higher performance, the second allows to run the Unity software on a different machine, which is a desirable feature in some setups. Furthermore, the networking layer that is created on the Simulator X side can be reused to connect other engines by applying the same approach.

Eventually, the decision to choose the networked solution was made. Since the standard serialization format that is provided by Java is not usable in this context, JSON (Ecma International, 2013) was chosen for serialization. This is especially reasonable since JSON-LD (Sporny, Longley, Kellogg, Lanthaler, & Lindström, 2013), which is based on JSON, can possibly be used in later implementations to facilitate the utilization of semantics.

Serializable Elements   Besides the format that is used for serialization, the elements to be serialized have to be identified. In order to utilize the rendering capabilities of Unity, a way to access existing assets in the scene as well as to instantiate new assets was created. For rendering aspects only the position, rotation, and scale are updated, whereas physical simulation involves the mass of an entity. Moreover, collision events are exchanged between both applications. In

```
val rotationConverter = new Converter(local.Rotation)(global.Transformation)
{
  def convert(i: ConstQuat4): ConstMat4f =
    ConstMat4f(rotationMat(Quat4(i.d, -i.a, -i.b, i.c)))

  def revert(i: ConstMat4f): ConstQuat4 = {
    val tmp = quaternion(Mat3(i))
    ConstQuat4(tmp.d, -tmp.a, -tmp.b, tmp.c)
  }
}
```

Listing 5.18: The rotation converter used by the Unity connection.

the ideal case, a C# counterpart to Simulator X would exist, which can handle the internal messages. Due to the prototypical nature of the connection, the intermediate step of wrapping Simulator X messages and serializing them into JSON strings is adopted.

Figure 5.9 exemplifies the connection between Simulator X and Unity. Besides the shown physics and sound component, any other component can be attached to Simulator X and, thus, to Unity.

Type Conversion

The type conversion mechanism is highly beneficial for the connection between Simulator X and Unity, since Simulator X does use matrices to represent object transformations, whereas Unity utilizes quaternions and vectors. Furthermore, Unity does apply a left-handed co-ordinate system, whereas the core representation of Simulator X assumes a right-handed coordinate system.

Listing 5.18 exemplifies the converter that is used by the Unity component. Although the conversion process is rather simple, changing the coordinate system is a common source of errors. With the centralization by means of converters this source is eliminated.

Asset / Aspect Connection

As mentioned above, two aspects are used for the connection to Unity: one for existing assets and one for those which shall be created at runtime.

The existing objects in the Unity scene are connected using the UnityExistingNode aspect. A C# script, which instantiates the Unity network server to which a Simulator X application connects, sends information about every game object in the Unity scene. The name of game objects also has to be provided in the UnityExistingNode aspect, wherefore it can be utilized to create a link between the Unity Game Object and the Simulator X entity. In order to do so, the Unity object ID and Simulator X UUID are sent to the Unity application which stores this information. Every EntityUpdate message that is sent afterwards will be applied to the game object that is linked in this way.

New objects are instantiated by utilization of the UnityAsset aspect. This aspect is used to instantiate an asset that is available in the loaded Unity scene, using the provided position,

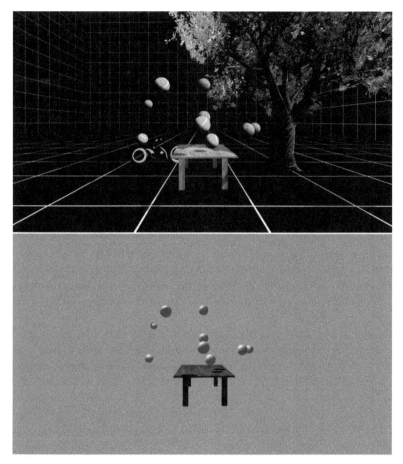

Figure 5.10: Running example with both Unity (top) and jVR renderer (bottom). Only the table and the jumping balls are synchronized, other objects in the Unity scene, e.g., the tree, the camera position, and the lights, are ignored by the Simulator X application.

orientation, and scale values. Similar to the `UnityExistingNode` aspect, the name of the asset and a pair of IDs are used to identify the entity at instantiation-time and at runtime, respectively.

State Updates

State updates are executed each time a value change occurs on either side of the connection. For Simualtor X, this is recognized by observing state variables and sending an `EntityUpdate` message for every value update. In Unity the process is more complex, since no notification mechanism for arbitrary values is provided. Currently, the `hasChanged` flag of the `transform` of every game object that is known to Simulator X is checked on a per-frame basis to determine if an `EntityUpdate` message has to be sent.

Besides property updates, both sides are notified about the removal of entities. When the connection is closed by the Simulator X application the Unity script resets the scene and waits for a new connection. In this way, the Unity application is used as a render server to which Simulator X applications can connect.

Events

The prototypical connection does only support collision events, which are instantly distributed to the opposite peer. A generic `SimXEvent` class has been implemented from which every new event class can derive. Afterwards, only event specific methods as well as serialization related functionality have to be implemented for the new event class, and its `Execute` method has to be called on each observation of the event.

Results

Figure 5.10 shows the running application. Adding the two above-mentions aspects is the only change that has to be made to make the Simulator X application (which is shown in the bottom figure) to use the Unity engine for rendering. A more detailed overview of these changes is presented in the context of a case study in the next chapter. The resulting scene is shown in the upper part of the figure.

In fact, both screenshots were taken simultaneously, wherefore both the `ShapeFromFile` aspects and the Unity aspects were added to the entity descriptions. Physics was simulated by the JBullet component in the Simulator X framework. Since neither the position of the camera nor the light in the two scenes were synchronized, shadows and distance to the objects slightly differ.

As shown by this example, Simulator X allows to create reusable simulation components from existing software. This does not only apply for single software libraries but also for complete engines, like Unity, and is achieved by means of the techniques proposed in this work.

5.6 Summary

In this chapter, the integration of the proposed techniques into the Simulator X framework was presented. Prior to that, the design decisions that have been taken at the beginning of its development were discussed. Out of these the adoption of the actor model and the integration of an ontology have already been reviewed before. In addition, the Simulator X framework is built using the Scala programming language. Especially its multi-paradigm support, integrated DSL support, as well as the conciseness of created code were found to be highly beneficial for reusable RIS applications.

Subsequently, the architecture elements of Simulator X that correspond to the elements of the component model presented in the previous chapter were discussed. Code examples from the Simulator X framework were provided to show its utilization in the context of a simple example. These indicated the readability, locality, and simplicity of application code.

The overview furthermore gave a hint of the low amount of work that is required to integrate a simulation module and the related aspects into an application: only one line has to be changed to integrate a simulation component and, depending on the formating, one or few more lines have to be changed for each entity description. This and related aspects will be reviewed in further detail in the next chapter.

Afterwards, in describing the framework's architecture elements, its facilities to support distributed computing, automatic type conversion, and state history were emphasized. Regarding the first aspect, the adoption of the actor model and its message-based architecture showed to be highly advantageous: no changes have to be made to a simulation component in order to execute it on a different computer in a networked application structure.

The described type conversion process is almost unnoticeable by component and application developers (after the respective converters have been defined), as was indicated by a further example. This is facilitated by the uniform access model that was presented in the previous chapter.

In combination with the uniform representation of the application state in the form of state variables the same model allowed to create a state history. This is highly beneficial for simulation modules that require information about states of the application that have been overwritten by more recent versions. Whereas the implementation of such a feature with a game engine or similar frameworks would require tremendous efforts, the implementation in Simulator X required only two aspects to be adjusted. Again, no changes had to be made to any simulation component.

Besides these functional features, the general structure of a Simulator X project was described and beneficial aspects for reusability discussed. The git version control software is used to maintain a determinate structure of component repositories. Such (sub-)repositories can be flexibly combined, allowing for reuse and frequent updates at the same time. The reluctance of developers to introduce dependencies into their programs is answered with the utilization of maven repositories, which allow to automatically resolve dependencies and obtain the required files.

Finally, components that regard the integration of additional sensors, interaction of decoupled AI modules, as well as preexisting, complex engines were exemplified. In all of these examples it could be observed that the coupling of simulation modules was reduced to a minimum: new sensor data can easily be used by modules that were part of an application before, AI modules can work together to achieve a common goal without being even aware of one another, and the prototypical creation of a simulation component that enables the utilization of a high-end game development framework has shown to be feasible.

Thus, use cases 1.2 and 1.3 where fully covered. Use case 1.1 has been accomplished in parts: the replacement of a rendering component from an existing application is yet to be shown. The following chapter will hence present a case study that continues the investigation of this use case. It furthermore presents different aspects that have been considered to further validate the applicability of the presented approach.

Chapter 6

Validation

Before software can be reusable it first has to be usable.

Ralph Johnson

6.1 Evaluating Reusability

As indicated in section 2.2.5, measuring the reusability of an IRIS framework is a complicated task, usually rather the reusability of (existing) software modules is evaluated. Yet, the developed methodology aims at supporting the process of creating such reusable components.

Due to the diversity of software modules that are applied in the field of RIS, evaluating the reusability of a single implemented component would yield unrepresentative results. Instead, the tasks that have to be performed to create and replace a component provide a much more meaningful impression of the results of this work. As indicated by the quotation from Ralph Johnson, a framework that is meant to foster reusability has to be usable in the first place. Therefore, the experiences of a framework's users as well as the projects that are achieved with it provide further indications for its utility.

Consequently, the following sections will take different views on the proposed methods as well as their implementation in the context of the Simulator X framework:

- A case study that expands on the integration of the Unity Engine, which was introduced in the previous chapter, is discussed to indicate the amount of work that arises with the creation, integration, and exchange of a simulation component.

- Different projects that utilize the Simulator X framework are presented to illustrate its usefulness in different fields of application.

- In the winter term 2014 a first usability study was conducted in a RIS course at the University of Würzburg, the results of which are discussed at the end of this chapter.

6.2 Case Study: Replacing a Rendering Component

One of the goals of this work is to enable the replacement of simulation components without affecting other parts of the application. Hence, this section evaluates the process of exchanging a component in the context of the Simulator X framework. To provide an example the jVR rendering component, which is provided with the framework, is meant to be exchanged by the Unity component that was introduced in section 5.5.4.

6.2.1 Creating a new Component

An outline of the component that establishes the connection to the Unity framework was already given in section 5.5.4. In the next paragraphs, different aspects to the implementation of this component are discussed.

The creation and integration of a Simulator X component, which can either wrap an existing simulation module or contain the desired functionality itself, is a 4 step process:

1. Create a component ontology.

2. Create aspects for the component.

3. Create a class that inherits from the abstract Simulator X Component class and implements the methods that are prescribed by the interfaces from section 4.5.3.

4. Integrate the component into an application.

Ontology File Every Simulator X component has to provide an OWL file that imports ontologies defining required concepts and component specific information (cf. section 3.4.1). The imported ontologies usually are limited to the basic descriptions ontology or to some other ontology, which imports that ontology.

Component specific knowledge especially comprises information on semantic types that are used by the component as well as by the aspects it provides. In the context of the Unity component this are the UnityAsset, UnityExistingNode, as well as types for translation, rotation, and scale. The OWL definitions for the Unity component are shown in listing A.6 in appendix A.

Aspects & Event Descriptions For Simulator X the two mentioned aspects as well as the required event descriptions are automatically generated from the ontology file. In the Unity module, which is implemented in form of a C# script included in a respective Unity application, these elements have to be implemented manually. This task is straightforward, since it only requires to map the associated messages to the creation of the represented objects and events. Nevertheless, it requires a considerable amount of work, which is indicated by the 449 lines of code that were written for this feature (cf. table 6.1).

Component Class In order to wrap a simulation module into a Simulator X component the interfaces that were presented in section 4.5.3 have to be implemented. The main aspects include setting up the module, synchronizing its internal state representation with the entity model of Simulator X, and forwarding events. This is facilitated by the concise interface that is provided by entities, state variables, and event descriptions.

The Lines of Code (LOC) that constitute the connection between Simulator X and Unity are shown in table 6.1. In the example of the Unity component the position, scale, and orientation of the rendered entities have to be synchronized with the simulation state, which is maintained by the Simulator X framework. This is achieved by implementing the methods from the EntityCreation and EntityControl interfaces, which manage the creation and maintenance of entities. On each creation of an entity the required information is sent to

Aspect	LOC Simulator X (Scala)	LOC Unity (C#)
Unity Component	265	129
(De)Serialization	209	183
Networking	102	267
Type Conversion	28	*
Aspects & Events	(115)	449
Total	719	1028

Table 6.1: Lines of Code analysis for the prototypical Unity component. Type conversion is performed in combination with the (de)serialization process in C# by directly creating the desired JSON strings.

the Unity module using said interfaces. Moreover, changes to the relevant state variables are observed by adding callbacks and sending update messages via the network connection. The event descriptions of the synchronized events are used to add further callbacks that also result in the emission of a respective message. The former is conducted in the enableAspect method, whereas latter is performed in the component's constructor.

In order to establish the reverse direction, messages that are received from the Unity module are propagated to the simulation state by means of the set and emit methods of the affected state variables and event descriptions. The same has to be achieved in the Unity script that is attached to the Unity application. The associated amount of code is listed in the row titled 'Unity Connection' in table 6.1.

Due to the adoption of a network-based approach further implementations regarding (de)serialization and networking code have to be performed. The amount of necessary program code is shown in the '(De)Serialization' and 'Networking' rows of table 6.1.

As discussed in section 5.5.4, the representation in Unity is different to the one adopted in Simulator X. At this point, the utilization of Simulator X's type conversion feature is highly beneficial, since program code that is used for conversion can be implemented in a centralized way. This relieves a later developer from coping with related issues. As shown in the 'Type Conversion' row of table 6.1, only 28 lines of code are necessary to achieve the conversion between both representations. In the implemented Unity script no conversion has to be performed, since the respective data types can easily be created from the serialized values, which are converted by Simulator X.

Integration into an Application The integration of a new component into an application is simplified by the structure of the Simulator X framework: since a component is entirely decoupled via messages, which are encapsulated in the software interfaces that were presented in section 4.5, only aspects have to be added. On the one hand, the component aspect has to be attached to the applicationConfiguration. On the other hand, each entity description that is used to instantiate an entity that shall be included in the component's simulation loop has to be added a respective aspect.

Consequently, one line of code is required for each entity description as well as for the instantiation of the component. Since the process of integrating a component into an application is also relevant for exchanging a component, more details are given in section 6.2.2.

Discussion

The implemented Unity component has a rather prototypical status, since only the creation of assets as well as the synchronization of a single event type have been implemented. As table 6.1 indicates, this was not achieved without effort. It is worth noting that nearly half of the lines of code are related to serialization and networking code, whereas only the other half is related to the creation of a reusable component, which was the essential aspect of this case study. Still, program code that is related to serialization can be reused when other modules are to be connected.

Utilizing the feature of code generation also shows its benefits: while the manual implementation of aspects and events resulted in 449 lines of code to be written on the Unity side, all of the 115 lines for Simulator X were generated from the ontology. Taking into account the fact that Scala code tends to be more concise than C# code, the benefits can be considered even higher than the plain numbers suggest.

The most important observation, however, is the fact that the utilization of the created component requires only one line of code per aspect that is utilized in an entity description. Since entity descriptions are largely generated from the ontology, the remaining efforts are vanishingly low: once a simulation component has been created, it can easily be reused in multiple applications.

In conclusion, these findings are in line with the observations of other researchers (cf. section 2.2.2). The creation of reusable software components requires huge amounts of work, whereas considerable advantages can subsequently be drawn from these efforts.

As shown in the next section, this is especially the case when a Simulator X component has to be exchanged by another one.

6.2.2 Exchanging Components

In the situation of an existing application, exchanging a simulation component involves the integration of a new component into the application logic. This commonly is achieved in a closely coupled manner, wherefore the application code has to be modified in many places.

In this work a component model and associated software interfaces have been defined that constrain the number of ways in which a component and an application can be interconnected. More precisely, three points of intersection exist:

1. entities that are retrieved by means of the world interface,

2. entities that have an aspect which belongs to the component, and

3. events that can be published and received.

Consequently, exchanging a component requires to consider updating the related aspects. The utilization of the world interface, however, is completely internal to a component, wherefore the application developer does not have to perform any modifications. Therefore, besides adding the component aspect to the list of used components, only the latter two items need to be considered for the integration of a component.

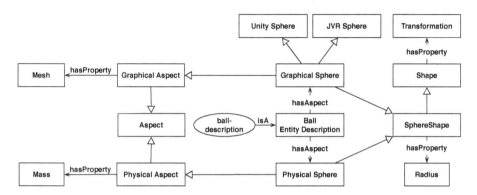

Figure 6.1: Simplified relations between concepts that are involved in the description of a virtual ball entity. It is sufficient to specify the ball-description to be an instance of the Ball Entity Description concept if either the Unity Sphere or the jVR aspect is present. Otherwise a HASASPECT relation has to be added in order to resolve the ambiguity.

Updating Entity Descriptions

As mentioned in section 5.2.6, each component provides a set of aspects that can be used in entity descriptions in order to include the component in the entity creation process. Since these aspects are described in the component's ontology file, this file initially has to be imported by the application's ontology file. This can be achieved by adding an `Import` statement, either manually or by using a graphical user interface (e.g., the protégé OWL editor created by the Stanford Center for Biomedical Informatics Research (2015)).

If the component is the only one that provides that aspect type, no further steps regarding the ontology have to be taken. This is owed to the fact that the aspects that match the entity description can automatically be determined by the code generation mechanism. If, on the other hand, multiple components of the same type are used in the application, the entity descriptions in the ontology have to be updated (cf. section 3.4.2). More specifically, the aspects that are associated to the descriptions have to be specified using the HASASPECT role. These concepts are visualized in figure 6.1.

The changes that have to be made to an existing program are exemplified in listing 6.1. The program is assumed to have utilized the jVR rendering component before, wherefore its component aspect (line 5) is part of the application configuration. Similarly, each entity description contains an aspect of the component (exemplified by the `ShapeFromFile` aspect in line 15). The application configuration and entity descriptions have to be adjusted to replace the jVR component by the Unity component. In the example this is achieved by replacing line 5 with line 7 and line 15 with line 17, respectively. It is also possible to utilize both components at the same time, in which case the whole content of listing 6.1 has to be used.

If an existing component is exchanged for one that provides the same functionality, chances are that the constructor parameters are compatible for the old and new aspects. However, often the parameter values have to be adapted, for example, if different assets are used and the paths to the associated files change. In this case, the entity descriptions have to be adjusted to maintain the applications operability. After the respective adjustments have been made, the replaced component will include the entities in its simulation loop as the previous one did.

```
 1   protected def applicationConfiguration = ApplicationConfig withComponent
 2      // physics component
 3      JBulletComponentAspect(physicsName, gravity) and
 4      // JVR renderer
 5      JVRComponentAspect(gfxName) and
 6      // Unity renderer
 7      UnityComponentAspect(unityName, "localhost", 8000)
 8
 9   // exemplary entity description
10   case class BallDescription(name : String, radius : Float, position : Vec3)
11      extends EntityDescription (name,
12      // physical aspect
13      PhysSphere(mass = 1f, transform = position, radius = radius),
14      // JVR aspect
15      ShapeFromFile( file = "ball.dae", scale = Vec3(radius*2f)),
16      // Unity aspect
17      UnityAsset( path = "ball", scale = Vec3(radius * 2f))
18   )
```

Listing 6.1: Exemplary code for adding, exchanging or removing a component. In the shown configuration the jVR renderer as well as Unity are used. Removing the lines associated with a component (i.e. lines 5 and 15 for jVR and lines 7 and 17 for Unity) results in the component's removal from the application.

Updating Events

Events are semantically linked to the occurrences they represent, wherefore possible incompatibilities mostly involve the symbols that identify the events. Due to being generated from the ontology, the events that a component emits and receives are inherently compatible to those used inside the application. A requirement for this is the assumption that all components share the same base ontology. However, it is possible that two components were developed based on different ontologies and thus symbols might differ. Consequently, equivalence assertions between concepts with different names but the same semantics have to be specified when such a component ontology is added to the application ontology.

In OWL this is possible by defining equivalent classes and individuals, wherefore a further ontology file that establishes a link between the ontology of the added component and the application ontology may have to be created. This task has to be carefully executed, since unexpected results can be obtained if incorrect assertions are made. Commonly, the ontologies that are provided by a component are limited in size, since they build on more general, common sense knowledge, which is contained in other ontology files. Moreover, the created connecting ontology can subsequently be reused each time the component is integrated into an application using the same application ontology. Therefore, the efforts put into its creation are worthwhile.

A problematic case, which cannot be solved without contributions of the component developers, is the situation in which the application depends on an event's payload that is not provided by the new component. In this case, either the application logic or the component has to be adapted. Assuming that the latter situation does not arise, compatibility of events either is a priori given or can be achieved by applying the above-mentioned steps.

Simulator X Component	LOC Module	LOC Component	Ratio
jVR Renderer	40294	2550	6.33%
JBullet Physics	29839	726	2.43%
LWJGL Sound	1955	429	21.94%

Table 6.2: Comparison between lines of code of Simulator X components and the associated simulation modules. For the LWJGL sound module only the code that is related to the OpenAL library was investigated.

6.2.3 Reuse in Simulator X

Applications that are created with the Simulator X framework use multiple simulation modules, which are wrapped into reusable simulation components. In this context, a module itself is reused 'as-is', wherefore the advantages of the approach can be evaluated by contrasting the lines of code that a module comprises with those that are used to integrate it into an application. Table 6.2 shows the results of this comparison for three prominent Simulator X components and the associated modules.

As mentioned in section 6.2.1, each entity description requires one additional line of code in which it is associated with the component by adding the respective aspect. The amount of code that is required for this depends on the number of different entities that are used in an application. Yet, it is rather small when compared to the size of the simulation component and especially to the wrapped module.

As indicated by the numbers in table 6.2, the integration of a simulation module into an application requires a lot less effort than its recreation. Yet, this does not reflect the actual gained benefits, since this view supposes that the whole module would have to be rewritten. This is only the case, if it is deeply integrated into a system and cannot be extracted (i.e. when it does not have the nature of a module at all). In contrast, it is rather the code that is used to integrate the module into a certain application which has to be reimplemented. As discussed in section 6.2.2, this task is simplified by the presented methods.

From a different point of view, the application code has to be adapted to the simulation modules that shall be integrated. This requires the creation of code for both the application logic and the connection to the simulation modules. The former is dependent on the particular application and hence hardly subject to reuse, whereas the latter clearly is.

Code coverage In order to evaluate the benefits of the proposed model, the amount of component code that is (re-)used by different applications can be measured. Table 6.3 shows the result of such measurements for two Simulator X applications:[13] a basic example application which features multiple balls bouncing on a rotating table, as well as the far more complex SiXton's Curse demonstration (Fischbach et al., 2011), which will be presented in section 6.3.1. A screenshot of the former was shown in the context of introducing the Unity component in section 5.5.4 on page 181. Table 6.3 contains the number of covered statements. This provides a more appropriate measure than the commonly used LOC metric, since a single line may contain multiple statements of arbitrary length or a statement might be spread over multiple lines of code.

---

[13] The contents of table 6.3 were created using the scoverage tool, available for download at http://scoverage.org.

	Total Stmts	Shared Invocations		Invocations Basic Example			Invocations SiXton's Curse		
	#	#	%	#	%T	%S	#	%T	%S
Core Component	10124	3383	33.42	3555	35.11	95.61	4155	41.04	81.42
jVR Renderer	3891	1357	34.88	1357	34.88	100.0	2278	58.55	59.57
JBullet Physics	1179	496	42.07	503	42.66	98.61	867	73.54	57.21
LWJGL Sound	707	326	46.11	352	49.79	92.61	471	66.62	69.21

Table 6.3: Number of statements of different Simulator X components (total number and number of those invoked in the context of the basic example as well as the SiXton's Curse application). %T and %S indicate the percentages regarding total statements and shared invocations. Measurements were performed by applying the *scoverage* tool during a typical run of each application.

The 'Total' column shows the overall number of statements that are present in the respective module, whereas the 'Shared Invocations' column lists the number (#) of statements that were invoked by both applications and the related percentage (%) regarding the total available statements . The remaining two columns show the number (#) of statements invoked by the respective application and the percentage to which these relate to the number of total statements (%T) as well as to the number of shared invocations (%S).

Since Simulator X is a research framework, the components are not optimized and hence often contain dead code. Therefore, the comparison of the reused total statements rather provides an indication of the reused percentage of a component than reliable data. For this reason, table 6.3 also relates the number of invoked statements to the number of shared invocations. These show the actual reuse rates between the two applications: the basic example application uses more than 90% of code of components that was also used by the SiXton's Curse application. Seen from the opposite direction, more than 57% of the code that is used by the simple example application was reused by the much more complex SiXton's Curse application.

Integration efforts Regarding the integration of components, SiXton's Curse utilizes 35 entity descriptions involving 693 lines of code (21,35% of 3246 lines of application code), whereas the basic example uses five entity descriptions involving 116 lines of code (41,28% of 281 lines of application code). These numbers are higher than the expected values, which are calculated by multiplying the number of entity descriptions with the number of components. This would result in 140 lines of code (except for 693 lines) for SiXton's Curse as well as 20 lines (instead of 115 lines) for the example application. The reason for this is that the entity descriptions are split into multiple lines (one per parameter of an aspect) to allow for higher readability.

Finally, table 6.4 shows the lines of code that were invoked in the context of both applications. These values were measured using the Coverage plugin of the IntelliJ IDEA IDE.[14] Except for the percentage of the JBullet component's code that was used by the SiXton's Curse application, they are in line with the measurements from table 6.3. The reason for this exception is assumed to be related to the ratio of statements per line in the part of code that is exclusively used by the SiXton's Curse application.

---

[14] IntelliJ IDEA is available via https://www.jetbrains.com/idea/.

	Total LOC	Invocations Basic Example		Invocations SiXton's Curse	
Core Module	7578	2939	38.78%	3228	42.60%
jVR Renderer	2550	946	37.10%	1466	57.49%
JBullet Physics	726	298	41.05%	436	60.06%
LWJGL Sound	429	244	56.88%	283	65.98%

Table 6.4: Lines of code of Simulator X components and their usage in the basic example as well as the SiXton's Curse application.

6.3 Developed Applications

The Simulator X framework has been the basis for multiple applications in diverse areas. Among these are multiple research demonstrations, exhibitions, and student projects. In the following sections the most prominent applications that have been created are presented.

6.3.1 Research Demonstrations

The Simulator X framework is designed to be used in various VR and MR setups. Thus, applications range from simple 2D touch interfaces to fully immersive 3D VEs.

SiXton's Curse

The framework was initially presented at the IEEE Virtual Reality conference in 2011 (Latoschik & Tramberend, 2011). At the same conference a research demonstration (Fischbach et al., 2011) was given to present the features of the prototype. The shown application involves the medieval city 'SiXton', which is being haunted by ghosts. A user, or rather a player, slips into the role of a magician, whose task is to keep the ghosts from achieving their goal of marooning the citizens. To achieve this goal, the ghosts gather powder kegs, which are distributed over the city, at the bridge that constitutes the only entrance to the town. Moreover, if a ghost is not carrying a barrel, it attacks the magician if he is in sight. When enough kegs are located at the bridge, they explode, destroy the bridge, and the game is lost. The magician can use three different spells to stop the ghosts. In order to cast a spell the user has to utter the correct phrase and perform the associated gesture.

As shown in figure 6.2, the application features 3D stereoscopic rendering. The user is tracked using an optical tracking system to allow for gesture recognition and correct perspective rendering. In addition, voice commands are recoded using a wireless microphone, and a Nintendo WiiRemote is used in order to navigate inside the virtual environment.

In the context of this application a component for simulating the behavior of the virtual ghosts was implemented. It includes a state machine, a path planning algorithm, and a module that controls the hovering-behavior of the ghosts.

The state machine manages the states of the ghosts and evokes certain behavior. If a ghost has no particular task, the world interface is queried for all barrel entities. If the state machine has no record about a barrel being involved in another ghost's behavior, the barrel becomes the idle ghost's target. For this purpose, its position state variable is observed. If the position is updated, e.g., because the magician pushed the barrel, a new path is planned and the

Figure 6.2: *SiXton's Curse* research demonstration at the IEEE VR '11 in Singapore.

ghosts behavior is updated. According to the newly planned path, the hovering-behavior module moves the virtual ghosts by applying impulses to the physically simulated ghost entities, eventually resulting in the desired movement. The notification is achieved by means of `ApplyImpulse` events, which are subscribed by the physics component.

Although the behavior component potentially can be split into the above-indicated three independent components, this was not the case when the application was implemented. Nevertheless, it is completely decoupled from other components: removing the associated aspect from the ghost entity description results in the ghost resting on the ground.

The inherently complex structure of the implemented application revealed the applicability of the taken design decisions. At the time of the publication these included symbol based access, the Scala programming language, and the utilization of the actor model.

The smARTbox

Whereas SiXton's Curse requires a complex hardware setup, the *smARTbox* (Fischbach, Latoschik, Bruder, & Steinicke, 2012) provides a portable setup (cf. figure 6.3). It consists of the smARTbox itself, which is a wooden box that features a back-projected multi-touch surface. Inside the box a stereoscopic 3D projector and the required sensors for the multi-touch functionality are located. Furthermore, it involves user-tracking by means of a Microsoft Kinect sensor.

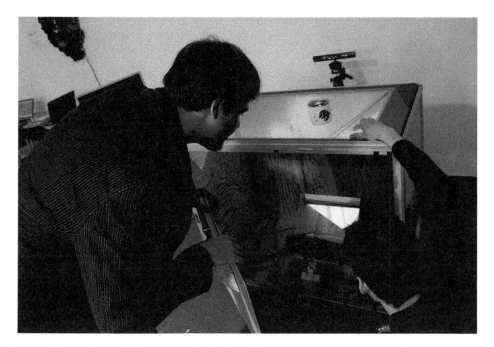

Figure 6.3: The *smARTbox* being presented at the ICEC '12.

Figure 6.3 shows the smARTbox running a virtual fishtank demonstration on the 11th International Conference on Entertainment Computing (ICEC 2012, Fischbach, Wiebusch, Latoschik, Bruder, and Steinicke (2012a)). The behavior of the fish is simulated using a swarm simulation component as well as a custom-made underwater physics component. Further components include the VRPN component and the jVR rendering component that are also used in the SiXton's Curse setup.

As indicated in section 6.2.2, exchanging the physics engine only required the instantiation of the engine as well as adjusting entity aspects. Since other components are not directly coupled to the physics engine, no further steps had to be taken.

In addition to the simulated fish, the touch-surface was used to detect interactions with the virtual water surface. The smARTbox served as a platform for different research demonstrations (Fischbach et al. (2012a) and Fischbach, Wiebusch, Latoschik, Bruder, and Steinicke (2012b)). As a part of this, the fishtank application was extended by the utilization of fiducial markers to allow for feeding the fish as well as by virtual reflections on the water surface utilizing the Kinect sensor.

XRoads

The most recent development that is based on the Simulator X framework is the Cross-Reality On A Digital Surface (XRoads) project (Giebler-Schubert, Zimmerer, Wedler, Fischbach, & Latoschik, 2013). It involves porting a board game to a multi-touch table and is performed in cooperation with the German games publisher *Pegasus Spiele*. XRoads is shown in figure 6.4.

Figure 6.4: *XRoads* being presented at the Spiel '14.

In the context of the project, new interaction techniques for virtual table tops are evaluated, wherefore different sensors (e.g., the *leap motion* controller) are attached to the digital surface. Furthermore, voice commands and the utilization of hand-held devices (i.e. smartphones and tablet-PCs) are supported by the XRoads application. The modular architecture of the Simulator X framework is highly beneficial for this intention, since it provides an abstract layer on which the sensor data can be applied. XRoads reuses the rendering component that was already used in the SiXton's Curse and the smARTbox demonstrations, even though only 2D graphics are rendered. An additional Graphical User Interface (GUI) component was implemented, which now is also used in the context of the SiXton's Curse application. The results of the XRoads project have been published in the form of research demonstrations by Fischbach, Zimmerer, Giebler-Schubert, and Latoschik (2014) and Zimmerer, Fischbach, and Latoschik (2014).

6.3.2 Exhibitions

Besides the research demonstrations mentioned in the section above, the XRoads project also was shown on the *Internationale Spieltage SPIEL* 2013 and 2014 in Essen as well as on the *Role Play Convention* 2013, 2014, and 2015 in Cologne. Each of these exhibitions lasted multiple days with visitors trying the applications all day long. In this way, the applications—and thus the concepts implemented in the Simulator X framework—were tested in a realistic scenario. The fact that Pegasus Spiele requested the demonstration for five times indicates that Simulator X -based applications are interesting not only in the research context but also for commercial projects.

In addition, both the smARTbox and the XRoads demonstration were successfully shown at the *Mainfranken-Messe* 2013 in Würzburg. This is especially noteworthy, since none of the developers who could have helped in case of any problems with the application was present at the fair.

6.3.3 Teaching-related Applications

As stated by the introductorily cited quote, usability is a requirement for reusable software. Especially in the context of the development of highly complex software, like VR applications, this is an ambitious goal. This is complicated further if developers do only have limited experience in the field of VR and programming in general. Thus, by the application of a VR research framework in the teaching context its usability was put to the acid test.

Courses

The Simulator X framework has been applied in multiple bachelor and master courses at the University of Würzburg. In this context, exercises ranged from the implementation of an AI-enhanced version of the *Pac-Man* game to a reimplementation of the *Put-that-there* application by Bolt (1980).

This approach has been practiced for multiple years, indicating the understandability and usability of the framework. The fact that some students do even dig deeper into the framework to extend its functionality supports this hypothesis.

Student Projects and Theses

In addition to public demonstrations of applications that were developed using the Simulator X framework, student projects and theses that utilized the framework were carried out. These include the development of new components (e.g., Eckstein, 2014) and applications. Some of these works were so successful that results could be published at peer-reviewed conferences (Fischbach, Treffs, et al. (2012), Fischbach, Neff, Pelzer, Lugrin, and Latoschik (2013) and Lugrin, Wiebusch, Latoschik, and Strehler (2013)).

6.4 Opinions: Questionnaires

As mentioned above, usability of a software framework is of high importance. In order to evaluate this aspect of the Simulator X framework, it was compared to three other frameworks from the fields of VR applications and computer games in a usability study. It has to be stressed that the performed study was not designed to reveal statistically significant results but rather is considered a prestudy, giving a first idea of the differences regarding the usability of the tested systems.

The most problematic issue in this context is to recruit a large number of participants who are willing to occupy themselves with the utilization of multiple RIS frameworks over a long time. On the one hand, this is due to a certain amount of expertise that a participant is required to have in the field of (RIS) application development and programming, which immensely reduces the amount of potential candidates. On the other hand, experts in this

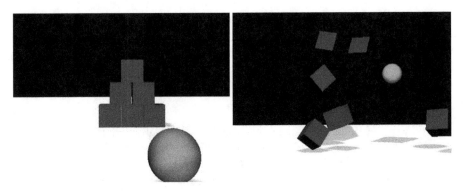

Figure 6.5: Example images shown to participants to indicate the goal of their task.

field usually are rare and often cannot afford the time that is necessary to participate in this kind of study. Both of this complicates the selection of a randomized set of participants a lot.

Thus—sacrificing the opportunity of generating statistically significant results—the participants of the *Realtime Interactive Systems* as well as the *3D User Interfaces* lectures, held in the winter term 2014 at the University of Würzburg, were given the opportunity to take part in the study. They were successively introduced to instantreality (Behr, Bockholt, & Fellner, 2011), Unity 4, Simulator X, as well as the Unreal Engine 4 and afterwards presented a questionnaire to evaluate each system.

The systems were discussed in the above mentioned order, spending four hours per week for three weeks on each of the frameworks. In this context, an introduction to basic functionality, user input, physics simulation, and the means to create an application that utilizes these features were covered. For all systems, except for instantreality, the topic of integrating audio feedback was covered additionally. At the end of each such introduction, the students were asked to implement a 'can knockdown' game, which had to feature a stack of six physically simulated boxes as well as a virtual ball that should be accelerated towards the boxes when a button is pressed.

In order to visualize the goal of their task, the participants were shown the two images from figure 6.5. After completing the task the participants were given as much time as they needed to complete the questionnaire.

After three months of introduction to the frameworks, the students had to choose one of the systems with the help of which they had to solve the task described by the IEEE Symposium on 3D User Interface (3DUI) contest 2011.[15] The goal was to create a 3D user interface with the help of which a virtual version of a cube puzzle could be solved. Students formed teams of three to five persons to complete this task. Starting with the announcement of the task, the students had 42 days to work on it.

After handing in their results, the participants were once more asked to fill out the questionnaire to evaluate the system they had chosen. The questionnaire is a composition of the NASA task load index (NASA TLX)[16], the questionnaire for the subjective consequences of

---

[15] The description of the 3DUI contest is available at http://conferences.computer.org/3dui/3dui2011/cfp-contest.html.
[16] The Paper and Pencil version of the NASA TLX questionnaire is available at http://humansystems.arc.nasa.gov/groups/tlx/downloads/TLXScale.pdf.

intuitive use (QUESI, Naumann & Hurtienne, 2010), as well as a free text field into which general comments could be inserted. Besides this opportunity to leave comments, the QUESI questions were also added text fields where comments could be added. The questionnaire was presented online.

Students were free to opt out of filling out the questionnaires. Furthermore, neither participating in the lectures nor in the exercises was mandatory, wherefore the number of completed questionnaires varies between the different systems.

The group of participants from the RIS lecture consisted of 21 students (3 females, 18 males), ten of which were between 21 and 23, eight between 24 and 26, and three between 27 and 30 years old. All of the participants were enrolled in the courses of study of either Human-Computer Interaction or Computer Science. Eight participants had not used a RIS framework before, whereas eleven had done so for 1.84 years on average ($SD = 0.99$) and two students stated to have used RIS frameworks for 13 and 15 years, respectively (which, due to their age, is assumed to be a misinterpretation of the question).

The group of 3DUI participants, which where evaluated anonymously to avoid influences from the grading process of the lecture, consisted of 19 students (2 females, 17 males). Nine of these were between 21 and 23, eight between 24 and 26, one between 27 and 30, and one between 31 and 40 years old. One group consisting of three participants used Simulator X, one group of five used the Unreal Engine 4, and the remaining eleven used Unity 4 for their project. Due to anonymity of responses, it is not possible to determine the sizes of the Unity 4 teams, since not all of the participants completed the questionnaires.

The users of the Simulator X framework had between one and four years experience in using the system for projects related to their studies before. They used it for 83.3 hours on average ($SD = 23.57$) to complete the 3DUI task. One of the five students who chose to use the Unreal Engine 4 stated to have had one year of experience using the Unreal engine, whereas others from that group were new to the system. Yet, one of the latter had been using a similar system for two years before. They spent 54 hours on average ($SD = 12.47$) to complete their 3DUI project. Only one of the Users of Unity 4 had used the system before (for two months). From those who were new to the system, six stated that they had been using similar systems for 3.17 years on average ($SD = 2.27$) before. Unity 4 was used for 96.8 hours on average ($SD = 54.70$) by students to complete their project.

In the following considerations, instantreality and the Unreal Engine 4 will not be considered for statistical evaluation. The former is the first system that was used to introduce the students to the type of applications and the can knockdown task, wherefore it includes the students' efforts to grasp the basics of the task instead of solely measuring the system's usability. The Unreal Engine 4 was evaluated by three and five participants according to their experiences in the can knockdown game and the 3DUI task, respectively, wherefore valid statistical results are not possible.

6.4.1 Results: NASA TLX

The results from the NASA TLX questionnaires that were used to evaluate the systems after their introduction are shown in figure 6.6a (except for the physical demand, which was considered inappropriate in this context). Due to the limited number of completed forms, especially for the unreal engine, the confidence intervals are rather extensive.

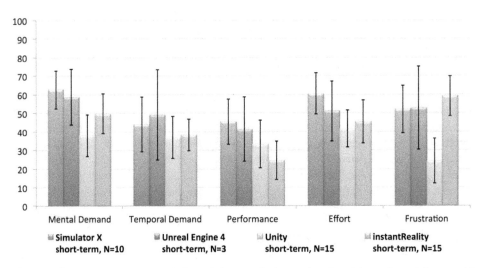

(a) Results after three introductory weeks for each framework. The number of participants for each framework is indicated by the values of N.

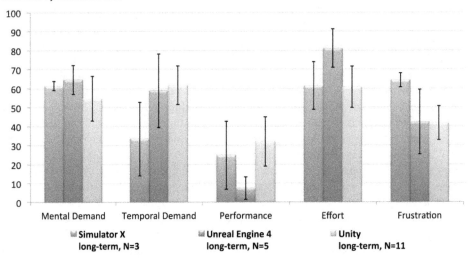

(b) Long-term results after completing the 3DUI project.

Figure 6.6: Results from the NASA TLX questionnaires, lower values indicate better results. The visualized whiskers indicate 95% confidence intervals. The visualized mean values as well as associated values for standard deviation are printed in appendix C.

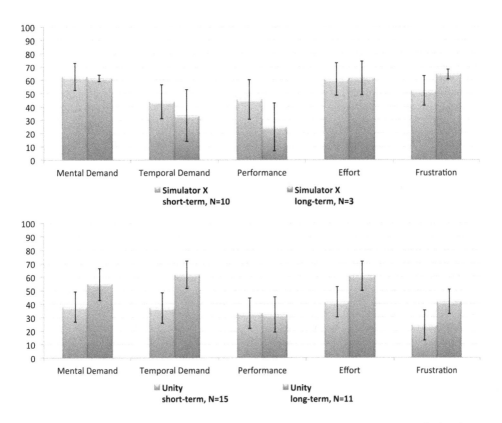

Figure 6.7: Comparison of short-term and long-term results from the NASA TLX questionnaire for Simulator X (top) and Unity (bottom). Whiskers indicate 95% confidence intervals.

According to a Shapiro-Wilk test the data retrieved for both Unity and Simulator X are normally distributed ($p = .05$), except for the frustration results for Unity. By the application of a Mann-Whitney U test significant differences to the disfavor of Simulator X in comparison to Unity were found regarding mental demand ($U = 28.5$, $p = .01078$) and frustration ($U = 31.5$, $p = .01684$). In contrast, participants estimated their performance to be considerably higher using Simulator X as compared to using instantreality.

The results of the NASA TLX questionnaires after completing the 3DUI contest task are shown in figure 6.6b. Due to the limited number of participants who used the Simulator X framework and the Unreal Engine 4 these results cannot be used for statistical analysis but rather provide an indication of long-term results. Again, a Shapiro-Wilk test shows the results for Unity to be distributed normally ($p = .05$).

Discussion Although these results are to the disfavor of Simulator X, some positive observations can be made. Whereas the first impression of the Simulator X framework on users, as compared to Unity 4, suggests to be more mentally demanding and to require higher efforts to achieve goals, this observation seems to vanish after a longer period of use.

Moreover, comparing the values of the initial NASA TLX results with those after the implementation of the 3DUI project puts the initial findings into perspective: as shown in figure 6.7, the negative results for the Simulator X framework did not change for the worse, whereas the positive findings for Unity declined. In fact, the application of the Mann-Whitney U test reveals significant changes for the categories of temporal demand ($U = 35.5, p = .01596$) and effort spent ($U = 39.5, p = .0271$).

The mean values and associated standard deviations that were obtained from the questionnaires are given in appendix C. All of the presented results have to be treated with caution due to the low number of completed questionnaires.

6.4.2 Results: QUESI

The QUESI is most often used to evaluate devices and graphical user interfaces, such as smartphones, operating systems, and websites. Yet, the measured features include elements such as 'subjective mental workload' (W), 'perceived achievement of goals' (G), 'perceived effort of learning' (L), 'familiarity' (F), and 'perceived error rate' (E), which are interesting for RIS frameworks, too. Although it was not initially designed to evaluate a software framework, the QUESI was applied to get an idea of its usability as perceived by the users.

Keeping in mind that the results only suggest a tendency, figure 6.8a presents the results from the questionnaires that were presented after the three-week introductions to the systems. A Shapiro-Wilk test indicated the results obtained for Simulator X and Unity to be normally distributed ($p = .5$). Similar to the results from the NASA TLX, Simulator X is observed to perform worse than Unity. In this regard, significant differences were found for all categories (see table 6.5).

Simulator X was also found to be in an inferior position compared to instantreality regarding perceived subjective workload, perceived effort of learning, and the QUESI total score.

Similar to the observations that were made with the NASA TLX results, these differences are mitigated when the systems are used over a longer period of time. Figure 6.8b contains the data that was obtained from the QUESI questionnaires that were filled out after the participants had finished the 3DUI contest task: no significant differences could be observed for any of the conditions between Simulator X and Unity.

Discussion The results found with the QUESI are largely in line with those obtained from the NASA TLX: Simulator X was observed to be in an inferior position to Unity, whereas no significant differences to the Unreal Engine 4 and instantreality could be detected. Similar to the NASA TLX results, long-term use of the systems was observed to mitigate differences in QUESI results.

	W	G	L	F	E	Total
U	18	24	10	31	27.5	12
p	.002	.005	.0003	.016	.009	.0005

Table 6.5: Whitney-Mann *U* test results for QUESI short-term result comparison between Simulator X and Unity.

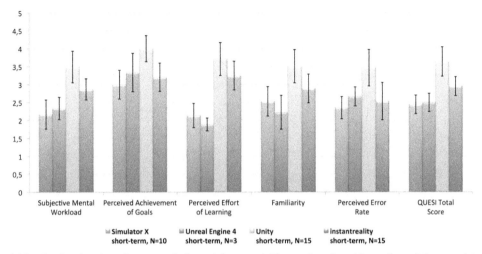

(a) Results after three introductory weeks for each framework. The number of participants for each framework is indicated by the values of N.

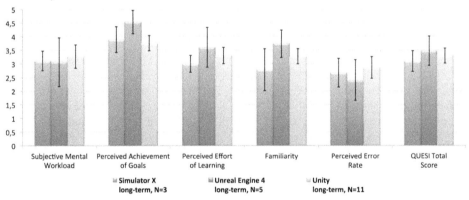

(b) Long-term results after completing the 3DUI project.

Figure 6.8: QUESI results, higher values indicate better results, whiskers indicate the 95% confidence intervals. The visualized mean values as well as associated values for standard deviation are printed in appendix C.

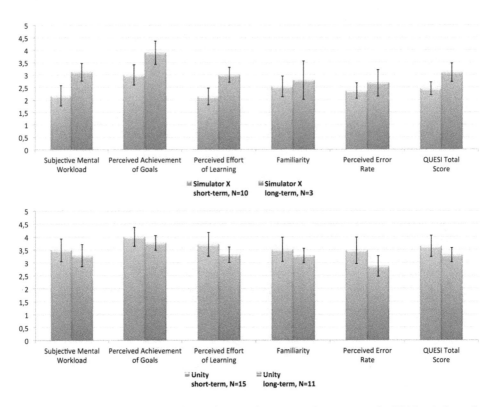

Figure 6.9: QUESI Simulator X (top) and Unity (bottom) short-term vs. long-term results. Whiskers indicate the 95% confidence intervals.

Moreover, the observations for the change of values regarding long-term use are similar to the ones made before. For both Simulator X and Unity the change in perceived usability is indicated by figure 6.9. In the same way as it was observed by the results of the NASA TLX, Simulator X compensates for the found differences from its initial evaluation by the QUESI questionnaire. Due to the very few users of the Simulator X framework, no statements according statistical significance can be made. Nonetheless, the results for the conditions 'subjective mental workload' and 'perceived learning effort' indicate mentionable improvements. Although a decrease of values for all QUESI conditions was observed for Unity, none of these were statistically significant.

6.4.3 User Comments

In order to gain insight into the reasons for the found differences for Simulator X, especially in comparison to Unity, the students' comments on the systems are reviewed. The collected statements are summarized in the next two paragraphs, whereas the next section will discuss them in combination with the previously mentioned findings.

Simulator X

Six participants provided comments on their experiences using Simulator X. One student mentioned that it is easy to integrate further hardware into an application and that Scala is easy to use. Furthermore, it was stated that Simulator X can easily be adjusted to fit different requirements and that the framework was stable. Finally, the fact that Simulator X is open source was welcomed, since this allowed modifications and adding custom-made components.

On the downside, especially the lack of documentation and a graphical editor was criticized. The complexity of the structure of a Simulator X project (cf. section 5.4) was felt to be very high. Using the callback-based way of accessing values was found to be difficult to use. Moreover, the request to buffer state values locally and thus allow for direct access was made by one student. Only indirectly related to Simulator X, the jVR component was mentioned to be inferior to those of other engines. Finally, participants faulted the amount of time that had to be spent compiling Simulator X applications as well as a lack of performance.

Unity 4

Four students provided comments on the Unity engine, which are summarized below. As opposed to Simulator X, the availability of documentation as well as the graphical editor of Unity was highly appreciated by the users. The opportunity to integrate program code into a self-contained C# file without being concerned about other aspects of the application was positively mentioned. The easy interaction with public member variables from created C# code, which can be modified in the editor at runtime, was stated to be favorable. Unity was furthermore described to "seem to be very intuitive." Finally, the facility to enable and disable single components through the editor was perceived to be beneficial.

As opposed to these positive observations, the free version of Unity was said to make the integration of additional plugins (especially to integrate sensors) difficult or even impossible. The fact that an external Integrated Development Environment (IDE) has to be used to work on program code was mentioned to be unfavorable, however, being able to close the Unity editor and continue programming, thereby decreasing performance requirements, was mentioned to be beneficial. One student stated that the navigation inside a scene using the Unity editor was inconvenient.

6.4.4 Discussion

The results that were obtained from the questionnaires show that Simulator X initially is more complicated to use than the other frameworks that were considered: significant differences regarding both, workload and perceived usability, were found. This was to be expected, since the commercial engines (Unity and the Unreal Engine 4) provide graphical editors, with the help of which the virtual environment can be modeled more easily.

As opposed to this, Simulator X can currently only be used by hardcoding initial values and does not provide a visual scene editor. Although the Scala programming language (used by Simulator X) bears some resemblance to Java and supports the OOP paradigm, C# (used by Unity) and C++ (used in the Unreal Engine 4) are even closer to languages students were used to (mostly Java). Furthermore, the high-end visual rendering capabilities of those engines make the created scenes much more appealing than the open source jVR renderer, which was developed in the context of a master thesis (Roßbach, 2010).

This was reflected by the opinions that participants expressed in the questionnaires: in general, Simulator X was observed to lack prototyping methods that allow to quickly create and test a virtual scene. Moreover, the definite lack of documentation was detrimental to the appraisal of Simulator X.

However, long-term use of Simulator X and Unity reduced the differences between the questionnaire results: while the values for Unity changed for the worse, the values for Simulator X changed for the better, in the end leaving no significant differences except for the level of frustration. The latter is supported by the comments that were left by participants: long compilation times, few documentation, and uncommon programming styles slowed down the use of the Simulator X framework.

On the other hand, the advantageous aspects of the commercial engines, especially involving the graphical editor, seem to become less beneficial when the task to be performed gets more complex. Especially the fact that the 3DUI task was rather concerned with the creation of application logic than with the creation of appealing VEs contributes to this.

It has to be stressed that the results only provide a biased comparison of the frameworks' usability, since too many factors (e.g., programming language, availability of graphical editors, differently experienced participants, etc.) affect the results. Moreover, the rather small set of participants prohibits statistically relevant assertions. Even though this is the case, the results provide a good indication that Simulator X can keep up with popular frameworks regarding the implementation of more complex applications.

The results obtained from the questionnaires are better than expected, considering the fact that Simulator X was compared with high-end game engines as well as the longstanding, highly-optimized software instantreality. Building on the comments that were given by the participants, the Simulator X framework can be improved to accomplish higher usability in the future.

6.5 Summary

This chapter was begun with the presentation of a case study, which explained the process of creating a component for the Simulator X framework. The approaches presented in the previous chapters allow to perform the creation in a simple four-step process, which was detailed in section 5.2.8. A lines-of-code analysis indicated the amount of work that arose during the creation of the prototypically implemented Unity component, which allows to use Unity's rendering and physical simulation capabilities in Simulator X applications.

Subsequently, the required steps to replace a component from an existing application were detailed. For this purpose an example was discussed, in which the jVR rendering component, which is commonly used in Simulator X applications, was exchanged for the above-mentioned Unity component. It was shown that simple adjustments to the application ontology as well as the modification of aspects in the entity descriptions that are used by the respective application is sufficient for the replacement process.

The case study was concluded with an analysis of reuse in the Simulator X framework. This analysis was performed by investigating the covered lines of code and statements that were invoked by two different applications. For the three examined simulation components as well as the Simulator X core component reuse rates between 34.88% and 73.54% regarding the components' statements as well as between 37.10% and 65.98% regarding the components' lines of code were observed. Comparing the statements of the components that were shared by the two applications, rates between 57.21% and 81.42% or between 92.61% and 100.0% (depending on the application the perspective of which was taken) were found.

Subsequently, an overview of the applications that have been developed with the Simulator X framework and presented on conferences and exhibitions was given. The diversity of application areas as well as used input and output devices indicated the framework's flexibility, and thus the applicability of the proposed approaches.

The chapter was concluded with the presentation of results from task load and usability questionnaires, which were filled in by students who worked with three prominent game engines and VR frameworks as well as with Simulator X. Although the low number of participants does not allow to draw statistically relevant conclusions, findings indicate that Simulator X is usable in a similar way that the other frameworks are. However, there are many opportunities for improvements, especially regarding support for users to get started using Simulator X. In this context, the comments that were given by the participants and discussed in section 6.4.3 provide a good starting point for future work.

This will be discussed in the following chapter, which at the same time presents the conclusion of this work.

Chapter 7

Conclusion

Of all the monsters that fill the nightmares of our folklore, none terrify more than werewolves, because they transform unexpectedly from the familiar into horrors. For these, one seeks bullets of silver that can magically lay them to rest.

No Silver Bullet
Frederick P. Brooks (1987)

7.1 Summary

Intelligent Realtime Interactive Systems (IRISs) and the highly specialized hardware devices they depend on are becoming evermore available. Consequently, their area of applications is growing and has already started to become a part of everyday life.

This results in a problem that researchers in the field of RIS and especially VR development have been experiencing for many years: specialized hardware devices, a huge number of closely interacting simulation modules, realtime requirements, highly specific use cases, and many more similarly challenging aspects result in the implemented software being specially tailored to particular needs. Like the werewolves from the above quoted metaphor by Frederick P. Brooks, these custom-made solutions can easily turn into unmanageable entities.

Due to its high complexity, such software becomes increasingly unmaintainable the older it gets and the more (unanticipated) adjustments are made. Similar problems have been known in the field of software engineering for a long time. There, different approaches, such as code-generators, Object-Oriented Programming, Component-Based Software Engineering, domain-engineering, and many more have been developed to address related issues.

In this work, a methodology that allows for the integration of a Knowledge Representation Layer (KRL) that augments architecture elements with ontologically grounded semantics was proposed. In order to be utilizable in program code, to reduce errors that could occur during manual translation, and to simply spare developers work, the KRL is generated from an OWL ontology.

Based on this KRL, a component model for reusable IRISs has been presented, which introduces semantic typing to the field of RISs. It furthermore provides a uniform access model that facilitates decoupling of simulation modules. By combining these techniques with the actor model the coupling between simulation modules is reduced to a minimum.

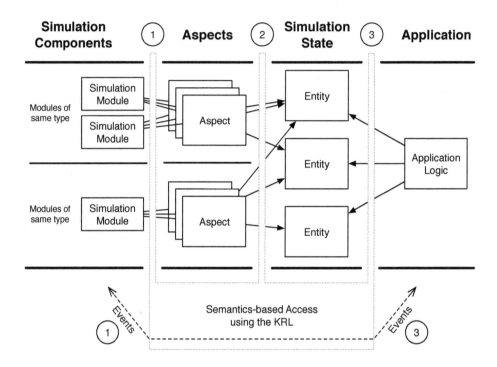

Figure 7.1: Three layers of decoupling: (1) decoupling simulation modules according to their functionality via aspects, (2) decoupling application content using aspects to describe entities, and (3) decoupling application logic by uniform access to entities. All communication is based on concepts and associated symbols that are grounded in the integrated KRL.

In this way, the proposed model allows to turn preexisting as well as new simulation modules into simulation components that can be loosely coupled, whereas they would otherwise have been closely coupled to create one of the above-mentioned custom-made software solutions. As a result, created simulation components can easily be added, removed, and replaced from a IRIS application and therefore are easy to reuse.

The proposed model and the underlying KRL provide a means for simulation components to access a shared simulation state. In doing so, components can act in a manner that is similar to the one known from blackboard model in the field of AI: new information is added to the blackboard (the simulation state) and then processed by other modules, which then make their own contributions. In this way, the simulation state becomes the interface between all participating actors.

It is apparent that this concept is especially beneficial for the integration of (symbolic) AI modules, which benefit from the added data, infer additional facts, and provide these to other modules via the shared state. In contrast to common approaches the model provides uniform access to meaningful information about the simulation state, no matter what source it originates from.

In the context of this work, the proposed methods were implemented in the Simulator X research framework, which is available to the public as an open source project.[17] Simulator X has been used in multiple research demonstrations, ranging from touch-table interaction to fully immersive VR setups. It furthermore provides the basis for the 'Quest – XRoads' game, which has been presented multiple times on different games fairs.

A case study was presented, which indicates the steps that are required for the previously mentioned tasks of adding, removing, and replacing simulation modules. It involved the prototypical creation of a module adapter for the Unity engine, a high-end development platform for computer games. By means of the implemented adapter, a reusable simulation component was created, which makes the high-quality rendering capabilities of Unity available for Simulator X applications. In the case study, the jVR rendering component, which is commonly used in Simulator X applications, was replaced by the Unity component, thereby demonstrating the applicability of the approach.

In general this answers the introductorily stated objectives (cf. section 1.4):

O1: Simulation modules are decoupled from one another and thus can be flexibly combined. As shown by layer 1 in figure 7.1, this is achieved by the concept of aspects, which allows each simulation component to maintain its own view on every entity, and the restriction of communication between components to the utilization of events.

O2: Aspects are closely related to the objective of decoupling application content from the simulation modules. Layer 2 in figure 7.1 indicates the composition of aspects to form entities, whereby simulation modules become replaceable without modifications to the application content.

O3: Finally, restricting communication between simulation components to messages (partly mediated by the shared simulation state, layer 3 in figure 7.1), application logic becomes loosely coupled to both simulation modules and the particular set of instantiated entities. In fact, the application logic can be regarded as a further simulation module, wherefore the three initial objectives are actually reduced to the first two.

All three layers and the event-based communication rely on concepts and symbols that are grounded in the KRL, which is stored in the form of an OWL ontology.

While the presented prototypical Unity adapter comprises more than 1700 lines of code, its utilization is much easier to achieve. For each type of entity that shall be affected by the Unity engine (i.e. that shall be rendered by Unity) one line of code has to be added, removed, or exchanged. Similarly, adding, removing, or replacing the Unity adapter requires to modify only one line of code. This matches previous observations from the field of software reuse: creating reusable software requires considerable efforts, whereas later benefits do more than compensate these initial efforts.

Making the assumption that a manual integration of the Unity engine into an existing project involving 10 types of entities would have required 400 lines of code (which is a highly optimistic estimation), the fifth application that is created in this setup would benefit from the proposed approach already. Considering the fact that software can be shared among and reused by multiple developers, these benefits become quite obvious.

---

[17] Simulator X is available at https://github.com/simulator-x

In order to get an idea of aspects regarding the usability of the model, Simulator X was additionally evaluated in a prestudy. Since long-term users of such frameworks are usually experts who cannot spare the time to participate in a long study, students were given this opportunity. Most of them were novices in creating RISs and had to gain expertise during the prestudy.

First results indicate that Simulator X is as easy (or as complex) to use as other high end frameworks and game engines, like Unity 4, the Unreal Engine 4, and instantreality. Moreover, results for short-term usage suggest that novice users are initially deterred by missing features, like a 3D editor or visual programming facilities. Yet, after a longer time of using a framework these features seem to become less important: compared to its short-term users, long-term users reported higher perceived workload for the Unity engine. In contrast, the corresponding values decreased after a longer use of Simulator X.

Although the proposed techniques have been developed in the context of IRISs, they can also be applied in the context of less complex systems: especially the enhanced capabilities of semantic reflection, e.g., in the form of semantic types and semantic traits, can be beneficial in any programming environment. This way, modularity and reusability can be facilitated in many other types of software.

7.2 Future Work

Despite the beneficial aspects that arise with the application of the presented component model and the underlying KRL, it after all is no silver bullet by means of which all problems of IRIS development can be laid to rest. This said, the approach bears potential to increase the silver content of IRIS frameworks.

In order to draw advantages from the proposed model, repositories of both reusable simulation components as well as ontologies are required, which provide functionality for different use cases. Besides complete components, this includes descriptions of semantic types, actions, entities, and events. Essentially, the more combinations of components are used and uploaded into publicly accessible repositories, the more benefits can be drawn.

Consequently, there is a variety of aspects that provide grounds for future work:

- **Ontology-related aspects:**
    - For each application area multiple components should be created. This way, an agreed upon ontology for each component type can be consolidated.
    - In the same way, pre-built ontologies for the combination of different components can be created. The positive aspect here is that such ontologies would not have to be created for others but would grow naturally with the adaption of a simulation module.
    - The creation of multiple OWL ontologies inevitably leads to ambiguous naming, use of different symbols for the same concept, and similar issues. This problem is not solely connected to the approaches developed in this work, nevertheless a solution or at least a means to reduce the related negative effects has to be found to reduce the amount of required manual adjustments.

- **Usability-related aspects:**

  – Although tools are available for editing ontologies, these usually are designed as general purpose applications. In contrast, the concepts that were presented in this work are limited in numbers, wherefore a specialized application that supports a developer in editing the ontology is conceivable. This way, the required amount of knowledge about the underlying concepts, especially regarding the OWL constructs, and thus the number of sources of errors can be reduced.

  – As observed in the conducted prestudy, the current lack of a graphical editor for VEs is perceived as rather deterring. While the implementation of such a tool would probably not exceed the features that are provided by the highly specialized tools in this area, the exploitation of the KRL can provide new ways of editing such content. For example, the semantic augmentation could allow for the utilization of multimodal interfaces in the context of the editor. Furthermore, searching for assets and utilizing information that is inferred from the currently defined properties can be supported.

  – Similar to a graphical editor for VE content, enhanced debugging features that involve semantic information about the entities can be implemented. For instance, different conditions for breakpoints could be specified more easily and semantic traits could be used to inspect the current application state.

  – Besides graphical editors, the identification of software development methods that increase the efficiency of developers using a system that adopts the proposed model would be highly useful. In this regard, especially the introduced aspect of semantic typing does constitute an interesting area of research. Moreover, it has to be evaluated which opportunities arise by further combination of the uniform access model and semantic traits regarding more sophisticated interfaces. In this way, a new of RIS programming might be achieved.

  – The conducted prestudy has only provided a first insight into the usability of the Simulator X framework as compared to other systems. However, the group of participants consisted of students with few or none experience in the area of RIS development. Future work has to involve the creation of an appropriate study design, selection or creation of reasonable questionnaires that are especially designed for the evaluation of such systems, and convoking experts from the field of RIS development in order to get more meaningful results.

- **Performance-related aspects:**

  – Simulator X has been used in different VR and MR applications that have been presented on multiple occasions (cf. section 6.3), indicating the general applicability of the proposed model. However, only few benchmarks have been performed (cf. Rehfeld, Tramberend, & Latoschik, 2014) and, due to the fact that Simulator X is a research platform, the implementation has not been optimized for high performance. Future work has to involve measurements of different implementation variants of the model, preferably using different programming languages and actor libraries.

- In RIS systems synchronization of the states between different modules is considered crucial. During the development of Simulator X, this requirement has shown to be not as critical as expected: often it was sufficient to run an application without any synchronization. Nevertheless, simple mechanisms to synchronize modules have been implemented, allowing for component synchronization on a per-frame basis. Further, yet unpublished efforts have been made to achieve synchronization on lower layers, for instance to allow the update of two state variables as an atomic operation (as viewed by the observing actors). This work has to be continued in the future to provide more advanced models of synchronization in actor-based RISs.

- Since the proposed methods build on the actor-model and its message-based communication, it is inherently capable of being used in distributed environments. Few work has been performed evaluating these capabilities (Rehfeld et al., 2013). Especially the effects of distribution on the underlying KRL need to be investigated in the future to ensure its utility in such areas of application.

- **Validation-related aspects:**

  - Up to now, the implemented applications either involved only few AI modules or were restricted in their complexity. For further validation of the approach more mature applications that highly depend on the utilization of multiple interacting AI modules have to be implemented. Especially (intelligent) multimodal interfaces (Latoschik & Fischbach, 2014) provide an interesting area of applications, which promises to be highly relevant regarding future user interfaces.

  - Most of the available reusability metrics are only suitable to a limited extend for the evaluation of RIS frameworks. New measures need to be developed, which provide framework developers with a means to evaluate frameworks before they are put to use.

This extensive list reveals the high potential for further research in the area of this work. Reasons for this include the few efforts that have been made to evaluate deeply integrated KRLs in RISs as well as the fact that related systems, like game engines, are largely developed in the commercial area, wherefore only few publications that extend over description of technical aspects exist.

As stated in the beginning of this work, the proposed methods are not limited to IRIS applications but can be used in many other fields of software engineering. Choosing from the presented techniques according to their needs, developers of applications in other areas can draw advantages of the presented results. Hence, in whatever direction future user interfaces, software, and hardware may develop, the odds are that the presented techniques can contribute to ease the humble programmer's task of satisfying ever-rising expectations.

Bibliography

Abaci, T., Ciger, J., & Thalmann, D. (2005). Planning with Smart Objects. In *The 13-th International Conference in Central Europe on Computer Graphics, Visualization and Computer Vision (WSCG) '2005* (pp. 25–28).

Acevedo-Feliz, D. (2014). VR Toolkits: Why do we keep reinventing the wheel? In *2014 IEEE Virtual Reality (VR)* (pp. 1–3). doi:10.1109/VR.2014.6802114

Allard, J., Gouranton, V., Lecointre, L., Limet, S., Melin, E., Raffin, B., & Robert, S. (2004). FlowVR: A Middleware for Large Scale Virtual Reality Applications. In M. Danelutto, M. Vanneschi, & D. Laforenza (Eds.), *Euro-Par 2004 Parallel Processing: 10th International Euro-Par Conference 2004. Proceedings* (pp. 497–505). Springer. doi:10.1007/978-3-540-27866-5_65

Allard, J., Gouranton, V., Lecointre, L., Melin, E., & Raffin, B. (2002). Net Juggler: running VR Juggler with multiple displays on a commodity component cluster. In *Virtual Reality, 2002. Proceedings* (pp. 273–273). IEEE. doi:10.1109/VR.2002.996534

Allard, J., Lesage, J.-D., & Raffin, B. (2010). Modularity for Large Virtual Reality Applications. *Presence: Teleoperators and Virtual Environments, 19*(2), 142–161. doi:10.1162/pres.19.2.142

Anastassakis, G. & Panayiotopoulos, T. (2011). Intelligent Virtual Environment Development with the REVE Platform: An Overview. In H. H. Vilhjálmsson, S. Kopp, S. Marsella, & K. R. Thórisson (Eds.), *Intelligent Virtual Agents: 10th International Conference, IVA 2011, Reykjavik, Iceland, September 15-17, 2011. Proceedings* (pp. 431–432). Springer. doi:10.1007/978-3-642-23974-8_48

Anastassakis, G. & Panayiotopoulos, T. (2012). A Unified Model for Representing Objects with Physical Properties, Semantics and Functionality in Virtual Environments. *Intelligent Decision Technologies, 6*(2), 123–137. doi:10.3233/IDT-2012-0129

Anastassakis, G., Panayiotopoulos, T., & Raptis, G. (2012). Towards a Methodology for Integrating Physics Engines with Virtual Environments: A Case Study Using the REVE Platform and the Vesper3D Physics Engine. In *Informatics (PCI), 2012 16th Panhellenic Conference on* (pp. 86–92). IEEE. doi:10.1109/PCi.2012.63

Aoyama, M. (1998). New Age of Software Development: How Component-Based Software Engineering Changes the Way of Software Development? In *1998 International Workshop on CBSE* (pp. 1–5).

Armstrong, D. J. (2006). The Quarks of Object-oriented Development. *Communications of the ACM, 49*(2), 123–128. doi:10.1145/1113034.1113040

Aylett, R. & Cavazza, M. (2001). Intelligent Virtual Environments - A State-of-the-art Report. In *Eurographics 2001 - STARs*. Eurographics Association. doi:10.2312/egst.20011046

Baader, F., Calvanese, D., McGuinness, D., Nardi, D., & Patel-Schneider, P. (Eds.). (2004). *The Description Logic Handbook: Theory, Implementation, and Applications*. Cambridge University Press. doi:10.2277/0521781760

Baader, F., Miličić, M., Lutz, C., Sattler, U., & Wolter, F. (2005). *Integrating Description Logics and Action Formalisms for Reasoning about Web Services* (LTCS-Report No. 05-02). Chair for Automata Theory, Institute for Theoretical Computer Science, Dresden University of Technology.

Bachmann, A., Kunde, M., Litz, M., & Schreiber, A. (2010). Advances in Generalization and Decoupling of Software Parts in a Scientific Simulation Workflow System. In *ADV-COMP 2010, The Fourth International Conference on Advanced Engineering Computing and Applications in Sciences* (pp. 34–38). IARIA.

Badler, N. I., Bindiganavale, R., Bourne, J. C., Palmer, M. S., Shi, J., & Schuler, W. (2000). A Parameterized Action Representation for Virtual Human Agents. In J. Cassell, J. Sullivan, S. Prevost, & E. F. Churchill (Eds.), *Embodied Conversational Agents* (pp. 256–284). MIT press.

Beck, F. & Diehl, S. (2011). On the Congruence of Modularity and Code Coupling. In *Proceedings of the 19th ACM SIGSOFT Symposium and the 13th European Conference on Foundations of Software Engineering* (pp. 354–364). ESEC/FSE '11. ACM. doi:10.1145/2025113.2025162

Behr, J., Bockholt, U., & Fellner, D. (2011). Instantreality — A Framework for Industrial Augmented and Virtual Reality Applications. In D. Ma, X. Fan, J. Gausemeier, & M. Grafe (Eds.), *Virtual Reality & Augmented Reality in Industry* (pp. 91–99). Springer. doi:10.1007/978-3-642-17376-9_5

Bieman, J. M. & Zhao, J. X. (1995). Reuse Through Inheritance: A Quantitative Study of C++ Software. *ACM SIGSOFT Software Engineering Notes, 20*(SI), 47–52. doi:10.1145/223427.211794

Bierbaum, A., Just, C., Hartling, P., Meinert, K., Baker, A., & Cruz-Neira, C. (2001). VR Juggler: A Framework for Virtual Reality Development. In *Virtual Reality, 2001. Proceedings. IEEE* (pp. 89–96). doi:10.1109/VR.2001.913774

Biermann, P. & Wachsmuth, I. (2003). An Implemented Approach for a Visual Programming Environment in VR. In *Proceedings Fifth Virtual Reality International Conference (VRIC 2003)* (pp. 229–234). Laval, France.

Biggerstaff, T. J. & Richter, C. (1989). Reusability Framework, Assessment, and Directions. In *Software reusability: vol. 1, concepts and models* (pp. 1–17). ACM. doi:10.1145/73103.73104

Boehm, B. W. (1987). Improving Software Productivity. *Computer, 20*(7), 43–57. doi:10.1109/MC.1987.1663694

Bolt, R. A. (1980). "Put-that-there": Voice and Gesture at the Graphics Interface. In *Proceedings of the 7th annual conference on computer graphics and interactive techniques* (pp. 262–270). SIGGRAPH '80. ACM. doi:10.1145/800250.807503

Bracha, G. & Cook, W. (1990). Mixin-based inheritance. In *Proceedings of the European Conference on Object-oriented Programming on Object-oriented Programming Systems, Languages, and Applications* (pp. 303–311). OOPSLA/ECOOP '90. ACM. doi:10.1145/97945.97982

Brooks, F. P. (1987). No Silver Bullet Essence and Accidents of Software Engineering. *Computer, 20*(4), 10–19. doi:10.1109/MC.1987.1663532

Buche, C., Querrec, R., De Loor, P., & Chevaillier, P. (2003). MASCARET: A Pedagogical Multi-Agent System for Virtual Environments for Training. In *Cyberworlds, 2003. proceedings. 2003 international conference on* (pp. 423–430). doi:10.1109/CYBER.2003.1253485

Cardelli, L. (1996). Bad Engineering Properties of Object-oriented Languages. *ACM Computing Surveys, 28*(4es). doi:10.1145/242224.242415

Cardino, G., Baruchelli, F., & Valerio, A. (1997, September). The Evaluation of Framework Reusability. *ACM SIGAPP Applied Computing Review, 5*(2), 21–27. doi:10.1145/297075. 297085

Carlsson, C. & Hagsand, O. (1993). DIVE A multi-user virtual reality system. In *Virtual Reality Annual International Symposium* (pp. 394–400). IEEE. doi:10.1109/VRAIS.1993.380753

Cavazza, M., Hartley, S., Lugrin, J.-L., & Le Bras, M. (2004). Qualitative Physics in Virtual Environments. In *Proceedings of the 9th International Conference on Intelligent User Interfaces* (pp. 54–61). IUI '04. ACM. doi:10.1145/964442.964454

Cavazza, M. & Palmer, I. (2000). High-level interpretation in virtual environments. *Applied Artificial Intelligence, 14*(1), 125–144. doi:10.1080/088395100117188

Cerny, M. (2012). Planning4J - Java API for AI planning. Retrieved April 7, 2015, from http://code.google.com/p/planning4j

Cheng, B. H. & Jeng, J.-J. (1997). Reusing analogous components. *IEEE Transactions on Knowledge and Data Engineering, 9*(2), 341–349. doi:http://doi.ieeecomputersociety.org/10.1109/69.591458

Chevaillier, P., Trinh, T.-H., Barange, M., De Loor, P., Devillers, F., Soler, J., & Querrec, R. (2012). Semantic Modeling of Virtual Environments using MASCARET. In *Workshop on Software Engineering and Architectures for Realtime Interactive Systems* (pp. 1–8). IEEE. doi:10.1109/SEARIS.2012.6231174

Clements, P. C. (2001). From subroutines to subsystems: Component-based software development. In G. T. Heineman & W. T. Council (Eds.), *Component-Based Software Engineering* (Chap. 11, pp. 189–198). Addison-Wesley.

Colburn, T. & Shute, G. (2011). Decoupling as a Fundamental Value of Computer Science. *Minds and Machines, 21*(2), 241–259. doi:10.1007/s11023-011-9233-3

Coninx, K., De Troyer, O., Raymaekers, C., & Kleinermann, F. (2006). VR-DeMo: a tool-supported approach facilitating flexible development of virtual environments using conceptual modelling. *Proceedings of Virtual Concept 2006.*

Council, B. & Heineman, G. T. (2001). Definition of a Software Component and Its Elements. In G. T. Heineman & W. T. Council (Eds.), (Chap. Definition of a Software Component and Its Elements, pp. 5–19). Addison-Wesley Longman Publishing Co., Inc.

Crytek. (2015). Cryengine. Retrieved February 15, 2015, from http://www.cryengine.com

De Troyer, O., Kleinermann, F., Pellens, B., & Bille, W. (2007). Conceptual Modeling for Virtual Reality. In *Tutorials, Posters, Panels and Industrial Contributions at the 26th International Conference on Conceptual Modeling* (Vol. 83, pp. 3–18). ER '07.

Devanbu, P., Brachman, R., Selfridge, P. G., & Ballard, B. W. (1991). LaSSIE: A Knowledge-based Software Information System. *Communications of the ACM, 34*(5), 34–49. doi:10.1145/103167.103172

Devanbu, P. & Jones, M. A. (1997). The Use of Description Logics in KBSE Systems. *ACM Transactions on Software Engineering and Methodology (TOSEM), 6*(2), 141–172. doi:10.1145/248233.248253

Dijkstra, E. W. (1972, October). The Humble Programmer. *Communications of the ACM, 15*(10), 859–866. doi:10.1145/355604.361591

Dijkstra, E. W. (1982). On the Role of Scientific Thought. In *Selected Writings on Computing: A Personal Perspective* (pp. 60–66). Springer New York. doi:10.1007/978-1-4612-5695-3_12

Ducasse, S., Nierstrasz, O., Schärli, N., Wuyts, R., & Black, A. P. (2006). Traits: A Mechanism for Fine-grained Reuse. *ACM Transactions on Programming Languages and Systems (TOPLAS), 28*(2), 331–388. doi:10.1145/1119479.1119483

Dusink, L. & van Katwijk, J. (1995). Reuse Dimensions. *ACM SIGSOFT Software Engineering Notes, 20*(SI), 137–149. doi:10.1145/223427.211828

Eckstein, B. (2014). *A Semantic Representation of Physical Objects and Processes in VR* (Master's thesis, Universität Würzburg).

Ecma International. (2013). *The JSON Data Interchange Format*. ECMA-404 (ECMA). 2013. Retrieved April 20, 2015, from http://www.ecma-international.org/publications/files/ECMA-ST/ECMA-404.pdf

Epic Games. (2015). Unreal Engine 4. Retrieved February 15, 2015, from https://www.unrealengine.com/

Ezran, M., Morisio, M., & Tully, C. (2002). *Practical Software Reuse*. Springer. doi:10.1007/978-1-4471-0141-3

Fayad, M. & Schmidt, D. C. (1997). Object-oriented Application Frameworks. *Communications of the ACM, 40*(10), 32–38. doi:10.1145/262793.262798

Ferrario, R., Guarino, N., Janiesch, C., Kiemes, T., Oberle, D., & Probst, F. (2011). Towards an Ontological Foundation of Services Science: The General Service Model. In *Wirtschaftsinformatik proceedings*.

Fichman, R. G. & Kemerer, C. F. (2001). Incentive compatibility and systematic software reuse. *Journal of Systems and Software, 57*(1), 45–60. doi:10.1016/S0164-1212(00)00116-3

Fikes, R. E. & Nilsson, N. J. (1971). STRIPS: A New Approach to the Application of Theorem Proving to Problem Solving. In *Proceedings of the 2nd International Joint Conference on Artificial Intelligence* (pp. 608–620). IJCAI'71. doi:10.1016/0004-3702(71)90010-5

Fischbach, M., Latoschik, M. E., Bruder, G., & Steinicke, F. (2012). smARTbox: Out-of-the-Box Technologies for Interactive Art and Exhibition. In *Proceedings of the 2012 Virtual Reality International Conference* (19, 19:1–19:7). VRIC '12. ACM. doi:10.1145/2331714.2331737

Fischbach, M., Neff, M., Pelzer, I., Lugrin, J.-L., & Latoschik, M. E. (2013). Input Device Adequacy for Multimodal and Bimanual Object Manipulation in Virtual Environments. In F. S. Marc Erich Latoschik Oliver Staadt (Ed.), *Virtuelle und Erweiterte Realität, 10. Workshop der GI-Fachgruppe VR/AR* (pp. 145–156). Informatik. Shaker Verlag.

Fischbach, M., Treffs, C., Cyborra, D., Strehler, A., Wedler, T., Bruder, G., … Steinicke, F. (2012). A Mixed Reality Space for Tangible User Interaction. In T. V. Christian Geiger Jens Herder (Ed.), *Virtuelle und Erweiterte Realität - 9. Workshop der GI-Fachgruppe VR/AR* (pp. 25–36). Shaker Verlag.

Fischbach, M., Wiebusch, D., Giebler-Schubert, A., Latoschik, M. E., Rehfeld, S., & Tramberend, H. (2011). SiXton's curse - Simulator X demonstration. In *2011 IEEE Virtual Reality Conference* (pp. 255–256). doi:10.1109/VR.2011.5759495

Fischbach, M., Wiebusch, D., Latoschik, M. E., Bruder, G., & Steinicke, F. (2012a). Blending Real and Virtual Worlds Using Self-reflection and Fiducials. In M. Herrlich, R. Malaka, & M. Masuch (Eds.), *Entertainment Computing - ICEC 2012: 11th International Conference, ICEC 2012, Bremen, Germany, September 26-29, 2012. Proceedings* (pp. 465–468). Springer. doi:10.1007/978-3-642-33542-6_54

Fischbach, M., Wiebusch, D., Latoschik, M. E., Bruder, G., & Steinicke, F. (2012b). smARTbox A Portable Setup for Intelligent Interactive Applications. In O. D. Harald Reiterer (Ed.), *Mensch & Computer* (pp. 521–524). Oldenbourg Verlag.

Fischbach, M., Zimmerer, C., Giebler-Schubert, A., & Latoschik, M. E. (2014). [DEMO] Exploring multimodal interaction techniques for a mixed reality digital surface. In *IEEE International Symposium on Mixed and Augmented Reality ISMAR* (pp. 335–336). doi:10.1109/ISMAR.2014.6948476

Frakes, W. B. & Fox, C. J. (1996). Quality improvement using a software reuse failure modes model. *IEEE Transactions on Software Engineering, 22*(4), 274–279. doi:10.1109/32.491652

Frakes, W. B. & Gandel, P. B. (1990). Representing reusable software. *Information and Software Technology, 32*(10), 653–664. doi:10.1016/0950-5849(90)90098-C

Frakes, W. B. & Kang, K. (2005). Software reuse research: status and future. *IEEE transactions on Software Engineering, 31*(7), 529–536. doi:10.1109/TSE.2005.85

Frakes, W. B. & Terry, C. (1996). Software Reuse: Metrics and Models. *ACM Computing Surveys (CSUR), 28*(2), 415–435. doi:10.1145/234528.234531

Frankel, D., Hayes, P., Kendall, E., & McGuinness, D. (2004). The model driven semantic web. In *1st International Workshop on the Model-Driven Semantic Web (MDSW2004)*.

Frécon, E. (2004). *DIVE on the Internet* (Doctoral dissertation, University of Göteborg).

Fröhlich, C. (2014). *Semantische Modellierung virtueller Umgebungen auf Basis einer modularen Simulationsarchitektur* (Doctoral dissertation, Bielefeld University).

Fröhlich, C. & Latoschik, M. E. (2008). Incorporating the Actor Model into SCIVE on an Abstract Semantic Level. In *IEEE VR Workshop on Software Engineering and Architectures for Realtime Interactive Systems* (pp. 61–64).

Gamma, E., Helm, R., Johnson, R., & Vlissides, J. (1994). *Design Patterns: Elements of Reusable Object-Oriented Software*. Addison-Wesley.

Garlan, D., Allen, R., & Ockerbloom, J. (1995). Architectural Mismatch or Why It's Hard to Build Systems out of Existing Parts. In *Proceedings of the 17th International Conference on Software Engineering* (pp. 179–185). ICSE '95. doi:10.1145/225014.225031

Geiger, C., Paelke, V., Reimann, C., & Rosenbach, W. (2000). A Framework for the Structured Design of VR/AR Content. In *Proceedings of the ACM Symposium on Virtual Reality Software and Technology* (pp. 75–82). VRST '00. ACM. doi:10.1145/502390.502405

Giebler-Schubert, A., Zimmerer, C., Wedler, T., Fischbach, M., & Latoschik, M. E. (2013). Ein digitales Tabletop-Rollenspiel für Mixed-Reality-Interaktionstechniken. In F. S. Marc Erich Latoschik Oliver Staadt (Ed.), *Virtuelle und Erweiterte Realität, 10. Workshop der GI-Fachgruppe VR/AR* (pp. 181–184). Shaker Verlag.

Griss, M. L. (1993). Software Reuse: From Library to Factory. *IBM Systems Journal, 32*(4), 548–566. doi:10.1147/sj.324.0548

Gruber, T. R. (1993). A translation approach to portable ontology specifications. *Knowledge Acquisition, 5*(2), 199–220. doi:http://dx.doi.org/10.1006/knac.1993.1008

Gui, G. & Scott, P. D. (2006). Coupling and Cohesion Measures for Evaluation of Component Reusability. In *Proceedings of the 2006 International Workshop on Mining Software Repositories* (pp. 18–21). MSR '06. ACM. doi:10.1145/1137983.1137989

Gutierrez, M., Vexo, F., & Thalmann, D. (2005). Semantics-based representation of virtual environments. *International Journal of Computer Applications in Technology, 23*(2-4), 229–238. doi:10.1504/IJCAT.2005.006484

Haefliger, S., Von Krogh, G., & Spaeth, S. (2008). Code Reuse in Open Source Software. *Management Science, 54*(1), 180–193. doi:10.1287/mnsc.1070.0748

Happel, H.-J., Korthaus, A., Seedorf, S., & Tomczyk, P. (2006). KOntoR: An Ontology-enabled Approach to Software Reuse. In *Proceedings of the 18th International Conference on Software Engineering And Knowledge Engineering* (pp. 349–354).

Happel, H.-J. & Seedorf, S. (2006). Applications of Ontologies in Software Engineering. In *Proceedings of the Workshop on Sematic Web Enabled Software Engineering on the ISWC* (pp. 5–9).

Harnad, S. (1990). The symbol grounding problem. *Physica D: Nonlinear Phenomena, 42*(1), 335–346. doi:10.1016/0167-2789(90)90087-6

Heinemann, L., Deissenboeck, F., Gleirscher, M., Hummel, B., & Irlbeck, M. (2011). On the Extent and Nature of Software Reuse in Open Source Java Projects. In K. Schmid (Ed.), *Top Productivity through Software Reuse: 12th International Conference on Software Reuse, ICSR 2011, Pohang, South Korea, June 13-17, 2011. Proceedings* (pp. 207–222). Springer. doi:10.1007/978-3-642-21347-2_16

Hendler, J. (2007). Where Are All the Intelligent Agents? *IEEE Intelligent Systems, 22*(3), 2–3. doi:10.1109/MIS.2007.62

Henning, M. (2006). The Rise and Fall of CORBA. *Queue, 4*(5), 28–34. doi:10.1145/1142031.1142044

Heumer, G., Schilling, M., & Latoschik, M. E. (2005). Automatic data exchange and synchronization for knowledge-based intelligent virtual environments. In *Virtual Reality Conference* (pp. 43–50). IEEE. doi:10.1109/VR.2005.1492752

Hewitt, C., Bishop, P., & Steiger, R. (1973). A Universal Modular ACTOR Formalism for Artificial Intelligence. In *Proceedings of the 3rd International Joint Conference on Artificial Intelligence* (pp. 235–245).

Hiebert, G. (2005). OpenAL 1.1 Specification and Reference. Retrieved April 30, 2015, from http://www.openal.org/documentation/openal-1.1-specification.pdf

Horridge, M. & Bechhofer, S. (2009). The OWL API: A Java API for Working with OWL 2 Ontologies. In *Proceedings of the 6th International Conference on OWL: Experiences and Directions - Volume 529* (pp. 49–58). OWLED'09. CEUR-WS.org.

Hristov, D., Hummel, O., Huq, M., & Janjic, W. (2012). Structuring Software Reusability Metrics for Component-Based Software Development. In *ICSEA 2012, The Seventh International Conference on Software Engineering Advances* (pp. 421–429).

Huhns, M. N. & Singh, M. P. (1997). Ontologies for agents. *IEEE Internet Computing, 1*(6), 81–83. doi:10.1109/4236.643942

ISO/IEC 25010. (2011). *Systems and Software Engineering – Systems and Software Quality Requirements and Evaluation (SQuaRE) – System and Software Quality models*. ISO/IEC 25010:2011 (ISO). 2011.

ISO/IEC 9126. (2001). *Software Engineering – Product Quality*. ISO/IEC 9126-1:2001 (ISO). 2001.

ISO/IEC/IEEE 24765. (2010). *Systems and Software Engineering – Vocabulary*. ISO/IEC/IEEE 24765:2010 (ISO). 2010.

Juarez, A., Schonenberg, W., & Bartneck, C. (2010). Implementing a low-cost CAVE system using the CryEngine2. *Entertainment Computing, 1*(3), 157–164. doi:10.1016/j.entcom.2010.10.001

Kallmann, M. (2001). *Object Interaction in Real-Time Virtual Environments* (Doctoral dissertation, École Polytechnique Fédérale de Lausanne).

Kalogerakis, E., Christodoulakis, S., & Moumoutzis, N. (2006). Coupling Ontologies with Graphics Content for Knowledge Driven Visualization. In *IEEE Virtual Reality Conference* (pp. 43–50). VR 2006. IEEE. doi:10.1109/VR.2006.41

Kapahnke, P., Liedtke, P., Nesbigall, S., Warwas, S., & Klusch, M. (2010). ISReal: An Open Platform for Semantic-Based 3D Simulations in the 3D Internet. In P. F. Patel-Schneider, Y. Pan, P. Hitzler, P. Mika, L. Zhang, J. Z. Pan, …B. Glimm (Eds.), *The Semantic Web – ISWC 2010: 9th International Semantic Web Conference, ISWC 2010, Shanghai, China, November 7-11, 2010, Revised Selected Papers, Part II* (pp. 161–176). Springer. doi:10.1007/978-3-642-17749-1_11

Kapolka, A., McGregor, D., & Capps, M. (2002). A Unified Component Framework for Dynamically Extensible Virtual Environments. In *Proceedings of the 4th International Conference on Collaborative Virtual Environments* (pp. 64–71). CVE '02. doi:10.1145/571878.571889

Kay, A. (2003, October). Turing Award Lecture. In *ACM Turing award lectures*. ACM. doi:10.1145/1283920.1961918

Kiczales, G., Hugunin, J., Hilsdale, E., Kersten, M., Palm, J., Lopes, C., … Isberg, W. (2003). *Aspect Oriented Programming*. Palo Alto Research Center.

Kim, Y. & Stohr, E. A. (1998). Software Reuse: Survey and Research Directions. *Journal of Management Information Systems, 14*(4), 113–147. doi:10.1080/07421222.1998.11518188

Kleinermann, F., De Troyer, O., Creelle, C., & Pellens, B. (2008). Adding Semantic Annotations, Navigation Paths and Tour Guides to Existing Virtual Environments. In T. G. Wyeld, S. Kenderdine, & M. Docherty (Eds.), *Virtual Systems and Multimedia* (pp. 100–111). Springer. doi:10.1007/978-3-540-78566-8_9

Kleinermann, F., De Troyer, O., Mansouri, H., Romero, R., Pellens, B., & Bille, W. (2005). Designing Semantic Virtual Reality Applications. In *Proceedings of the 2nd INTUITION International Workshop* (pp. 5–10).

Klusch, M., Gerber, A., & Schmidt, M. (2005). Semantic Web Service Composition Planning with OWLS-Xplan. In *AAAI Fall Symposium on Semantic Web and Agents*.

Ko, A. J., Abraham, R., Beckwith, L., Blackwell, A., Burnett, M., Erwig, M., … Wiedenbeck, S. (2011). The State of the Art in End-user Software Engineering. *ACM Computing Surveys (CSUR), 43*(3), 21:1–21:44. doi:10.1145/1922649.1922658

Krötzsch, M. (2012). OWL 2 Profiles: An Introduction to Lightweight Ontology Languages. In T. Eiter & T. Krennwallner (Eds.), *Reasoning Web. Semantic Technologies for Advanced Query Answering: 8th International Summer School 2012, Vienna, Austria, September 3-8, 2012. Proceedings* (pp. 112–183). Springer. doi:10.1007/978-3-642-33158-9_4

Krueger, C. W. (1992). Software reuse. *ACM Computing Surveys (CSUR), 24*(2), 131–183. doi:10.1145/130844.130856

Kuck, R., Wind, J., Riege, K., & Bogen, M. (2008). Improving the Avango VR/AR Framework: Lessons Learned. In *Virtuelle und Erweiterte Realität: 5. Workshop der GI-Fachgruppe VR/AR* (pp. 209–220). Shaker Verlag.

Lamport, L. (1978, July). Time, Clocks, and the Ordering of Events in a Distributed System. *Communications of the ACM, 21*(7), 558–565. doi:10.1145/359545.359563

Latoschik, M. E. (2005). A User Interface Framework for Multimodal VR Interactions. In *Proceedings of the 7th international conference on Multimodal interfaces* (pp. 76–83). ICMI '05. ACM. doi:10.1145/1088463.1088479

Latoschik, M. E. (2015). engineering Real-Time Interactive Systems. Tutorial on IEEE VR 2015 conference. Retrieved April 16, 2015, from https://www.hci.uni-wuerzburg.de/eris/01-real-time-interactive-systems-150325-handout.pdf

Latoschik, M. E., Biermann, P., & Wachsmuth, I. (2005). Knowledge in the Loop: Semantics Representation for Multimodal Simulative Environments. In A. Butz, B. Fisher, A. Krüger, & P. Olivier (Eds.), *Smart Graphics: 5th International Symposium, SG 2005, Frauenwörth Cloister, Germany, August 22-24, 2005. Proceedings* (pp. 25–39). Springer. doi:10.1007/11536482_3

Latoschik, M. E. & Fischbach, M. (2014). Engineering Variance: Software Techniques for Scalable, Customizable, and Reusable Multimodal Processing. In M. Kurosu (Ed.), *Human-Computer Interaction. Theories, Methods, and Tools: 16th International Conference, HCI International 2014, Heraklion, Crete, Greece, June 22-27, 2014, Proceedings, Part I* (pp. 308–319). Springer. doi:10.1007/978-3-319-07233-3_29

Latoschik, M. E. & Fröhlich, C. (2007a). Semantic Reflection for Intelligent Virtual Environments. In *2007 IEEE Virtual Reality Conference* (pp. 305–306). doi:10.1109/VR.2007.352514

Latoschik, M. E. & Fröhlich, C. (2007b). Towards Intelligent VR: Multi-Layered Semantic Reflection for Intelligent Virtual Environments. In *Proceedings of the International Conference on Computer Graphics Theory and Applications* (pp. 249–259). doi:10.5220/0002081302490259

Latoschik, M. E., Fröhlich, C., & Wendler, A. (2006). Scene Synchronization in Close Coupled World Representations Using SCIVE. *International Journal of Virtual Reality, 5*(3), 47–52.

Latoschik, M. E. & Schilling, M. (2003). Incorporating VR databases into AI knowledge representations: A framework for intelligent graphics applications. In *Proceedings of the Sixth IASTED International Conference on Computer Graphics and Imaging* (pp. 79–84).

Latoschik, M. E. & Tramberend, H. (2010). Engineering Realtime Interactive Systems: Coupling & Cohesion of Architecture Mechanisms. In *Proceedings of the 16th Eurographics Conference on Virtual Environments & Second Joint Virtual Reality* (pp. 25–28). EGVE - JVRC'10. Eurographics Association. doi:10.2312/EGVE/JVRC10/025-028

Latoschik, M. E. & Tramberend, H. (2011). Simulator X: A Scalable and Concurrent Architecture for Intelligent Realtime Interactive Systems. In *2011 IEEE Virtual Reality Conference* (pp. 171–174). doi:10.1109/VR.2011.5759457

Leach, R. J. (2012). *Software Reuse: Methods, Models, Costs.* AfterMath.

Lee, E. A. (2006). The Problem with Threads. *Computer, 39*(5), 33–42. doi:10.1109/MC.2006.180

Lenat, D. B., Guha, R. V., Pittman, K., Pratt, D., & Shepherd, M. (1990). Cyc: Toward Programs with Common Sense. *Communications of the ACM, 33*(8), 30–49. doi:10.1145/79173.79176

Lewis, M. & Jacobson, J. (2002). Game Engines in Scientific Research. *Communications of the ACM, 45*(1), 27–31. doi:10.1145/502269.502288

Limet, S., Robert, S., & Turki, A. (2009). FlowVR-SciViz: A Component-Based Framework for Interactive Scientific Visualization. In *Proceedings of the 2009 Workshop on Component-Based High Performance Computing* (17, 17:1–17:9). CBHPC '09. ACM. doi:10.1145/1687774.1687791

Luck, M. & Aylett, R. (2000). Applying Artificial Intelligence to Virtual Reality: Intelligent Virtual Environments. *Applied Artificial Intelligence, 14*(1), 3–32. doi:10.1080/088395100117142

Lugrin, J.-L. & Cavazza, M. (2007). Making Sense of Virtual Environments: Action Representation, Grounding and Common Sense. In *Proceedings of the 12th International Conference on Intelligent User Interfaces* (pp. 225–234). IUI '07. ACM. doi:10.1145/1216295.1216336

Lugrin, J.-L., Charles, F., Cavazza, M., Le Renard, M., Freeman, J., & Lessiter, J. (2012). CaveUDK: A VR Game Engine Middleware. In *Proceedings of the 18th ACM symposium on Virtual Reality Software and Technology* (pp. 137–144). VRST '12. ACM. doi:10.1145/2407336.2407363

Lugrin, J.-L., Wiebusch, D., Latoschik, M. E., & Strehler, A. (2013). Usability Benchmarks for Motion Tracking Systems. In *Proceedings of the 19th ACM Symposium on Virtual Reality Software and Technology* (pp. 49–58). VRST '13. ACM. doi:10.1145/2503713.2503730

Manhas, S., Vashisht, R., Sandhu, P. S., & Neeru, N. (2010). Reusability Evaluation Model for Procedure Based Software Systems. *International Journal of Computer and Electrical Engineering, 2*(6), 1107–1111.

Mannuß, F., Hinkenjann, A., & Maiero, J. (2008). From Scene Graph Centered to Entity Centered Virtual Environments. In M. E. Latoschik, D. Reiners, R. Blach, P. Figueroa, & R. Dachselt (Eds.), *IEEE VR 2008 Workshop on Software Engineering and Architectures for Realtime Interactive Systems* (pp. 37–40). Shaker Verlag.

Manola, F. & Miller, E. (2004). *RDF primer.* World Wide Web Consortium. Retrieved December 15, 2014, from http://www.w3.org/TR/rdf-primer/

Martin, D., Burstein, M., Hobbs, J., Lassila, O., McDermott, D., McIlraith, S., … Payne, T. (2004). OWL-S: Semantic markup for web services. W3C member submission. Retrieved April 30, 2015, from http://www.w3.org/Submission/OWL-S/

Maslow, A. H. (2004). *The Psychology of Science: A Reconnaissance.* (p. 15). Maurice Bassett.

Matuszek, C., Cabral, J., Witbrock, M. J., & DeOliveira, J. (2006). An Introduction to the Syntax and Content of Cyc. In *AAAI Spring Symposium: Formalizing and Compiling Background Knowledge and Its Applications to Knowledge Representation and Question Answering* (Technical Report SS-06-05, pp. 44–49).

McCain, R. (1985). Reusable Software Component Construction: A Product-Oriented Paradigm. In *5th computers in aerospace conference* (pp. 125–135). American Institute of Aeronautics and Astronautics. doi:10.2514/6.1985-5068

McDermott, D. & Dou, D. (2002). Representing Disjunction and Quantifiers in RDF. In I. Horrocks & J. Hendler (Eds.), *The Semantic Web — ISWC 2002: First International Semantic Web Conference Sardinia, Italy, June 9–12, 2002 Proceedings* (pp. 250–263). Springer. doi:10.1007/3-540-48005-6_20

McDermott, D., Ghallab, M., Howe, A., Knoblock, C., Ram, A., Veloso, M., … Wilkins, D. (1998). *PDDL—The Planning Domain Definition Language* (tech. rep. No. CVC TR-98-003/DCS TR-1165). Yale Center for Computational Vision and Control.

McIlroy, M. D. (1968). Mass-Produced Software Components. In P. Naur & B. Randell (Eds.), *Software Engineering: Report on a Conference sponsored by the NATO Science Committee, Garmisch, Germany, 7th to 11th October 1968* (pp. 79–85). Scientific Affairs Division, NATO.

Metral, C., Falquet, G., & Cutting-Decelle, A. F. (2009). Towards Semantically Enriched 3D City Models: An Ontology-based Approach. *Academic Track of GeoWeb 2009 - Cityscapes, International Archives of Photogrammetry, Remote Sensing and Spatial Information Sciences (ISPRS), XXXVIII-3-4/C3).*

Meyer, B. (1987). Reusability: The Case for Object-Oriented Design. *IEEE Software, 4*(2), 50–64. doi:10.1109/MS.1987.230097

Mili, A., Mili, R., & Mittermeir, R. T. (1998). A Survey of Software Reuse Libraries. *Annals of Software Engineering, 5*(1), 349–414.

Mili, H., Mili, F., & Mili, A. (1995). Reusing Software: Issues and Research Directions. *IEEE Transactions on Software Engineering, 21*(6), 528–562. doi:10.1109/32.391379

Mohagheghi, P. & Conradi, R. (2007). Quality, Productivity and Economic Benefits of Software Reuse: A Review of Industrial Studies. *Empirical Software Engineering, 12*(5), 471–516. doi:10.1007/s10664-007-9040-x

Morisio, M., Ezran, M., & Tully, C. (2002). Success and failure factors in software reuse. *IEEE Transactions on Software Engineering, 28*(4), 340–357. doi:10.1109/TSE.2002.995420

Motik, B., Grau, B. C., Horrocks, I., Wu, Z., Fokoue, A., & Lutz, C. (2012). *OWL 2 Web Ontology Language: Profiles* (W3C Recommendation No. REC-owl2-profiles-20121211). W3C. Retrieved April 30, 2015, from http://www.w3.org/TR/owl2-profiles/

Naumann, A. & Hurtienne, J. (2010). Benchmarks for Intuitive Interaction with Mobile Devices. In *Proceedings of the 12th International Conference on Human Computer Interaction with Mobile Devices and Services* (pp. 401–402). MobileHCI '10. ACM. doi:10.1145/1851600.1851685

Neches, R., Fikes, R. E., Finin, T., Gruber, T., Patil, R., Senator, T., & Swartout, W. R. (1991). Enabling technology for knowledge sharing. *AI magazine, 12*(3), 36–56. doi:10.1609/aimag.v12i3.902

Nesbigall, S., Warwas, S., Kapahnke, P., Schubotz, R., Klusch, M., Fischer, K., & Slusallek, P. (2011). ISReal: a platform for intelligent simulated realities. In J. Filipe, A. Fred, & B. Sharp (Eds.), *Agents and Artificial Intelligence: Second International Conference, ICAART 2010, Valencia, Spain, January 22-24, 2010. Revised Selected Papers* (pp. 201–213). Springer. doi:10.1007/978-3-642-19890-8_15

Nickel, U., Niere, J., & Zündorf, A. (2000). The FUJABA Environment. In *Proceedings of the 22nd international conference on Software engineering* (pp. 742–745). ICSE '00. ACM. doi:10.1145/337180.337620

Nierstrasz, O., Gibbs, S., & Tsichritzis, D. (1992). Component-oriented Software Development. *Communications of the ACM, 35*(9), 160–165. doi:10.1145/130994.131005

Nii, H. (1986). The Blackboard Model of Problem Solving and the Evolution of Blackboard Architectures. *AI Magazine, 7*(2), 38–53. doi:10.1609/aimag.v7i2.537

Oberle, D. (2014). Ontologies and Reasoning in Enterprise Service Ecosystems. *Informatik-Spektrum, 37*(4), 318–328. doi:10.1007/s00287-014-0785-5

Oberle, D., Lamparter, S., Grimm, S., Vrandečić, D., Staab, S., & Gangemi, A. (2006). Towards Ontologies for Formalizing Modularization and Communication in Large Software Systems. *Applied Ontology, 1*(2), 163–202.

Object Management Group. (2013). *MOF Support for Semantic Structures.* formal/2013-04-02 (OMG). 2013. Retrieved April 20, 2015, from http://www.omg.org/spec/SMOF/1.0/

Odersky, M., Altherr, P., Cremet, V., Emir, B., Maneth, S., Micheloud, S., ... Zenger, M. (2006). *An Overview of the Scala Programming Language* (LAMP-REPORT No. 2006-001). École Polytechnique Fédérale de Lausanne (EPFL).

Orkin, J. (2004). Symbolic Representation of Game World State: Toward Real-Time Planning in Games. In *Proceedings of the AAAI Workshop on Challenges in Game Artificial Intelligence* (Vol. 5).

Otto, K. A. (2005a). Semantic Virtual Environments. In *Special Interest Tracks and Posters of the 14th International Conference on World Wide Web* (pp. 1036–1037). WWW '05. ACM. doi:10.1145/1062745.1062856

Otto, K. A. (2005b). Towards Semantic Virtual Environments. In *Workshop Towards Semantic Virtual Environments (SVE'05)* (pp. 47–56).

Parnas, D. L. (1972). On the Criteria to Be Used in Decomposing Systems into Modules. *Communications of the ACM, 15*(12), 1053–1058. doi:10.1145/361598.361623

Pellens, B. (2007). *A Conceptual Modelling Approach for Behaviour in Virtual Environments Using a Graphical Notation and Generative Design Patterns* (Doctoral dissertation, Vrije Universiteit Brussel, Brussels, Belgium).

Peters, S. & Shrobe, H. E. (2003). Using Semantic Networks for Knowledge Representation in an Intelligent Environment. In *Proceedings of the First IEEE International Conference on Pervasive Computing and Communications* (pp. 323–329). PerCom '03. doi:10.1109/PERCOM.2003.1192756

Ponder, M. (2004). *Component-Based Methodology and Development Framework for Virtual and Augmented Reality Systems* (Doctoral dissertation, EPFL, Lausanne). doi:10.5075/epfl-thesis-3046

Ponder, M., Papagiannakis, G., Molet, T., Magnenat-Thalmann, N., & Thalmann, D. (2003). VHD++ Development Framework: Towards extendible, component based VR/AR simulation engine featuring advanced virtual character technologies. In *Computer Graphics International* (pp. 96–104). doi:10.1109/CGI.2003.1214453

Potok, T. E., Vouk, M., & Rindos, A. (1999). Productivity analysis of object-oriented software developed in a commercial environment. *Software: Practice and Experience, 29*(10), 833–848. doi:10.1002/(SICI)1097-024X(199908)29:10<833::AID-SPE258>3.0.CO;2-P

Prieto-Díaz, R. (1989). Software Reusability: Vol. 1, Concepts and Models. In T. J. Biggerstaff & A. J. Perlis (Eds.), (Chap. Classification of Reusable Modules, pp. 99–123). ACM. doi:10.1145/73103.73107

Prieto-Díaz, R. (1993). Status Report: Software Reusability. *IEEE Software, 10*(3), 61–66. doi:10.1109/52.210605

Radatz, J., Geraci, A., & Katki, F. (1990). IEEE standard glossary of software engineering terminology. *IEEE Std, 610121990*, 121990.

Ravichandran, T. & Rothenberger, M. A. (2003). Software Reuse Strategies and Component Markets. *Communications of the ACM, 46*(8), 109–114. doi:10.1145/859670.859678

Bibliography

Rehfeld, S., Tramberend, H., & Latoschik, M. E. (2013). An actor-based distribution model for Realtime Interactive Systems. In *2013 6th Workshop on Software Engineering and Architectures for Realtime Interactive Systems (SEARIS)* (pp. 9–16). doi:10.1109/SEARIS. 2013.6798103

Rehfeld, S., Tramberend, H., & Latoschik, M. E. (2014). Profiling and Benchmarking Event- and Message-passing-based Asynchronous Realtime Interactive Systems. In *Proceedings of the 20th ACM Symposium on Virtual Reality Software and Technology* (pp. 151–159). VRST '14. ACM. doi:10.1145/2671015.2671031

Riaz, M., Mendes, E., & Tempero, E. (2009). A Systematic Review of Software Maintainability Prediction and Metrics. In *Proceedings of the 2009 3rd International Symposium on Empirical Software Engineering and Measurement* (pp. 367–377). ESEM '09. IEEE Computer Society. doi:10.1109/ESEM.2009.5314233

Rich, C. & Feldman, Y. A. (1992, June). Seven Layers of Knowledge Representation and Reasoning in Support of Software Development. *IEEE Transactions on Software Engineering*, 18(6), 451–469. doi:10.1109/32.142869

Roßbach, M. (2010). *Die jVR Graphics Engine* (Master's thesis, Beuth Hochschule für Technik Berlin).

Rugaber, S. (2000). The use of domain knowledge in program understanding. *Annals of Software Engineering*, 9(1-2), 143–192. doi:10.1023/A:1018976708691

Russell, S. & Norvig, P. (2010). *Artificial Intelligence: A Modern Approach*. Prentice Hall Series in Artificial Intelligence. Prentice Hall.

Salisbury, J. o. (1159). *The metalogicon*.

Sametinger, J. (1997). *Software Engineering with Reusable Components*. Springer Berlin Heidelberg. doi:10.1007/978-3-662-03345-6

Shaw, C., Green, M., Liang, J., & Sun, Y. (1993). Decoupled Simulation in Virtual Reality with the MR Toolkit. *ACM Transactions on Information Systems (TOIS)*, 11(3), 287–317. doi:10.1145/159161.173948

Shaw, C., Liang, J., Green, M., & Sun, Y. (1992). The Decoupled Simulation Model for Virtual Reality Systems. In *Proceedings of the SIGCHI Conference on Human Factors in Computing Systems* (pp. 321–328). CHI '92. ACM. doi:10.1145/142750.142824

Shaw, M. (1995). Architectural Issues in Software Reuse: It's Not Just the Functionality, It's the Packaging. In *Proceedings of the 1995 Symposium on Software Reusability* (pp. 3–6). SSR '95. ACM. doi:10.1145/211782.211783

Shearer, R., Motik, B., & Horrocks, I. (2008). HermiT: A Highly-Efficient OWL Reasoner. In A. Ruttenberg, U. Sattler, & C. Dolbear (Eds.), *Proceedings of the 5th International Workshop on OWL: Experiences and Directions (OWLED 2008 EU)*.

Sherif, K. & Vinze, A. (2003). Barriers to Adoption of Software Reuse: A Qualitative Study. *Information & Management*, 41(2), 159–175. doi:10.1016/S0378-7206(03)00045-4

Sindre, G., Conradi, R., & Karlsson, E.-A. (1995). The REBOOT Approach To Software Reuse. *Journal of Systems and Software*, 30(3), 201–212. doi:10.1016/0164-1212(94)00134-9

Sirin, E., Parsia, B., Grau, B. C., Kalyanpur, A., & Katz, Y. (2007). Pellet: A Practical OWL-DL Reasoner. *Web Semantics: science, services and agents on the World Wide Web*, 5(2), 51–53. doi:10.1016/j.websem.2007.03.004

Soto, M. & Allongue, S. (2002). Modeling Methods for Reusable and Interoperable Virtual Entities in Multimedia Virtual Worlds. *Multimedia Tools and Applications, 16*(1), 161–177. doi:10.1023/A:1013249920338

Sowa, J. F. (2000). Ontology, metadata, and semiotics. In B. Ganter & G. W. Mineau (Eds.), *Conceptual Structures: Logical, Linguistic, and Computational Issues: 8th International Conference on Conceptual Structures, ICCS 2000, Darmstadt, Germany, August 14-18, 2000. Proceedings* (pp. 55–81). Springer. doi:10.1007/10722280_5

Sporny, M., Longley, D., Kellogg, G., Lanthaler, M., & Lindström, N. (2013). *JSON-LD 1.0 - A JSON-based Serialization for Linked Data*. W3C. Retrieved April 30, 2015, from http://www.w3.org/TR/json-ld/

Stanford Center for Biomedical Informatics Research. (2015). Protégé. Retrieved March 25, 2015, from http://protege.stanford.edu

Steed, A. (2008). Some Useful Abstractions for Re-Usable Virtual Environment Platforms. In M. E. Latoschik, D. Reiners, R. Blach, P. Figueroa, & R. Dachselt (Eds.), *IEEE VR Workshop on Software Engineering and Architectures for Realtime Interactive Systems* (pp. 33–36). Shaker Verlag.

Sugumaran, V. & Storey, V. C. (2003). A Semantic-based Approach to Component Retrieval. *SIGMIS Database, 34*(3), 8–24. doi:10.1145/937742.937745

Taylor, R. M., Hudson, T. C., Seeger, A., Weber, H., Juliano, J., & Helser, A. T. (2001). VRPN: A Device-independent, Network-transparent VR Peripheral System. In *Proceedings of the ACM Symposium on Virtual Reality Software and Technology* (pp. 55–61). VRST '01. ACM. doi:10.1145/505008.505019

Taylor, R. M., Jerald, J., VanderKnyff, C., Wendt, J., Borland, D., Marshburn, D., … Whitton, M. C. (2010). Lessons about Virtual Environment Software Systems from 20 Years of VE Building. *Presence: Teleoperators and Virtual Environments, 19*(2), 162–178. doi:10.1162/pres.19.2.162

Tobies, S. (2001). *Complexity results and practical algorithms for logics in knowledge representation* (Doctoral dissertation, RWTH Aachen).

Tracz, W. (1988). Software Reuse Myths. *SIGSOFT Software Engineering Notes, 13*(1), 17–21. doi:10.1145/43857.43859

Tracz, W. (1995). Confessions of a Used-program Salesman: Lessons Learned. In *Proceedings of the 1995 Symposium on Software Reusability* (pp. 11–13). SSR '95. ACM. doi:10.1145/211782.211785

Tramberend, H. (1999). Avocado: A Distributed Virtual Reality Framework. In *Virtual Reality, 1999. Proceedings., IEEE* (pp. 14–21). doi:10.1109/VR.1999.756918

Tutenel, T., Bidarra, R., Smelik, R. M., & Kraker, K. J. D. (2008, December). The role of semantics in games and simulations. *Comput. Entertain. 6*(4), 57:1–57:35. doi:10.1145/1461999.1462009

Typesafe Inc. (2015). Akka for Scala. Retrieved April 30, 2015, from http://akka.io

Unity Technologies. (2015). Unity. Retrieved March 15, 2015, from http://www.unity3d.com

Van Vliet, H. (1993). *Software Engineering: Principles and Practice*. John Wiley & Sons, Ltd.

van Hoff, A. (2015). JmDNS. Retrieved April 30, 2015, from http://jmdns.sourceforge.net/

Vinoski, S. (1997). CORBA: Integrating Diverse Applications within Distributed Heterogeneous Environments. *IEEE Communications Magazine, 35*(2), 46–55. doi:10.1109/35.565655

Völkel, M. & Sure, Y. (2005). RDFReactor-From Ontologies to Programmatic Data Access. In *Poster proceedings of the 4th international semantic web conference* (p. 55).

W3C OWL Working Group. (2009). *OWL 2 Web Ontology Language Document Overview* (W3C Recommendation No. REC-owl2-overview-20091027). W3C. Retrieved April 30, 2015, from http://www.w3.org/TR/owl2-overview/

W3C SPARQL Working Group. (2013, March). *SPARQL 1.1 Overview* (W3C Recommendation No. REC-sparql11-overview-20130321). W3C. Retrieved April 30, 2015, from http://www.w3.org/TR/sparql11-overview/

Washizaki, H., Yamamoto, H., & Fukazawa, Y. (2003). A metrics suite for measuring reusability of software components. In *Ninth International Software Metrics Symposium, 2003. Proceedings* (pp. 211–223). IEEE. doi:10.1109/METRIC.2003.1232469

Wiebusch, D., Fischbach, M., Latoschik, M. E., & Tramberend, H. (2012). Evaluating Scala, Actors, & Ontologies for Intelligent Realtime Interactive Systems. In *Proceedings of the 18th ACM symposium on Virtual Reality Software and Technology* (pp. 153–160). VRST '12. ACM. doi:10.1145/2407336.2407365

Wiebusch, D. & Latoschik, M. E. (2012). Enhanced Decoupling of Components in Intelligent Realtime Interactive Systems using Ontologies. In *2012 5th Workshop on Software Engineering and Architectures for Realtime Interactive Systems (SEARIS)* (pp. 43–51). IEEE. doi:10.1109/SEARIS.2012.6231168

Wiebusch, D. & Latoschik, M. E. (2014). A Uniform Semantic-based Access Model for Realtime Interactive Systems. In *2014 IEEE 7th Workshop on Software Engineering and Architectures for Realtime Interactive Systems (SEARIS)* (pp. 51–58). IEEE. doi:10.1109/SEARIS.2014.7152801

Wiebusch, D. & Latoschik, M. E. (2015). Decoupling the Entity-Component-System Pattern using Semantic Traits for Reusable Realtime Interactive Systems. In *2015 IEEE 8th Workshop on Software Engineering and Architectures for Realtime Interactive Systems (SEARIS)*. IEEE.

Wiebusch, D., Latoschik, M. E., & Tramberend, H. (2010). Ein Konfigurierbares World-Interface zur Kopplung von KI-Methoden an Interaktive Echtzeitsysteme. In *Virtuelle und Erweiterte Realität: 7. Workshop der GI-Fachgruppe VR/AR* (pp. 47–58). Shaker Verlag.

Wingrave, C. A. & LaViola, J. J. (2010). Reflecting on the Design and Implementation Issues of Virtual Environments. *Presence: Teleoperators and Virtual Environments, 19*(2), 179–195. doi:10.1162/pres.19.2.179

Wooldridge, M. (2009). *An Introduction to MultiAgent Systems.* John Wiley & Sons Ltd.

Würsch, M., Ghezzi, G., Reif, G., & Gall, H. C. (2010). Supporting Developers with Natural Language Queries. In *Proceedings of the 32nd ACM/IEEE International Conference on Software Engineering - Volume 1* (pp. 165–174). ICSE '10. ACM. doi:10.1145/1806799.1806827

Yao, H. & Etzkorn, L. (2004). Towards a Semantic-based Approach for Software Reusable Component Classification and Retrieval. In *Proceedings of the 42nd Annual Southeast Regional Conference* (pp. 110–115). ACM-SE 42. ACM. doi:10.1145/986537.986564

Ziaka, E., Vrakas, D., & Bassiliades, N. (2011). Translating Web Services Composition Plans to OWL-S Descriptions. In *ICAART 2011 - Proceedings of the 3rd International Conference on Agents and Artificial Intelligence, Volume 1 - Artificial Intelligence* (pp. 167–176).

Zimmerer, C., Fischbach, M., & Latoschik, M. E. (2014). Fusion of Mixed-Reality Tabletop and Location-Based Applications for Pervasive Games. In *Proceedings of the Ninth ACM International Conference on Interactive Tabletops and Surfaces* (pp. 427–430). ITS '14. ACM. doi:10.1145/2669485.2669527

Appendix A

OWL Definitions

Common Elements

Property Representation

```
Declaration(Class(core:DataType))
Declaration(Class(core:SemanticValue))

SubClassOf(core:Entity core:SemanticValue)

Declaration(ObjectProperty(core:hasDataType))
ObjectPropertyDomain(core:hasDataType core:SemanticValue)
ObjectPropertyRange(core:hasDataType core:DataType)

Declaration(DataProperty(core:hasId))
FunctionalDataProperty(core:hasId)

Declaration(DataProperty(core:hasValue))
DataPropertyDomain(core:hasValue core:SemanticValue)
DataPropertyRange(core:hasValue xsd:string)

Declaration(DataProperty(types:hasTypeString))
DataPropertyDomain(core:hasTypeString core:DataType)
DataPropertyRange(core:hasTypeString xsd:string)

Declaration(AnnotationProperty(core:hasAnnotation))
```

Listing A.1: OWL Definitions for Properties

```
Declaration(Class(core:HasPart))
Declaration(Class(core:Relation))

Declaration(ObjectProperty(core:hasPart))

SubClassOf(core:HasPart core:Relation)
SubClassOf(core:Relation core:SemanticValue)

Declaration(ObjectProperty(core:hasObject))
ObjectPropertyDomain(core:hasObject core:Relation)
ObjectPropertyRange(core:hasObject core:SemanticValue)

Declaration(ObjectProperty(core:hasSubject))
ObjectPropertyDomain(core:hasSubject core:Relation)
ObjectPropertyRange(core:hasSubject core:SemanticValue)

Declaration(AnnotationProperty(core:hasPredicate))

AnnotationAssertion(core:hasPredicate core:HasPart core:hasPart)
```

Listing A.2: OWL Definitions for Relations

```
Declaration(Class(core:ValueDescription))

Declaration(ObjectProperty(core:basedOn))
ObjectPropertyDomain(core:basedOn core:ValueDescription)
ObjectPropertyRange(core:basedOn core:ValueDescription)

Declaration(ObjectProperty(core:hasProperty))
ObjectPropertyRange(core:hasProperty core:SemanticValue)

Declaration(ObjectProperty(basicDescriptions:describesProperty))
ObjectPropertyDomain(basicDescriptions:describesProperty
    core:ValueDescription)
ObjectPropertyRange(basicDescriptions:describesProperty core:SemanticValue)

Declaration(ObjectProperty(core:providesProperty))
ObjectPropertyDomain(core:providesProperty core:Aspect)
ObjectPropertyRange(core:providesProperty core:ValueDescription)

Declaration(ObjectProperty(core:requiresProperty))
ObjectPropertyDomain(core:requiresProperty core:Aspect)
ObjectPropertyRange(core:requiresProperty core:ValueDescription)

SubObjectPropertyOf(ObjectPropertyChain(core:providesProperty
    basicDescriptions:describesProperty) core:hasProperty)
SubObjectPropertyOf(ObjectPropertyChain(core:requiresProperty
    basicDescriptions:describesProperty) core:hasProperty)
```

Listing A.3: OWL Definitions for Property Descriptions

Entity Representation

```
Declaration(Class(core:Aspect))
Declaration(Class(core:Entity))
Declaration(Class(basicDescriptions:EntityDescription))

SubClassOf(core:Entity core:SemanticValue)

Declaration(AnnotationProperty(core:overridesProvide))

Declaration(ObjectProperty(core:hasAspect))
ObjectPropertyRange(core:hasAspect core:Aspect)
```

Listing A.4: OWL Definitions for Entity Descriptions

```
Declaration(Class(core:Application))
Declaration(Class(core:Component))
Declaration(Class(core:Event))

Declaration(ObjectProperty(core:usesComponent))

Declaration(ObjectProperty(core:providesEvent))
ObjectPropertyDomain(core:providesEvent core:Component)
ObjectPropertyRange(core:providesEvent core:Event)

Declaration(ObjectProperty(core:requiresAspect))
ObjectPropertyDomain(core:requiresAspect core:Component)
ObjectPropertyRange(core:requiresAspect core:Aspect)

Declaration(ObjectProperty(core:requiresEvent))
ObjectPropertyDomain(core:requiresEvent core:Component)
ObjectPropertyRange(core:requiresEvent core:Event)

Declaration(ObjectProperty(core:supportsAspect))
ObjectPropertyRange(core:supportsAspect core:Aspect)

Declaration(ObjectProperty(core:usesComponent))
ObjectPropertyDomain(core:usesComponent core:Application)
ObjectPropertyRange(core:usesComponent core:Component)

SubObjectPropertyOf(ObjectPropertyChain(core:usesComponent
    core:supportsAspect) core:supportsAspect)
SubObjectPropertyOf(ObjectPropertyChain(core:usesComponent
    core:requiresAspect) core:requiresAspect)
```

Listing A.5: OWL Definitions for Components

Unity Component

```
Prefix(core:=<http://www.hci.uni-wuerzburg.de/ontologies/simx/SimxCoreOntology.owl#>)
Prefix(desc:=<http://www.hci.uni-wuerzburg.de/ontologies/simx/concepts/BasicDescriptions.owl#>)
Prefix(types:=<http://www.hci.uni-wuerzburg.de/ontologies/simx/concepts/BasicTypes.owl#>)
Prefix(unity:=<http://www.hci.uni-wuerzburg.de/ontologies/simx/ components/renderer/Unity/Unity.owl#>)

Ontology(<http://www.hci.uni-wuerzburg.de/ontologies/simx/components/renderer/Unity/Unity.owl>
Import(<http://www.hci.uni-wuerzburg.de/ontologies/simx/components/renderer/SimxRenderer.owl>)

Declaration(Class(unity:Unity))
SubClassOf(unity:Unity types:GraphicsComponent)

Declaration(NamedIndividual(unity:UnityComponent))
ClassAssertion(unity:Unity unity:UnityComponent)
DataPropertyAssertion(core:inPackage unity:UnityComponent "simx.components.renderer.unity")

Declaration(NamedIndividual(unity:Unity_RotationDescription))
ClassAssertion(ObjectSomeValuesFrom(desc:describesProperty types:Rotation) unity:Unity_RotationDescription)
ObjectPropertyAssertion(core:forComponent unity:Unity_RotationDescription unity:UnityComponent)
ObjectPropertyAssertion(core:hasDataType unity:Unity_RotationDescription
    types:simplex3d.math.floatx.ConstQuat4f)

Declaration(NamedIndividual(unity:Unity_ScaleDescription))
ObjectPropertyAssertion(core:basedOn unity:Unity_ScaleDescription desc:SirisCore_ScaleDescription)
ObjectPropertyAssertion(core:forComponent unity:Unity_ScaleDescription unity:UnityComponent)
ObjectPropertyAssertion(core:hasDataType unity:Unity_ScaleDescription types:simplex3d.math.floatx.ConstVec3f)

Declaration(NamedIndividual(unity:Unity_TransformationDescription))
ObjectPropertyAssertion(core:basedOn unity:Unity_TransformationDescription
    desc:SirisCore_TransformationDescription)
ObjectPropertyAssertion(core:forComponent unity:Unity_TransformationDescription unity:UnityComponent)
ObjectPropertyAssertion(core:hasDataType unity:Unity_TransformationDescription
    types:simplex3d.math.floatx.ConstVec3f)

Declaration(NamedIndividual(unity:Unity_UnityAsset))
ClassAssertion(types:ShapeFromFile unity:Unity_UnityAsset)
```

```
ObjectPropertyAssertion(core:forComponent unity:Unity_UnityAsset unity:UnityComponent)
ObjectPropertyAssertion(core:requiresProperty unity:Unity_UnityAsset desc:SirisCore_TransformationDescription)
ObjectPropertyAssertion(desc:hasCreateParameter unity:Unity_UnityAsset desc:SirisCore_ScaleDescription)
ObjectPropertyAssertion(Annotation(core:hasAnnotation types:File) desc:hasCreateParameter
    unity:Unity_UnityAsset desc:SirisCore_StringDescription)

Declaration(NamedIndividual(unity:Unity_UnityExistingNode))
ClassAssertion(renderer:ExistingNode unity:Unity_UnityExistingNode)
ObjectPropertyAssertion(core:forComponent unity:Unity_UnityExistingNode unity:UnityComponent)
ObjectPropertyAssertion(core:requiresProperty unity:Unity_UnityExistingNode
    desc:SirisCore_TransformationDescription)
ObjectPropertyAssertion(Annotation(core:hasAnnotation types:Offset) desc:hasCreateParameter
    unity:Unity_UnityExistingNode desc:SirisCore_TransformationDescription)
ObjectPropertyAssertion(desc:hasCreateParameter unity:Unity_UnityExistingNode desc:SirisCore_NameDescription))
```

Listing A.6: Unity Component OWL Content

Action Representation

```
Declaration(Class(actions:Action))
Declaration(Class(actions:Parameter))

Declaration(ObjectProperty(actions:hasEffect))
ObjectPropertyDomain(actions:hasEffect actions:Action)
ObjectPropertyRange(actions:hasEffect core:Relation)

Declaration(ObjectProperty(actions:hasParameter))
ObjectPropertyDomain(actions:hasParameter actions:Action)
ObjectPropertyRange(actions:hasParameter actions:Parameter)

Declaration(ObjectProperty(actions:hasPrecondition))
ObjectPropertyDomain(actions:hasPrecondition actions:Action)
ObjectPropertyRange(actions:hasPrecondition core:Relation)

Declaration(ObjectProperty(actions:hasReturnValue))
ObjectPropertyDomain(actions:hasReturnValue actions:Action)
ObjectPropertyRange(actions:hasReturnValue core:Property)

Declaration(ObjectProperty(actions:implementedBy))
ObjectPropertyDomain(actions:implementedBy actions:Action)

Declaration(ObjectProperty(actions:objectof-effect))
ObjectPropertyDomain(actions:objectof-effect actions:Parameter)
ObjectPropertyRange(actions:objectof-effect core:Relation)

Declaration(ObjectProperty(actions:objectof-precondition))
ObjectPropertyDomain(actions:objectof-precondition actions:Parameter)
ObjectPropertyRange(actions:objectof-precondition core:Relation)

Declaration(ObjectProperty(actions:subjectof-effect))
ObjectPropertyDomain(actions:subjectof-effect actions:Parameter)
ObjectPropertyRange(actions:subjectof-effect core:Relation)

Declaration(ObjectProperty(actions:subjectof-precondition))
ObjectPropertyDomain(actions:subjectof-precondition actions:Parameter)
ObjectPropertyRange(actions:subjectof-precondition core:Relation)

Declaration(AnnotationProperty(actions:hasPredicate))

SubObjectPropertyOf(ObjectPropertyChain(actions:hasParameter
    actions:objectof-effect) actions:hasEffect)
SubObjectPropertyOf(ObjectPropertyChain(actions:hasParameter
    actions:objectof-precondition) actions:hasPrecondition)
SubObjectPropertyOf(ObjectPropertyChain(actions:hasParameter
    actions:subjectof-precondition) actions:hasPrecondition)
SubClassOf(ObjectIntersectionOf(ObjectSomeValuesFrom(actions:hasPrecondition
    core:Relation) ObjectSomeValuesFrom(actions:hasEffect core:Relation))
    actions:Action)

SubObjectPropertyOf(ObjectPropertyChain(actions:hasParameter
    actions:subjectof-effect) actions:hasEffect)
```

Listing A.7: OWL Definitions for Action Representation

Appendix B

Interfaces

Dispatch

```
                «interface»
               EventDispatch
publish(event : Event, receiver : EventHandler)
publish(event : Event)
```

Figure B.1: The EventDispatch interface used in the component model.

Registry

```
                          «interface»
                           Registry
+ getComponent(name : String) : SimulationComponent
+ getComponent(name : String, type : GroundedSymbol) : SimulationComponent
+ getComponents(type : GroundedSymbol) : SimulationComponent[*]
+ registerComponent(component : SimulationComponent)
+ getEntities(annotations : GroundedSymbol[*]) : Entity[*]
+ registerEntity(annotations : GroundedSymbol[*], entity : Entity)
+ provideEvent(eventDescription : EventDescription, publisher : EventPublisher)
+ requestEvent(eventDescription : EventDescription, subscriber : EventHandler)
```

Figure B.2: The Registry interface used in the component model.

IActionAccess

```
                «interface»
               IActionAccess
+ execute(parameters : SemanticValue[*]{ordered})
```

Figure B.3: The IActionAccess interface used in the component model.

Appendix C

Questionnaire Results

NASA TLX

	IR (15)		SimX (10)		UE 4 (3)		Unity 4 (15)	
	Mean	SD	Mean	SD	Mean	SD	Mean	SD
Mental Demand	49.73	21.10	62.60	16.53	58.67	13.20	38.00	22.26
Temporal Demand	39.13	16.74	43.90	23.73	49.00	21.40	36.93	22.33
Performance	24.47	20.24	45.30	19.60	41.33	15.33	33.20	25.34
Effort	45.33	22.91	60.50	17.81	51.00	14.31	41.53	19.70
Frustration	59.07	21.17	51.90	20.57	52.67	19.77	24.13	23.92

Table C.1: NASA TLX short-term results. IR = instantreality, SimX = Simulator X, UE 4 = Unreal Engine 4

	SimX (3)		UE 4 (5)		Unity 4 (11)	
	Mean	SD	Mean	SD	Mean	SD
Mental Demand	61.33	2.05	64.60	8.69	54.64	20.11
Temporal Demand	33.33	17.13	58.80	22.19	61.64	17.25
Performance	24.67	15.84	7.40	6.80	32.00	22.10
Effort	61.33	11.15	81.00	11.58	60.73	18.45
Frustration	64.33	3.30	42.20	19.36	41.55	15.17

Table C.2: NASA TLX long-term results. SimX = Simulator X, UE 4 = Unreal Engine 4

QUESI

	IR		SimX		UE 4		Unity 4	
	Mean	SD	Mean	SD	Mean	SD	Mean	SD
subjective mental workload	2.87	0.59	2.17	0.65	2.33	0.31	3.49	0.44
perceived achievement of goals	3.20	0.78	3.00	0.65	3.33	0.53	4.00	0.36
perceived effort of learning	3.24	0.79	2.13	0.54	1.89	0.18	3.71	0.46
familiarity	2.89	0.80	2.53	0.67	2.22	0.47	3.51	0.46
perceived error rate	2.53	1.02	2.35	0.50	2.67	0.27	3.47	0.51
QUESI total score	2.95	0.52	2.44	0.41	2.49	0.25	3.64	0.41

Table C.3: QUESI short-term results. IR = instantreality, SimX = Simulator X, UE 4 = Unreal Engine 4

	SimX (3)		UE 4 (5)		Unity 4 (11)	
	Mean	SD	Mean	SD	Mean	SD
subjective mental workload	3.11	0.31	3.07	1.02	3.27	0.72
perceived achievement of goals	3.89	0.42	4.53	0.50	3.76	0.47
perceived effort of learning	3.00	0.27	3.60	0.83	3.03	0.50
familiarity	2.78	0.69	3.73	0.57	3.27	0.47
perceived error rate	2.67	0.47	2.40	0.86	2.86	0.68
QUESI total score	3.09	0.33	3.47	0.61	3.29	0.47

Table C.4: QUESI long-term results. SimX = Simulator X, UE 4 = Unreal Engine 4

www.ingramcontent.com/pod-product-compliance
Lightning Source LLC
LaVergne TN
LVHW080114070326
832902LV00015B/2585